IN A SUMMER SWELTER

The Charles Manson Murders

Simon Davis

Birriebungie Press

Published by Birribungie Press, P.O. Box 456,
Gerringong, New South Wales, Australia, 2534.

National Library of Australia Cataloguing-in-Publication entry:

Creator: Davis, Simon, author
Title: In A Summer Swelter

ISBN: 978-0-6481252-0-4 (pbk)

Subjects: TRUE CRIME/Murder/General
               LAW/Ethics and Professional Responsibility
               SOCIAL SCIENCE/Criminology

Also available as an ebook: 978-0-6481252-1-1 (ebk)

Cover design and typesetting by Publicious Book Publishing
Published in collaboration with Publicious Book Publishing.
www.publicious.com.au

The author's royalties will be shared, after expenses, with government and community
programs for street kids and victims of domestic violence and homelessness, all of
which were themes weaving in and out of the subject events.

ACKNOWLEDGMENTS

Thank you to the following people for their contributions to this book:

My wife, Kathryn, solicitor, to whom this book is dedicated. This project would never have been completed, nor even started, without her encouragement, support and advice about law and writing.

Crown prosecutor Trevor Bailey, who doubles as my brother-in-law, for working on the manuscript with me and steering me away from legal error. Whatever error remains is of my making.

Sasha Shearman, barrister and sister-in-law, for huge moral support and dropping things in an instant to get cases and other materials to me.

U.S. attorney David Hull for giving his time to debate and explore various matters, both factual and legal. David improved my thinking about important matters. Again, any remaining error is entirely mine.

Andy McDermott and team at Publicious Book Publishing Services for the cover design, printing, general guidance on all things publishing, and being great to work with.

Patrick Danaher for his professional editing and expert guidance.

Lorraine Wheeler for help with editing, organising ideas and shaping the book.

Office of the District Attorney for the County of Los Angeles, for assistance with transcripts and other primary source material.

www.cielodrive.com for assistance with primary material and transcripts.

The family canines, Joe Rokocoko (better known as "Joey"), Goldie and cousin Happy for watching every move.

TABLE OF CONTENTS

CAST OF CHARACTERS

MANSON FAMILY - Males	ALIAS
MANSON, Charles Milles	Jesus Christ, The Soul, Charles Summers, Charles Willis Manson, Charles Maddox, The Wizard, JC, The Gardener, The Devil.
BAILEY, Laurance Edward	Larry, Little Larry, Larry Jones
BROWN, Kenneth Richard	Scott Bell Davis, Scott
DAVIS, Bruce McGregor	Bruce McMillan, George McGregor, Jack Paul
DECARLO, Danny	Donkey Dan, Daniel Romeo, Richard Allen Smith
GROGAN, Steven	Clem Tufts, Scramblehead, Grant Mollan
HAUGHT, John Philip	Zero
LANE, Robert Ivan	Soupspoon
VANSICKLE, William Joseph	Bill Vance, William Rex Cole, David Lee Hamic
POSTON, Brooks	
THOMPSON, Vern Edward	Vern Plumlee
TODD, Hugh Rocky	Randy Morglea
WALLEMAN, Thomas John	T.J., T.J. the Terrible
WATKINS, Paul Alan	Little Paul
WATSON, Charles	Tex, Charles Montgomery, Mad Charlie, Chuck

MANSON FAMILY – Females   ALIAS

MANSON FAMILY – Females	ALIAS
ATKINS, Susan Denice	Sadie Mae Glutz, Sexy Sadie, Donna Kay Powell, Sharon King.
BAILEY, Ella Jo	Yeller, Yellerstone, Ella Beth Sinder
BARTELL, Susan	Country Sue
BRUNNER, Mary	Mother Mary, Mary Manson, Marioche, Linda Dee Moser, Christine Marie Euchts
COOPER, Sherry Ann	Simi Valley Sherry
COTTAGE, Madeline	Linda Baldwin, Little Patty
FROMME, Lynette	Squeaky, Red, Elizabeth Elaine Williamson
GILLIES, Catherine	Cappy, Capistrano, Cathy Myers, Patricia Anne Burke, Patti Sue Jardin
GOOD, Sandra	Sandy, Blue, Sandra Collins Pugh
HOYT, Barbara	Barbara Rosenburg
KASABIAN, Linda Darleen	Linda Christian, Yana the Witch, Linda Chiochios
KRENWINKEL, Patricia	Katie, Big Patty, Marnie Reeves, Mary Ann Scott, Cathran Patricia Smith
LAKE, Dianne	Snake, Dianne Bluestein
LUTESINGER, Kathryn	Catherine Lynn Drake, Katy, Kitty
MOOREHOUSE, Ruth Ann	Ouisch, Ruth Ann Huebelhurst, Ruth Ann Smack, Rachel Sue Morse
PITMAN, Nancy Laura	Brenda Sue McCann, Brindle, Cydette Perell
SCHRAM, Stephanie	

SHARE, Catherine — Gypsy, Manon Minette, Kathleen Diane Shore, Catherine Ann James, Jessica Beth Tracy

SINCLAIR, Collie — Sheery Andrews

SMITH, Claudia Leigh

VAN HOUTEN, Leslie Sue — Lulu, Leslie Marie Sankston, Leslie Sue, Leslie Owens, Louella Maxwell Alexandria, Morning Flower

VON AHN, Dianne — Mary Ann Schwarm

WILDEBUSH, Joan — Juanita Wildebush

MANSON FAMILY - Children	ALIAS	BIRTH DATE	PARENTS
DECARLO, Dennis	Dennis Smith	1967	Danny DeCarlo
FRIEDMAN, John	26 March 1959		
GLUTZ, Zezozoze Zadfrack		7 October 1968	Susan Atkins
KASABIAN, Tanya		February 1968	Linda Kasabian
MANSON, Valentine Michael	Pooh Bear, Michael		
	Shawn Manson, Sunstone Hawk	1 April 1968	Charles Manson/ Mary Brunner
PUGH, Ivan S.	Elf, Chosen	16 September 1969	Sandra Good

POLICE

BLACKBURN, Clifford	Police officer.
BOEN, Jerome	Police fingerprints
BURDICK, A.H.	Police lieutenant, polygraph examiner
DOLAN, Harold	Police fingerprints
DRYNAN, Thomas	Police officer, testified against Atkins in penalty phase of first Tate/LaBianca trial.
DUNLOP, Donald	Sheriff, discovered Manson hiding under building on 16 August 1969 raid.
GLEASON, William	Deputy Sheriff, conducted raid on Spahn Ranch 16/8/69
GUENTHER, Charles	Police sergeant, fingerprints
GUTIERREZ, Manuel	Police sergeant
LEE, William	Police ballistics
MCGANN, Michael	Police sergeant
MCKELLAR, William	Police sergeant, arrested Krenwinkel in Alabama
PURSELL, Jim	Police officer, arrested Manson, et al, 13 October 1969.
WARD, Donald	Inyo County Sheriff
WATSON, Michael	Police officer
WHITELEY, Paul	Police sergeant

PROSECUTION ATTORNEYS

BUGLIOSI, Vincent	Deputy District Attorney ("DA"), Los Angeles County, prosecuted Manson, Watson, Atkins, Krenwinkel and Van

	Houten for Tate/LaBianca murders in 1970/71.
FOWLES, Frank	DA, Inyo County
KATZ, Burt	Deputy DA, LA County, prosecuted Beausoleil for Hinman murder.
KAY, Steven	Deputy DA, LA County, assisted Bugliosi in prosecution of Manson, Watson, Atkins, Krenwinkel and Van Houten for Tate/LaBianca murders. Prosecuted Van Houten in re-trials in 1977/78.
MUSICH, Donald	Deputy DA, LA County, assisted Bugliosi in prosecution of Manson, Watson, Atkins, Krenwinkel and Van Houten for Tate/LaBianca murders in 1970/71.
STOVITZ, Aaron	Head of Trials Division, DA's Office, LA County, co-prosecutor with Bugliosi for part of prosecution of Manson, Atkins, Krenwinkel and Van Houten for Tate/LaBianca murders in 1970/71.
YOUNGER, Evelle	DA, LA County

DEFENCE ATTORNEYS

BALL, Joseph	Investigated Manson's competence to represent himself in December 1969.

BARNETT, Donald	Represented Van Houten 10 December 1969 to 19 December 1969, replaced by Marvin Part
CABALLERO, Richard	Represented Atkins 10 December 1969 to 6 March 1970, replaced by Daye Shinn.
CARUSO, Paul	Represented Atkins 10 December 1969 to 6 March 1970, replaced by Daye Shinn.
FITZGERALD, Paul	Represented Manson 11 December 1969 to 24 December 1969. Represented Krenwinkel 24 March 1970 to end of trial on 19 April 1971.
HOLLOPETER, Charles	Represented Manson 6 March 1970 to 19 March 1970.
HUGHES, Ronald	Represented Manson 19 March 1970 to c22 March 1970. Represented Van Houten 17 July 1970 to 30 November 1970.
KANAREK, Irving	Represented Manson c22March 1970 to 19 April 1971.
KEITH, Maxwell	Represented Van Houten 3 December 1970 to 19 April 1971. Represented Van Houten in re-trials in 1977 and 1978.
PART, Marvin	Represented Van Houten 19 December 1969 to 6 February 1970, replaced by Ira Reiner
REINER, Ira	Represented Van Houten 6 February 1970 to 17 July 1970.
SALTER, Leon	Represented Beausoleil 1969 and 1970.
SHINN, Daye	Represented Atkins 11 March 1970 to 19 April 1971.

MISCELLANEOUS

ALEXANDER, Judge A.	Trial judge, second Tate/ LaBianca trial (Watson's trial)
ALTOBELLI, Rudy	Owner of 10050 Cielo Drive
BARRETT, Samuel	Manson's parole officer in 1969
BEAUSOLEIL, Robert	Aka Bobby, aka The Frenchman, aka Jason Lee Daniels, aka Cupid, convicted murderer of Gary Hinman.
BICKSTON, Robert	Witness at Shea trial, prospective employer of Shea.
BINDER, Jerry	Witness at Shea trial
BISHOP, George	Writer, observer in court
BRANDEN, Nathaniel	Psychologist
BROWN, Dr Claude	Psychiatrist, examined Krenwinkel 24 December 1969.
CHAPMAN, Winifred	Housekeeper/cleaner at 10050 Cielo Drive, discovered bodies.
CHOATE, Judge Raymond	Trial judge at Manson's trial for Hinman and Shea murders.
CROCKETT, Paul	Prospector in Death Valley area, to whom Paul Watkins and Brooks Poston defected from Family in mid-1969 before murders.
CROWE, Bernard	Aka Lotsapoppa, drug dealer, shot by Manson 1 July 1969, survived.
DALTON, David	Rolling Stone journalist
DAVIS, Ivor	Journalist, in-court observer, author of Five to Die.
DEERING, Dr Harold	Psychiatrist, testified as to Dianne Lake's competence to testify.

DELL, Judge George — Presided over some of the pre-trial motions and arraignments in Tate/LaBianca and Hinman trials.

DORGAN, Joe — Boyfriend of Suzanne Struthers, discovered Leno LaBianca's body

FAITH, Professor Karlene — Writer, academic/researcher at California Institute for Women 1972.

FELTON, David — *Rolling Stone* journalist

FLETCHER, Kit — Friend of Atkins, to whom Atkins made admissions.

FLYNN, Juan — Ranch hand at Spahn Ranch.

FOKIANOS, John — Newspaper vendor, last person to see LaBiancas alive apart from killers.

FOLGER, Abigail — Coffee heiress, friend of the Polanskis, partner of Voytek Frykowski, murdered 9 August 1969.

FRYKOWSKI, Wojiciech — Aka "Voytek", friend of the Polanskis, partner of Abigail Folger, murdered 9 August 1969.

GARRETSON, William — Occupant of guest house at 10050 Cielo Drive.

GRAHAM, Virginia — Inmate at Sybil Brand Institute to whom Atkins made admissions.

GUERRERO, Frank — House painter at 10050 Cielo Drive.

HATAMI, Sharokh — Sharon Tate's photographer

HEARST, Dennis — Delivered bicycle to 10050 Cielo Drive on 8 August 1969.

HINMAN, Gary — Musician, murdered 27 July 1969.

HOCHMAN, Dr Joel S. — Psychiatrist

HUGHES, Veronica	Aka Ronnie Howard, Shelley Nadell, inmate at Sybil Brand Institute to whom Atkins made admissions
IRELAND, Timothy	Resided near 10050 Cielo Drive, heard screams.
IRWIN, Mike	Aka Mike Erwin, friend of Gary Hinman.
JAKOBSON, Gregg	Music agent.
KATSUYAMA, David	Deputy Medical Examiner, conducted autopsies of Hinman and the LaBiancas.
KEENE, Judge William	Presided over some of the pre-trial motions and arraignments in the Tate/LaBianca and Hinman trials.
KOENIG, Charles	Employee of Standard Oil Company, found Rosemary LaBianca's wallet in service station toilet.
KRELL, Glenn	Friend of Gary Hinman
KRONER, Rosina	Aka Luella, former girlfriend of Tex Watson
LABIANCA, Leno	Businessman, murdered 10 August 1969.
LABIANCA, Rosemary	Business woman, wife of Leno, murdered 10 August 1969
LANCE, Victor	Witness at Shea trial.
LIVSEY, Dr Clara	Medical doctor, prosecution consultant on re-trial of Leslie Van Houten, author of *The Manson Women*.
LOMAX, Edward	Ex-employee of Hi Standard, manufacturer of gun which killed Sebring and Parent.

MAUPIN, Sgt. William	Court officer whom Manson sought to bribe.
MELCHER, Terry	Music producer, lived at 10050 Cielo Drive until late 1968.
NOGUCHI, Thomas	LA County Coroner, conducted autopsies on victims from 10050 Cielo Drive
OLDER, Judge Charles H.	Trial judge, first Tate/LaBianca trial
PARENT, Steven	Visitor to 10050 Cielo Drive, murdered 9 August 1969.
PEARL, Ruby	Spahn Ranch Manager
POLANSKI, Roman	Husband of Sharon Tate
RETZ, Frank	Witness at Shea trial, prospective purchaser of Spahn Ranch.
ROSE, Al	Administrator of Haight Ashbury Free Clinic.
SANDERS, Ed	Musician, author of *The Family*.
SEBRING, Jay	Hairdresser, murdered 9 August 1969.
SHEA, Donald	Aka Shorty, Ranch hand at Spahn Ranch, murdered circa 30 August 1969
SHEA, Judge	Trial judge at Bobby Beausoleil's first trial.
SKRDLA, Dr Blake	Psychiatrist
SMITH, Dr David	Medical doctor, Haight Ashbury Free Clinic, treated Family members.
SMITH, Dr Roger	Criminologist, Manson's first parole officer in San Francisco, 1967.
SPAHN, George	Owner of Spahn Ranch where Family mostly based in 1969.

SPRINGER, Al	Member of Straight Satans motorbike gang.
STARR, Randy	Ranch hand at Spahn Ranch.
STEVENSON, Jo	Friend of Atkins, to whom Atkins made admissions.
STRUTHERS, Frank	Son of Rosemary LaBianca
STRUTHERS, Suzanne	Daughter of Rosemary LaBianca
SWARTZ, Johnny	Ranch hand, owner of yellow Ford used by Family in Tate/LaBianca murders
TATE, Sharon	Actor, wife of Roman Polanski, murdered 9 August 1969.
TRUE, Harold	Lived next door to 3301 Waverley Drive.
TUBICK, Herman	Foreman of jury at first Tate/laBianca trial.
VARGAS, Tom	Gardener at 10050 Cielo Drive
WALKER, Roseanne	Inmate at Sybil Brand Institute to whom Atkins made admissions
WEBER, Rudolph	Resident near 10050 Cielo Drive, in a different street, chased Watson, et al, from his property.
WEISS, Steven	Found gun used at 10050 Cielo Drive.
WILSON, Dennis	Member of Beach Boys.
ZAMORA, William	Juror, later wrote book about trial.

.

INTRODUCTION

Background

In the summer of 1969, Los Angeles suffered some of the wildest and most vicious murders in the annals of crime, committed by a group of young people known as the Manson Family[1]. The leader of the group was Charles Manson. Upon arrest, Manson would identify himself as "Charles Manson, also known as Jesus Christ", although he would later announce in court he hadn't decided what he was or who he was. The group gave the appearance of peaceful hippies living a communal lifestyle, but appearances can be deceptive, as were many facets of this case.

The murders generated hysterical publicity and still command attention. Some of the victims were Hollywood celebrities, including actor Sharon Tate and one Jay Sebring, hairdresser to the stars. Ms Tate was the wife of film director Roman Polanski, who was overseas at the time. The murders appeared random and without motive. The savagery was extreme. One victim, Frykowski, endured 51 stab wounds, two gun shots and 13 blows to the head. Ms Tate, eight months pregnant, was stabbed and suspended by rope from a roof rafter. Rosemary LaBianca was stabbed 41 times.

Charles Manson has many supporters who complain about his conviction. Most of it is polemic rather than objective analysis. As time goes by and memories fade, some of this commentary seems

---

1. The group was not a biological family.

to be gaining a foothold. Additionally, at least two former Manson Family members, Susan Atkins and Patricia Krenwinkel, have spoken in the not-too-distant past of receiving fan mail from young people glorifying the events as "cool". Both women have denounced such communications.

My background is that I obtained degrees in Law and Arts (sociology, history) at Macquarie University, Sydney, Australia, in 1984. I then practiced as a solicitor and barrister until 2014. One of the acquired skills of a trial lawyer is the ability to draw inferences from the way in which a court case is conducted by the various parties. Many of the facts about these events have been misinterpreted or misreported out of a lack of understanding about the way the trials were conducted. An understanding of the trials – for example, choices of topics and questions for cross-examination, nature of objections, and so on – leads to a better understanding of the murders. That is what this book is about.

A close look at the Tate/LaBianca trial also ties up some of the loose ends that have always attended this story, and dispels some of the myths that have grown, and continue to grow. It also yields a story which has never been fully, or adequately, told of how Manson attempted to save himself at the expense of his female co-defendants.

I shall also explore the enduring mystery of how the other Family members, who gave the appearance of young people from average middle class backgrounds, undisposed to criminality, came to be savage murderers. This involves the issue of brainwashing. Given the nature of the relationship between Manson and his followers, the central forensic tension in this case has always, unavoidably, been assessing the level of his culpability as against their culpability. The more he was culpable, the less they were, in particular the convicted females Atkins, Krenwinkel and Van Houten. This tension was obscured at the first Tate/LaBianca trial because Manson engineered that all of the defence lawyers were in fact following his instructions in pursuit of a so-called "united defence". As will be seen, this was a scam perpetrated by Manson with a view to securing his own acquittal, whilst ensuring the other defendants went to the gas chamber.

The various trials and appeals will be considered, and also material that has become available since, including admissions and statements by Manson and other Family members. Emphasis will be given to primary sources, in particular the trial transcripts where available. Transcripts are generally repositories of "truth" about events. Cross-examination, in particular, is the ultimate fact checker. Court cases tend to be purpose-built for the promotion of truth. They are not always successful at this, but they usually are.

One problem in the narrative has been the treatment of the so-called Helter Skelter motive. Helter Skelter was alleged by the prosecution to be a race war which Manson prophesised, and the murders were allegedly his attempt to ignite the war. If one looks at the treatment of the murders by the media, and various writers since, one could be forgiven for thinking the Helter Skelter motive was the sole basis of the prosecution of Manson for the Tate/LaBianca murders. On the other hand, primary sources such as transcripts and appeal judgments, and indeed the law itself, make it plain that Helter Skelter was not the sole basis of the prosecution.

Manson's supporters argue the Helter Skelter motive was too "far out" to be believable. Some say it was made up by the prosecution. This is developed into the proposition that the whole prosecution was not to be believed. The law actually was (and still is) that the prosecution did not have to prove motive. It is puzzling so much has been written about something the prosecution didn't have to prove. It is equally puzzling why a prosecutor would make up something he did not have to prove. This book will undertake a review of the arguments that have arisen over Helter Skelter and endeavour to come to a better understanding of how it operated in the conviction of Manson.

For readers already familiar with the Manson story, I will develop other points which are somewhat novel and perhaps bound to surprise, such as:

1. the Hinman murder (not Tate) was, arguably, the first of the cold-blooded murders designed to ignite Helter Skelter;

2. there was egregiously unethical conduct on the part of the defence lawyers (in collusion with Manson) in the first

Tate/LaBianca trial, arguably to the point of criminality. As a result, the female defendants Atkins, Krenwinkel and Van Houten almost certainly did not get a fair trial.

Methodology

There are four things to be said about the method of this book.

First, most of the literature on these events concerns itself with the infamous Tate/LaBianca murders. However, Tate/LaBianca was book-ended by two other homicides for which Manson was convicted, and a shooting incident for which he escaped charges. All of these events occurred in July and August 1969. It is best to deal with all of the events, and in chronological order (notwithstanding the trials occurred out of order).

Secondly, I have studied and practiced law in New South Wales, Australia, but not in California. The relevant law in each jurisdiction is, by and large, the same. Both jurisdictions have common law origins and traditions. I have researched Californian criminal law to the extent of satisfying myself that little, or nothing, turns on whatever distinctions may exist. I apologise in advance for any significant points of distinction which may have been lost on me.

Thirdly, I have not interviewed the participants in the subject events. There are two reasons. First, meeting and greeting is not conducive to impartiality. Secondly, my research has left me with little confidence in the ability of the protagonists to accurately remember the events. And there is now available contemporaneous material including early confidential interviews with Family members, not to mention audio and video records from which sensible observations of demeanour are possible. It is important to recognise that what these people said at the time of the events is more probative than what they may say 47 years later [2]. In any event, applying normal

---

2. With respect, an excellent discussion of the problems associated with memory can be found in *Nominal Defendant v. Cordin* [2017] NSWCA 6, per Davies J at paragraphs 165 to 167. For further discussion about memory and other fact finding considerations, see Appendix 1.

principles about the weight to be accorded certain types of evidence (see Appendix 1), I found this case reasonably easy to sort out without needing to interview anybody. Some of the lay commentaries on the case give the impression it was a maze of complex factual considerations, but it wasn't (except, arguably, the Hinman murder for reasons which will become apparent when that incident is considered).

Finally, nothing in this book should be interpreted as an argument about the pending parole entitlements of any of the convicted murderers. That the female defendants did not get a fair trial would be one consideration in a judgment about parole entitlement, but there are other considerations that will not receive attention in this book.

Personal Reflections

I was a child of the 1960's, turning nine years old in August 1969. I have no memory of the subject events.

By 1976, I was a 16 year old Beatles fan looking for anything I could read about that group. I came across prosecutor Bugliosi's book, *Helter Skelter*[3]. I recognised that part of the title as a Beatles song but quickly discovered the book was about a different group, the Manson Family, and some grizzly murders. Bugliosi had prosecuted the killers. I was determined to buy something, so this would do.

As I read the book, I became scared by the descriptions and randomness of the killings. I became sensitive to the sound of rustling bushes outside my bedroom window, even though I was thousands of miles from Los Angeles. I was absorbed with the book, but I couldn't get the thread of Helter Skelter. Yes, the Family talked and talked about it, but did they actually do these crazy murders because of it? I assumed I just didn't get it. I was also troubled by how the killers (except Manson himself) seemed to come from the same type of conventional home life as me. Again, I didn't understand it. After

---

3. Bugliosi, V. and Gentry, C., *Helter Skelter: The True Story of the Manson Murders*, W.W. Norton and Co., 1974.

I finished reading that book, life took over and I didn't give much thought to the Manson murders.

In 1990, I was a 30 year old lawyer making plans to renovate my house. Scratching around in the dirt under the floor, I came across a crusty yellowed old newspaper, the Sydney *Daily Mirror,* dated 3 December 1969. I shone a torch on it. It bore a large headline: *"CRAZED HIPPIES MURDER 11"* and sub-headings *"Sharon Tate begged for baby's life"* and *"Police round up devil cult".* Squeezed in the 18 inch sub-floor space, I read the story which occupied several pages.

Twenty four years later, now in semi-retirement, I came across Charles Manson again. A book with his face on the cover lunged up at me from a lower shelf in a book shop. It was called *Manson: The Life and Times of Charles Manson* by Jeff Guinn[4]. After reading that book, I still felt puzzled by Helter Skelter and the young killers. My mind raced to the then topical actions of ISIS and other extreme groups whose teenage children tape bombs to themselves in order to kill others. All in the name of a cause.

I began to wonder if my legal experience might unravel my teenage confusion. The story had reached out to me enough times that I now had to reach out to the story. It also occurred to me that no independent trial lawyer has ever written about these murders or the accompanying trials. I read some of the material put out by Manson's sympathisers and supporters. I was intrigued as to whether there was any merit in what they had to say. That intrigue didn't last long. But other important questions arose, such as how and why this tragedy occurred. And what was the role of the lawyers, especially those for the defence? I came to think the story should not be left to future generations in the haphazard state of the present commentary. The story is important enough to deserve some historical accuracy so it can be judged appropriately for what it really was.

---

4. Guinn, J., *Manson: The Life and Times of Charles Manson,* Simon & Schuster, 2013.

CHAPTER 1: THE FAMILY

"you couldn't meet a nicer bunch of people"

Leslie Van Houten describes the Manson
Family to Sergeant Michael McGann[5]

Charles Manson and the Beginnings

Charles Milles Manson was born in Cincinnati, Ohio, on 12 November 1934[6]. His childhood was unsettled. He never met his father, whose identity was a mystery. His mother was sentenced to a lengthy prison term when he was only five years old. He came under the care of relatives. It is hard to detect anything untoward about the care given by the relatives. It was strict. There was an emphasis on religion. Young Charles didn't like these aspects.

Things started unravelling by 1943 (age nine) when Charles began stealing in the home environment. In 1944, his mother was released from prison but she felt incapable of caring for her son. In 1947, she arranged for him to be placed at the Gibault School for Boys in Indianapolis. Manson ran away from Gibault several times. On one occasion he returned to his mother, who promptly sent him back. By early 1948 (13 years old), he was committing armed robberies. After two weeks of this activity, he was caught and sentenced to reform

5. Record of interview dated 26 November 1969, sourced from www.cielodrive.com.

6. By some accounts, Manson was born on 11 November, but 12 November was probably the correct date.

school – Indiana Boys School in Plainfield, Indiana – where he arrived in early 1949.

Young Charlie was not a model inmate. Psychiatric assessment in June 1951 (16 years old) found a *"marked degree of rejection, instability, and psychic trauma"* in his past. He had such a sense of rejection and inferiority about his mother that he had to *"suppress any thoughts about her"*. He had *"developed certain facile techniques for dealing with people"* which *"for the most part consisted of a good sense of humour"* and an *"ability to ingratiate himself"*[7].

In January 1952, at the Natural Bridge Honor Camp (reform school), Charlie was caught sodomising another boy while holding a razor blade to the boy's throat. He had been due for parole before this incident, but instead was transferred to the Federal Reformatory at Petersburg, Virginia. Between January and August 1952, he committed eight serious disciplinary offences, three involving homosexual acts. He was considered *"dangerous"* and *"shouldn't be trusted across the street"*. He had definite *"assaultive tendencies"*. It was decided to send him to the maximum security Federal Reformatory at Chillicothe, Ohio, where he arrived on 22 September 1952 (age 17)[8].

Over the next year or so, Charlie's behaviour fluctuated although generally improved. He was paroled in May 1954 (age 19). After another series of misadventures and crimes, he was returned to custody in March 1956. Various custodial assessments around this period referred to his inability to control himself and a tendency to *"cut up"* and misbehave in large groups. He was capable of positive adjustment, but was erratic, moody and a very difficult case.

It was reported Charlie indulged himself in a number of philosophical pursuits, including Scientology and Freemasonry. He reached the Scientology state of "theta clear" meaning freedom from past trauma and negative emotion. At some stage he read Dale

7. Report of Dr Block, based on an assessment on 29 June 1951.
8. Bugliosi, *Helter Skelter*, p.194.

Carnegie's *How to Win Friends and Influence People.* A staff assessment at McNeil Island Penitentiary, Washington, reported:

> *"He hides his loneliness, resentment, and hostility behind a façade of superficial ingratiation . . . An energetic, young-appearing person whose [verbalisation] flows quite easily, he gestures profusely and can dramatize situations to hold the listener's attention"*[9]

Charlie would certainly become a master of easy flowing verbalisation. He was, and is, garrulous in the extreme. Much of it is mumbo jumbo. Even Family members would later say they sometimes found it hard to understand him. Some years later he would explain his philosophy in an interview with *Rolling Stone* magazine as being *"Don't think . . . I don't believe in words"* to which the interviewer replied: *"If you don't believe in words, why do you use so many of them?"*[10].

One feature of Manson's years of incarceration was his enthusiasm for the subject of pimping. He learned that successful working girls often had father hang-ups and responded well to a mixture of affection and, on the other hand, just enough violence to remind them who was boss. The trick was to make the girls fear you and love you at the same time[11]. It seems he had more than a passing interest in the exploitation of women for financial benefit. During 1958/9, Manson enjoyed about a year of freedom during which he engaged himself in pimping. There followed another arrest, and incarceration.

Annual jail review in September 1964 reported Manson as having *"an intense need to call attention to himself . . . remains emotionally*

9. Quoted in Bugliosi, *Helter Skelter,* p.200.

10. Dalton D., Felton, D., "Year of the Fork, Night of the Hunter", *Rolling Stone*, no.61, 25 June 1970, p.36.

11. Guinn, J., *Manson*, pp.57 to 58.

insecure and tends to involve himself in various fanatical interests"[12]. One of his interests, said by some reports to be an obsession, was guitar playing, and with that came the flavour of the times – the Beatles.

Upon his release from the Terminal Island correctional facility in Los Angeles in March 1967, Manson was a 32 year old man. Since 1948 (age 14) he had only experienced two and a half years outside of reform school or prison. And that time was occupied with pimping and petty crime.

After release, Manson found his way to San Francisco where he met 23 year old Mary Brunner. A sexual relationship developed. By August 1967, Manson had a veritable harem of other young women in addition to Brunner who travelled around together in a bus. Manson was sexually active with all of these women, and they harboured little resentment about sharing his attention. Manson was able to create this happy state of affairs by applying techniques of flattery and ingratiation. He also developed a father-figure line. An account of his modus operandi was given by Susan Atkins (aka Sadie Mae Glutz) in her evidence at a Grand Jury proceeding:

> " . . . a man walked in and had a guitar with him and all of a sudden he was surrounded by a group of girls. . . . he started to play music . . . he sounded like an angel . . . and I asked him if I could play his guitar and I wanted to get some attention from him . . . he handed me the guitar and to myself I thought 'I can't play this', and then he looked at me and said 'You can play that if you want to'. Now he had never heard me say 'I can't play this', I only thought it. . . . it blew my mind because he was inside my head and I knew that he was something that I had been looking for. . . I went down and kissed his feet. . . . [and] a day or so later . . . he told me to take off my clothes [and he] . . .

---

12. Bugliosi, *Helter Skelter,* p.202.

stood me in front of the mirror and I turned away and he says, 'Go ahead and look at yourself, there is nothing wrong with you. You are perfect. You have always been perfect'. He says 'This is in body form. You were born perfect and everything that has happened to you from the time you were a child all the way up to this moment has happened perfectly. You have made no mistakes. The only mistake you have made are the mistakes that you thought that you made. They were not mistakes' . . . [A]nd he said 'have you ever thought about making love with your father?' I said 'yes I thought that I would like to make love with my father'. . . he said 'All right, when we are making love imagine in your imagination that I am your father' . . . and it was a very beautiful experience"

The father theme resonated with many of the girls recruited into the Family. Linda Kasabian disliked her step-father. Lynette Fromme (aka Squeaky) had a father hang up when Manson came across her in 1967. Nancy Pitman (aka Brenda McCann) claimed she had been kicked out of home by her father when 16 years old. Sandra Good alleged she had been disowned by her father.

If there wasn't a father hang-up, Charlie had an impressive repertoire of other pick-up lines such as this one he used on Catherine Share (aka Gypsy):

"He looked me straight in the eye and pierced my eyes and said 'This is your dream girl, start living it'. And I was fascinated . . . he said I belonged with him and that we were one and pulled me in immediately. I never left. Everybody was drawn to him . . . we felt that he had a corner on the truth"[13]

---

13. *Most Evil: Charles Manson*, Discovery Channel, 2006.

San Francisco was the hippie mecca of the so-called summer of love of 1967 into which Manson had landed. Evidently he wasn't the only person with criminal form arriving in the city:

> *"You may recall a song the lyrics of which were 'If you come to San Francisco, you'd better wear a flower in your hair'. By 1967, if you came to San Francisco you needed to wear a .45 in your belt. It had changed that fast. The kids were still coming from all over the United States with the same sort of expectations but the welcoming committee was very very different"*[14]

As will be seen, the kids arriving in San Francisco also arrived loaded up with their parents' credit cards. It will be seen that Manson's scamming of the credit cards of his followers' parents knew no bounds. In one of several arrests in 1969, he was found hiding under a building and as he emerged a pile of credit cards fell from his shirt pockets. Some have suggested that the first year or two of the Family's existence was an adventure of peace and love. To some of his followers it may have seemed that way, but in truth Manson was interested in exploitation, both sexual and financial.

At some stage the fledgling group was called, or called itself, the Family[15]. Most Family members were female and younger than Manson. Most were teenagers or in their early 20's and were drop-outs, runaways, or searching for "the truth". They were a nomadic group of travellers until August 1968 when they settled, more or less, at a disused movie set called Spahn Ranch on the outskirts of Los Angeles owned by an aging gentleman George Spahn. The Ranch was still something of an ongoing concern. Ranch hands were employed. Horses were rented out for riding in the surrounding countryside.

---

14. Dr Roger Smith, Manson's parole officer in San Francisco, interviewed on *Charles Manson: Serial Killer*, Entertainment Channel, 2000.

15. Susan Atkins said at a Grand Jury proceeding on 5 December 1969 that *"[A]mong ourselves we called ourselves the Family, a Family like no other Family"*.

The arrangement was that the Family could stay there in return for attending to Ranch maintenance.

There have been numerous estimates of the size of the Family. The lines of Family membership were blurred. There weren't membership cards. There were members who were hard core, and others who were less committed. There were comings and goings. By most accounts, the men had more freedom to come and go than the women. For example, Bruce Davis and Charles "Tex" Watson spent periods away during the winter of 1968/69. The women rarely left. If they did, they weren't away for long. The perception seems to have been that the women outnumbered the men. By my reckoning, the male contingent of the Family numbered about eight or nine, and the Family total was between 20 and 30 persons at any one time.

There were also at least five children. The Family purported to hold the children in high esteem, partly because of a pseudo-philosophical belief that they had not yet been corrupted by the establishment and it was desirable to preserve their purity.

Leadership

Manson was earlier described as the leader of the Family. However, because the question of leadership was a lynchpin of the trial case against him, it is worthy of attention. It will be seen that anyone who joined the Family expecting an egalitarian hippie commune would be disappointed. Many have testified, or written, about the extent of Manson's control at the Ranch. He once told prosecutor Vincent Bugliosi that he even knew what the mice were doing at the Ranch[16]. Far from a hippie commune, it was in reality a dictatorship. Professor Karlene Faith has described Manson as *"typical of cult leaders in that he was totalitarian, at first in a soft voice, later aggressively"*[17].

---

16. Bugliosi, *Helter Skelter,* p.609.
17. Faith, K., *The Long Prison Journey of Leslie Van Houten*, Northeastern University Press, 2001, p.36.

Danny De Carlo was a member of the Straight Satans motorbike gang who frequently hung out with the Family. The female Family members referred to him as "Donkey Dan", which was apparently an allusion to an outstanding anatomical feature. By most accounts, DeCarlo had become a bona fide Family member by mid-1969. He would later testify at the Tate/LaBianca trial that the girls worshipped Charlie and they said Charlie knew all and saw all. DeCarlo observed that Manson would tell the Family when it was time to eat, no-one was to be served until he was seated and during dinner he would do all the talking.

Charles "Tex" Watson would later corroborate DeCarlo in testimony at his own trial and add *"nobody ever went to sleep before [Charlie] did or nobody ever got out of bed before he did"*.

Linda Kasabian would testify that Manson was the *"head"* of the Family and on joining the group she was told to never ask *"why?"*. She never saw anyone refuse to do what he said, and *"we always wanted to do anything and everything for him"*.

An outsider, Gregg Jakobson, was a frequent visitor to the Ranch in connection with helping Manson secure a recording contract. Jakobson would testify that Charlie *"absolutely"* dominated the Family.

Dr David Smith of the Haight-Ashbury Free Clinic knew Manson and the Family well. He was, in effect, at least in 1967/68, the Family doctor. Clinic administrator Al Rose spent some time living with the Family. Rose and Smith subsequently had published an article in which they described Manson as *"an extroverted, persuasive individual [who] served as absolute ruler of this group-marriage commune. What he approved was approved by the rest of the group. What he disapproved was forbidden"*[18].

The evidence in the Tate/LaBianca trial was littered with references to Manson's domination and control, too many to set out here. The Court of Appeals of California (hereafter "the appeal court") summarised it this way:

18. David E. Smith and Alan J. Rose (1970) *The Group Marriage Commune: A Case Study, Journal of Psychoactive Drugs*, 3:1, 115-119, DOI:10.1080/02791072.1970.10471368., p.116.

"Without doubt, Manson was the leader of the Family. The scope of his influence ranged from the most simple to the most complex of matters. He decided where the Family would stay; where they would sleep; what clothing they would have, and when they would wear it; when they would take their evening meal; and when they would move.

. . .

Manson's position of authority was firmly acknowledged. It was understood that membership in the Family required giving up everything to Manson and never disobeying him. His followers . . . were compliant. They regarded him as infallible . . ."[19]

The main voices against all of this have been (i) Manson himself and (ii) various Family members who testified that Manson was not the leader. As will be seen, this testimony was fabricated, having been scripted by Manson. This was so obvious that it only reinforced that Manson was the leader.

Finance

The Family had various sources of finance.

First, pursuant to a philosophical mantra of *"everything that's yours is mine, and everything that's mine is yours"*, Manson appropriated any sources of finance brought to the Family by new members. It was not a reciprocal arrangement as the mantra might be taken to suggest. New members gave up everything they owned as the price of admission to the Family. Linda Kasabian was leaned on to steal $5,000 from an acquaintance. Juanita Wildebush was required to hand over $10,000. Sandra Good handed over $5,000.

---

19. *People v. Manson & Ors.* [1976] 61 Cal. App. 3d 123, pp. 127 to 128.

Another source of cash was Dennis Wilson of the Beach Boys. Although not a Family member, Wilson was estimated to have contributed, directly or indirectly, $100,000 to the Family coffers.

Another revenue stream involved Family members falsely indicating to their parents an intention to return home, and requesting the plane or train fare. The money went to Charlie. Parents' homes were burgled and credit cards plundered.

Prostitution was lucrative. Manson pimped the girls. Their sex was offered by him in exchange for favours he needed from other people. The Spahn Ranch wasn't so much a commune as a brothel. Paul Watkins would later write:

> "[Manson] spoke like a pimp. There was never any doubt that the girls <u>belonged</u> to him and that their favours were a gift, not from them, but from Charlie . . .
> . . . [we had] mechanics rebuilding Harleys, diesels, and dune buggies round the clock. We paid them, and paid them well – in money, dope, and all the sex they could handle."[20]

Lynette Fromme was pimped to George Spahn as part of the maintenance deal at the Ranch[21]. She was also pimped to Paul Fitzgerald, one of the defence attorneys at the first Tate/LaBianca trial, which will be considered in more detail in a later chapter.

Patricia Krenwinkel (Katie) would later tell an interviewer:

> "Charlie used sex for, number one, when people would come and he wanted power over them then he would offer them whatever women he had and he had certain women he always put out front which he called his street girls. They were the ones that he thought were the most beautiful, the

20. Watkins, P., with Soledad, G., *My Life With Charles Manson,* Bantam Books Inc., 1979, pp.150, 155.
21. Bugliosi, *Helter Skelter,* pp.145 and 185; Guinn, *Manson,* p.173.

ones that would be the most enticing . . . he was an excellent pimp"[22]

The appeal court said the following:

"Manson ordered one of the male members of the Family, Paul Watkins, to get more females and bring them to him. Instructing the female members of the Family to provide sexual favours to members of the commune, and to do the same for outsiders for the purpose of recruiting new members, Manson also directed them to deny favours if enlistment seemed unlikely"[23]

Supplies of food were obtained by sifting through garbage dumpsters containing discarded food from supermarkets:

" . . . the supermarkets all over Los Angeles throw away perfectly good food every day . . . but the food is still good, and us girls used to go out and do garbage runs [we would pick up this food and take it back to the Ranch] and cut out the blue spots and check it over to see that it was good food"[24]

Theft, in particular credit card theft, was a major activity of the Family. Susan Atkins (Sadie Mae Glutz) said the following before a Grand Jury:

"Q. Did Charlie ever ask you girls to steal anything for him . . .?
A. No, I took it upon myself. I was – we'd get programmed to do things.
Q. Programmed by Charlie?

22. *A Turning Point*, ABC TV, 1994.
23. *People v. Manson & Ors.* [1976] 61 Cal. App. 3d 123, pp.127 to 128.
24. Susan Atkins' testimony at Grand Jury proceeding, 5 December 1969.

A. *By Charlie, but it's hard for me to explain it so that you can see the way – the way I see the words that would come from Charlie's mouth would not come from inside him it would come from what I call the infinite.*

Q. *Well, what did he indicate to you with respect to stealing goods at all?. . .*

A. *He just said that we needed credit cards and we need that and we could use some of this.*

Q. *When he said that you assumed you had to go out and get them for him?*

A. *Yes, and also anything that we saw we needed . . . [Once] there was an automobile parked on the side of the road. I opened the door and looked inside the glove compartment and saw some credit cards. I reached in and took them.*

Q. *Did you use those credit cards?*

A. *Personally myself I did not.*

Q. *Did you turn the credit cards over to Charlie?*

A. *I turned them over to Charlie, yes . . . Charlie always told us 'You do what you want to do. If you do not want to do it, do not do it'. But when he would ask me to do something I felt I had to go ahead and do it because I know he would do the same thing for me otherwise he wouldn't ask me to do it"[25]*

Bruce Davis and Paul Watkins would later confirm the credit card (and other) theft[26]. Tex Watson would later recall that in the summer of 1969: *"[W]e began stealing anything we could get our hands on: money, credit cards, traveler's checks, dune-buggie parts. It was all for Helter Skelter"[27].*

There were also "creepy-crawl" missions in which Manson and/or Family members would dress in dark clothes, randomly enter houses

---

25. Ibid.

26. Davis' Parole Hearing, 4 October 2012; Watkins, *My Life With Charles Manson*, p.152.

27. Watson, C., as told to Chaplain Ray, *Will You Die For Me?*, Revell, a division of Baker Publishing Group, 1978, p. 122, used by permission.

with occupants asleep and steal things and re-arrange furniture. Some have said these missions were straight burglaries. Others have said they were undertaken to spook people for the sake of it. Others have suggested they were dress rehearsals for entering homes to inflict violence.

There was drug business too. A drug deal on 1 July 1969, dealt with in the next chapter, netted the Family about $2,400, which would have been good money in 1969[28]. It is difficult to assess the precise extent of the dealing. The deal on 1 July was a rather shambolic Keystone Cops type of affair that suggested they weren't exactly major players in the Los Angeles drug scene.

Drugs

Drug use was a significant part of Family life. LSD trips were regular, probably once per week, maybe more. However, Smith and Rose doubted that drug use amounted to a major health problem at the Ranch[29].

It seems that drugs played little part in the murder spree of July/ August 1969. Bruce Davis has dismissed drugs as a direct factor in the murders in which he was involved: *"We didn't take – I didn't take drugs especially to do this"*[30]. Patricia Krenwinkel would later say, against interest, that she was not drug affected during the murders she committed[31].

Atkins and Watson probably consumed speed prior to the Tate/ LaBianca killings. Atkins has never seriously attempted to blame her actions on speed. Watson, on the other hand, has been inconsistent on this issue. At his trial in 1971, he mentioned speed but only fleetingly to the extent of claiming to have consumed it. A defence

28. The net proceeds of this crime vary according to who is telling the story. I will refer to it as $2,400.
29. David E. Smith and Alan J. Rose (1970) *The Group Marriage Commune: A Case Study, Journal of Psychoactive Drugs,* 3:1, 115-119, DOI:10.1080/02791072.1970.10471368., at page 118.
30. Parole Hearing, 4 October 2012.
31. History given to Dr Claude Brown, 24 December 1969.

psychiatrist, Dr Ira Frank, testified about the "preservation" effect of speed as an explanation of the multitude of stab wounds inflicted. The preservation theory postulates that speed promotes a pattern of repeated, or preserved, physical motions. Dr Frank proposed that this type of physical repetition could have explained the enormous number of stab wounds inflicted, particularly on the victim Frykowski. It can be assumed the jury was not impressed by Dr Frank's evidence for Watson was convicted.

In his memoir published in 1978, Watson spoke of taking a *"couple of deep snorts of speed"* before Tate and speed and a *"light tab of acid"* before LaBianca[32]. In 2016, at a parole hearing, he came out with this: *". . . I knew I couldn't do what [Manson] was asking me to do unless I took [speed]"*. This was tantamount to saying that speed caused him to commit the murders. His attorney, doubtless nervous about this being interpreted as a rejection of responsibility for the murders, then repaired things with this statement: *"He can't blame drugs. He acknowledges having ingested drugs so that he could commit the offences. He knew in advance that he was going to commit them but he said 'hey, listen, I got to make this effective'. So yeah, drugs had something to do with it but he's not blaming drugs"*.

The preservation theory continues to be the subject of debate and speculation. But it remains just that, speculation, in the absence of expert pharmacological (toxicological) evidence. And there cannot ever be such evidence in this case because none of the usual factual parameters have ever been established – for example, dosage, mode of administration, physical characteristics of person, precise make-up of the drug, time of ingestion, half-life of the drug, and so on. I have conferred with, examined and cross-examined toxicologists and never known one prepared to express an opinion in the absence of those sorts of basic factual parameters. In short, the evidence is all unsatisfactorily anecdotal.

A relative of one of the victims spoke at Watson's 2016 parole hearing and quoted a Dr Barbara Fries, who had addressed herself to

---

32. Watson, *Will You Die For Me?*, pp. 137 and 145. There was also a somewhat cryptic reference to the effects of speed at p.140, which I confess I do not understand.

the Watson drug issue in a report: *"It is not defensible to say Charles Watson was influenced immediately or chronically changed by LSD or speed. No drug has ever produced a sustained psychotic state that would cause a person to carry out organized activity as in these murders with regard to the planning, the targeting, murdering, painting messages in blood, wiping out the crime scene free of fingerprints, not to mention escaping capture and hiding from authorities"*[33].

Perhaps the final word should go to Family member Linda Kasabian who saw Watson in action during the Tate murders and testified that he appeared calm, clear headed and not hallucinating.

Several Family members have blamed drugs as an antecedent cause of the killings. Leslie Van Houten (Lulu) has referred to the cumulative effect of LSD ingestion. Bruce Davis has said he was *"sure that drugs lubricated the way"*[34]. In reply to a parole board member's question about whether he was under the influence of drugs during any of the murders Davis said: *"I would say residually as psychedelic drugs and other drugs have an accumulative effect on your psych, on mine yes"*[35]. This was argued by the defendants at the first Tate/LaBianca trial. The argument was, even if they weren't stoned, nevertheless the residual effects of the LSD would have been operative. But this was rebutted by expert evidence to the effect that regular users of LSD build up a tolerance so that repeated use does not create a cumulative effect at all. Instead, the regular user will progressively become less vulnerable to the drug's effects. Furthermore, LSD is not generally associated with violent behaviour.

That said, LSD may have been an indirect factor in a different way. Arguably, it was a pre-condition to Manson's ability to manipulate Family members. It would seem impossible to rule out the role of drugs, in particular LSD, in facilitating the almost super-natural hold that Manson had over his followers.

There are also theories floating around to the effect that the victims of the Tate/LaBianca killings and the murderers were involved

---

33. Parole hearing, 27 October 2016.
34. Parole hearing, 4 October 2012.
35. Ibid.

together in some sort of drug conspiracy. I have communicated with several of the propagators of these theories and have asked them to supply evidence but none has been forthcoming. Plenty of theories, innuendos, speculations, but no evidence. I was told the "*connections*" (presumably between victims and killers) would "*rock my socks off*". But my socks are still on and I have not come across any evidence for drug crime in my other research.

As already touched upon, the one drug deal about which much is known was the deal on 1 July. This will be discussed in more detail in the following chapter. Suffice to say at this stage, the Family engaged a person who was a well-known drug dealer by the name of Crowe to put up the money. I cannot find anywhere any evidence that the Family itself put up amounts of money for drug business, or indeed manufactured or sold drugs itself. There were no drug manufacturing laboratories or equipment at the Spahn Ranch. It appears the drug activity was confined to purchasing, and probably never in the sorts of quantities which would bespeak commercial activity, but would rather suggest personal consumption. And indeed the deal on 1 July was not a deal designed to secure money or drugs for further drug business – it was in fact a burn aimed at stealing money from a known drug dealer for a purpose (Helter Skelter) far removed from drug business.

I cannot presently recall even seeing any statements to support the drug allegations, let alone anyone being cross-examined on statements. I read many thousands of pages of transcripts in my research and found barely a single word from any witness referable to drug business in relation to any of the murders. It would be expected it would have been one of the first things said by the defendants in the overall circumstances of these murders and trials if there was any truth in it. There were none of the other usual evidentiary accoutrements of drug crime – no admissions, no witnesses, no payments, no money trails, no agreed amounts or costs, no high electricity costs or meter bypassing, no drug trade paraphernalia such as drug labs. There were quantities of the drug MDA found in the blood of two of the victims, Folger and Frykowski, but nowhere near such quantities that would suggest drug business warranting (five) wild murders (the Tate killings), nor indeed even suggestive of those persons being drug intoxicated. I am driven to conclude the drug conspiracy theories ought to be discarded as false distractions that take the focus away from the real issues.

The drug theories and rumours about the victims actually surfaced soon after the murders, with Roman Polanski feeling compelled to issue a media statement of denial in late 1969. It was regrettable that the media's treatment of the case drove Polanski to feel so compelled. It is unhelpful, to put it mildly, that rumours to the same effect continue to bubble away to this day. Without the production of some good evidence after 47 years, they ought not be taken seriously. They can only offend the families of the victims who must endure their deceased relatives being slandered by fringe element conspiracy theories. Needless to say, Mansonites gladly jump on the bandwagon of this drug speculation because it tends to demonise the victims and correspondingly mitigate the criminality of the convicted murderers, in particular Charles Manson.

Health

The lifestyle and conditions at the Spahn Ranch were not conducive to good health. Hygiene was "*poor*" to non-existent[36]. There were chronic skin infections and other problems. During a raid on the Ranch on 16 August 1969, police found a dish of fecal matter in an icebox in the Ranch trailer (caravan).

Smith and Rose wrote:

> "*Communicable diseases ranging from upper respiratory problems to gonorrhoea are rampant. Hepatitis and food poisoning also occur with great frequency*"[37]

---

36. Bruce Davis, Parole hearing 6 September 2007, citing an earlier 2005 Parole Consideration Hearing report giving Davis' description of conditions at the Ranch.

37. David E. Smith and Alan J. Rose (1970) *The Group Marriage Commune: A Case Study, Journal of Psychoactive Drugs*, 3:1, 115-119, DOI:10.1080/02791072.1970.10471368., p.118.

Professor Karlene Faith has contended that many of the Family members were hypoglycaemic, based upon numerous accounts of candy bar consumption. This might be right, although unprovable. Faith also referred to a number of features of Family life which would have been detrimental to sound judgment making – poor diet, erratic sleep patterns, giving sex on demand, coping with sexually transmitted diseases, drugs and isolation[38]. It would be hard to disagree with this, although impossible to quantify.

There were also numerous physical injuries resulting from violent assaults perpetrated by Manson, considered in more detail in due course. It seems that no medical treatment was sought for these injuries.

There were mental health issues. Later assessment of this in the cases of the accused killers would be prevented by Manson forbidding psychiatric examination and forbidding the running of psychiatric defences. However, enough would be said, and is now known, to state that the mental health of at least the killers was questionable, to say the least.

There were at least three childbirths, two of which were apparently without medical intervention. Despite the rhetoric about the paramountcy of the children, their health was poor. The babies were described as suffering from severe sunburn and malnutrition when the Family was eventually rounded up in October 1969. Linda Kasabian would later testify the children were not well looked after and methods used to stop them crying included forcefully covering their mouth by hand or blocking their noses until they stopped.

Misogyny

Manson believed women were born to serve men. Paradoxically, the female Family members supported Manson's misogyny. Susan Atkins would later testify before a Grand Jury that it *"was up to us girls . . . to*

---

38. Faith, *The Long Prison Journey of Leslie Van Houten*, p.17.

take care of our men" and *"Charlie is the only man I have ever met . . . that is a complete man. He will not take any back talk from a woman. He will not let a woman talk him into doing anything. He is a man".*

Brooks Poston would later tell Inyo County Sheriff Don Ward:

> *"One of Charlie's basic creeds, is that all girls are for, is to fuck, or make love. And, that's all they're for, and that's — there's no crime, there's no sin, that everything's alright. . . 'Cause God put woman there to take care of man, and that's all woman was supposed to do. Take care of him and tend to his wants at all times. And she wasn't supposed to give any opinions or talk to the man or say anything"*[39]

Gregg Jakobson would testify that Manson had explained the function of a woman was to have babies and serve men.

Violence

Violence was a constant feature of Family life. Because Manson and his supporters have proclaimed life at Spahn Ranch was a love-in, with one writer recently describing Manson as a non-assaultive type of guy[40], it is necessary to set out some of the accounts of violence.

Patricia Krenwinkel would later recall: *"I remember when I laughed at him once and he jerked me by the hair and said 'You won't ever laugh at me again'. And then I started watching him beat Mary [Brunner] . . . and threatening to do that to anyone who ever had a problem with him"*[41].

Stephanie Schram testified about a beating inflicted by Manson with the butt of a rifle severe enough to knock her to the ground.

Linda Kasabian would later testify that she saw Manson strike Dianne Lake several times. Ignoring the instruction to never ask

---

39. Transcript of interview, 3 October 1969, by courtesy of Los Angeles District Attorney's office ("LADA").

40. Stimson, G., *Goodbye Helter Skelter,* The Peasenhall Press, 2014.

41. Parole hearing, 7 July 2004.

"*why?*", Kasabian asked Catherine Share who said Lake had wanted to be beaten and Manson was merely obliging her. Lake was only 16 years old. Lake herself would testify: "*when I was about 20 minutes into a trip Charlie got up and slugged me in the mouth . . .*". And "*Charlie hit me with a chair leg and kicked and whipped me with a cord*".

Share's explanation of the assault on Lake became a standard retort by Family members, on behalf of Manson, to accusations of his violence. One of Manson's chief lieutenants, Sandra Good, would later testify about a beating inflicted on Stephanie Schram:

> "*Well, once she provoked Charlie into hitting her, and he hit her, and she came running up to the girls and said 'Ah, he finally hit me; I finally got some attention' and she was very pleased. . . She was gleeful, like a little kid, for getting attention from her daddy for doing something she thought was wrong . . . she was gleeful about it. 'Guess what he finally hit me!'*"

Paul Watkins would later write about an assault upon Susan Atkins. After an exchange between Atkins and Manson at the dinner table (about the quality of a salad dressing prepared by Atkins):

> "*[Manson] grabbed her by the arm and started slapping her. 'I don't listen to that kind of talk. You can just take that shit on down the road. Dig what I'm saying!'.*
>
> *[Atkins] cried out . . . [and] grappled with Charlie until he pinned her arms against the side of the bar 'I'll break your goddam fingers off! Let go, dammit!'.*
>
> *'Stop it Charlie . . . stop it!' Her breathing came in short gasps.*
>
> *Finally he forced her to the floor, bending her fingers back against her hand. She groaned, but he wouldn't let go . . .*"[42]

---

42. Watkins, *My Life With Charles Manson*, p.70.

Watkins also recalled an assault upon Nancy Pitman during a music session. Charlie demanded she sing. Pitman asked what she should sing. Manson tugged her hair and she said *"Ahhhh"*, apparently in pain. Manson said: *"That's a sound . . . now try something else"* and he yanked her hair again. She then sang[43]. Watkins also recalled *"many such outbursts from Charlie – sometimes verbal, sometimes physical . ."*. Watkins later said Manson taught them to submit to his violence because resistance meant they had not surrendered their egos[44].

Brooks Poston would later testify: *". . . after I saw [Manson] knock down a couple of girls, it became pretty well evident that if he wanted them to do something that he wanted it done"*.

There are more accounts of Manson's violence in various books and transcripts. Most of it seems to have occurred during 1969. It escalated during the summer. On 6 June, Manson *"beat the shit out of"* Ranch hand Randy Starr in front of Gregg Jakobson and music producer Terry Melcher[45]. On 1 July, rather than repay a Family drug debt, Manson opted to shoot the creditor, causing serious injuries. On 27 July, he violently attacked an acquaintance of the Family, Gary Hinman, with a sword. On about 30 August, he led other Family members in stabbing Ranch hand, Donald Shea, to death. All of these crimes will be examined in later chapters.

Prosecutor Vincent Bugliosi would later write that he struggled to find a sustained history of violence in Manson's background[46]. But this was in a part of his book ostensibly devoted to the state of his investigations by November 1969. At that stage, little or none of the violence at Spahn Ranch would have been documented.

---

43. Ibid, p.158.

44. Ibid, p. 71.

45. Gregg Jakobson, quoted in Dalton D., Felton, D., "Year of the Fork, Night of the Hunter", *Rolling Stone,* no.61, 25 June 1970, p.40.

46. Bugliosi, *Helter Skelter,* p. 203.

Isolation

Manson forbade Family members discussing their pasts and generally ordained that they sever, or vacate, their past lives. This was part of the reason for the name changes according to Susan Atkins, who would later testify: "*In order for me to be completely free in my mind I had to be able to completely forget the past. The easiest way to do this is to . . . change identity by doing so with a name [change] . . ."*[47]. Patricia Krenwinkel would later recall: "*No one was allowed to have their old name because their old name belonged to the past*"[48].

The women were forbidden from carrying cash. Birthdays were given up. Wrist watches were forbidden. Calendars and books were banned. Contact with biological families was forbidden unless it was to request money for the Family.

Juan Flynn would later testify that Manson explained he had to remove the programming forced upon Family members by their (biological) families, schools and churches. Manson told Flynn that to rid one's self of ego you had to give up your parents and just blank yourself out.

Charles "Tex" Watson would later testify: "*There was no wrong. Everything was perfect . . . there was no mistake . . . there was no thought of any wrong at all. There was no thought in our heads. All the thought was gone*".

Leslie Van Houten spoke at some length at her 2016 parole hearing about the attraction of having someone else do her thinking for her. And Catherine Share would later recall:

> "*[Charlie would] say 'thinking is stinking, don't think any more, be like a little child, be like me'. If you even wanted to question or talk about anything you couldn't do it 'cos you weren't supposed to think*"[49]

---

47. Evidence to Grand Jury 5 December 1969.
48. Parole hearing 17 July 1978.
49. *Most Evil: Charles Manson*, Discovery Channel, 2006.

Share has also said:

> *"When you isolate someone or a group of people and there's no newspapers, there's no television, there's no parents, no family, [the leader] becomes, you know, the newscaster, the prophet, the father, mother, everything. I thought [Manson] had a clear line to God and God spoke through him"*[50]

This topic is, however, not without complication. Despite Share's statement, there was access to a television. After the Tate murders, Family members gathered around to watch the news – of what they had done.

Another question is the extent to which Family members were locked in to staying. Some claim they were virtually imprisoned at the Ranch. But others came and went. It appears the men had more freedom to do as they pleased. They were able to carry cash. They had no baby caring responsibilities. The mothers of the babies would have found it impossible to get away. When Mary Brunner tried to leave with her child, she was beaten badly[51]. One of Stephane Schram's beatings also resulted from expressing a desire to leave. Susan Atkins was warned that if she tried to leave she'd be hung upside down and have her throat slit as an example to everyone else[52].

Manson wasn't the only enforcer. Tex Watson joined in. Linda Kasabian would later testify that Cathy Gillies had once absconded from the Ranch to the beach *"and she came back in the afternoon . . . Tex was there and he told her if she ever left again to ask first and he said something like her life meant nothing to him"* and next time he would kill her[53].

---

50. Ibid.

51. Atkins-Whitehouse, *The Myth of Helter Skelter*, p.12.

52. Record of interview with attorneys Caballero and Caruso, 1 December 1969, sourced from www.cielodrive.com.

53. Kasabian's testimony at Tex Watson's trial in 1971.

Charlie's Death Trip

By many accounts, Manson was obsessed with the subject of death. For Charlie, there actually was no death, death was love and death was just a "change". He also repeatedly sought pledges from Family members about death: *"will you die for me?"*[54].

Watson would later recall Manson's death games:

> *"Sometimes Charlie would gather us all together . . . and have us imagine a rich piggie [member of the white establishment] sitting in a chair in the middle of the circle we'd form. 'Imagine we just yanked this pig out of his big car and stuck him here', Charlie would instruct us . . . we'd usually drop acid, and after a while Charlie got in the habit of quietly talking about things that might happen, things that could be done to this imaginary piggie – things like tying him up, stabbing him, going into his house and murdering all his family and getting all his money, or frightening him into willing everything he had to us and then killing him. We'd all follow Charlie's lead and imagine the butchery and the terror, and even though it was all just a game, the images stayed locked in our brains after the game was over"* [55]

Killing was not just the subject of games. It was also part of the study curriculum. Stephanie Schram described to Sheriff's Officers William Gleason and George Palmer what has come to be referred to as Manson's "murder school":

> *"Schram: [Charlie] gave us a lesson on how to stab people and – He said . . . we'll take them and we'll, we'll chop them up and we'll have to learn how to, how to put their*

---

54. Patricia Krenwinkel interview with Dianne Sawyer, *A Turning Point*, ABC TV, 1994.
55. Watson, *Will You Die For Me?*, pp. 121 to 122.

> bodies in places where people aren't going to see them
> and how, and he said that, you know, he asked if
> everybody could do it.
>
> . . .
>
> Palmer: Well, what did Charlie say about this — how to kill
>   people? Did he —
> Schram: Well, he acted, he looked at me and he said 'Are you okay,
>   you can do it?' . . . I said 'If it really came upon me to
>   kill somebody I wouldn't know how' you know and he says
>   'Well you have to' you know and he showed me gotta get
>   them from here to here [sic].
> Palmer: Well how did he show you? . . .
> Schram: He had a knife and he said, and he used me for a
>   demonstration . . . [he said] 'if you're going to cut them
>   from their neck cut them from one side to the other' and
>   if you stick the knife inside be sure to wiggle it around so
>   you can get a lot of —
> Palmer: Yeah, get a lot as much as you can. Did he ever say just
>   sticking it straight into him in the neck. Did he show you
>   the different areas —
> Schram: No, but he said 'Stick it straight into their ear, or in their
>   eyes if you can . . ."[56]

Barbara Hoyt would later recall that Tex Watson took some of the
murder classes:

> "He demonstrated how to stab a person. He told us 'don't just
> stick the knife in and out'. He said 'bring it up when you
> cut someone so that you cut up more stuff', and he made us
> practice"[57]

---

56. Record of interview dated 4 December 1969, courtesy of LADA.
57. *The Manson Women*, Biography Series, Entertainment Channel.

Paul Watkins would later testify Charlie was always preaching love, but he really had no idea what it was, and *"death is Charlie's trip, it really is"*.

The Failed Record Deal

As mentioned, Manson learned guitar in prison. He also wrote songs. There were differing views of his talent. During 1968 and 1969 he tried to secure a recording contract. Gregg Jakobson evidently thought Manson had something to offer and arranged auditions with record producer Terry Melcher who had worked with the Byrds and other big name acts[58]. The auditions were unsuccessful. It appears Manson wasn't told anything specifically, but rather it was left on a *"don't call me, I'll call you"* basis.

Melcher, Jakobson and Dennis Wilson were close acquaintances. Manson hung around with all three during 1968 and 1969. In 1968, the Beach Boys recorded one of Manson's songs, *Cease to Exist*, but changed the title and some of the lyrics. They did not credit Manson. Dennis Wilson was credited as the song writer. But the song was not successful. The information about this is vague but by some accounts Manson was ropable about his song being plundered, which was understandable. The failure of his auditions, and the loss of his song, are said to have fuelled Manson's anti-establishment anger which, as will be seen, was well on the rise in any event during 1969.

Philosophy

Manson's philosophies found expression in a series of oxymora: *"no sense makes sense"* . . . *"we are all one"* . . . *"you are me and I am you"* . . . *"what's yours is mine and mine is yours"* . . . *"there is no bad, everything is good"* . . . *"death is unimportant, it is only a change"* . . . *"there is no right or wrong, everything is all right"* . . . *"killing is*

58. Melcher was the son of movie star Doris Day.

all right". The philosophies called for an abdication of the moral distinctions that usually sanction human beings against harmful undertakings. They were, in effect, a call to a variety of criminal activities.

One of Manson's philosophies was that of "the now"[59]. He eschewed concepts of time, past and future. Witnesses would later testify that Helter Skelter was meant to happen "now" or *"any minute"*[60]. Killing people was bringing them to "the now". Catherine Share would later suggest that "the now" helped precipitate the murders in July and August 1969. Manson could not afford any more delay in his "now" race war apocalypse lest he lose his Messianic credibility with the group. Share would later say:

> *". . . if you tell people for three straight years everyone's going to go crazy. And they go to town and people are . . . going to the movies, and going to the beach, and having fun, and it's still not happening, if you're wrong about that, maybe you're wrong about everything else"*[61]

Charlie had other philosophies too. He certainly wasn't a one dimensional guru. But much of it was puerile gibberish. For example, Brooks Poston told Inyo County police:

> *"And I heard [Manson] comment once, that wouldn't it be nice if . . . we could just stay in bed forever and make love. And not to have to worry about eating. Because eating wasn't important. It was only a way to get out your sexual interests, like smoking cigarettes. And he said that everything stemmed from sex . . . everything was vaginal, or, or penial. And that it all stemmed from sex. Everything you did was make*

59. The "now" is said to have been a common youth philosophy of the 1960's. It certainly became one of Charlie's favourites.
60. Testimony of Gregg Jakobson.
61. *Most Evil: Charles Manson*, Discovery Channel, 2006.

love. From putting, uh, a screw into a, into a fixture. From putting a cigarette into your mouth. From drinking a coffee, to opening a door, to getting in a car, to sweeping. Anything you did was sex – from his viewpoint. And he was, telling everyone there, that is what it stemmed from – that, that's all it was. Everything was making love, and that is what God really wanted you to do, because that's why he gave men a nutsack and a peter, and girls, a pussy – as he puts it" [62]

It seems incredible that this was the man whom the Family members saw as the diviner of "the truth" and "*more than anything else he was the only one that any of us ever felt that he knew what he was doing*"[63].

It may have been that only select people were exposed to the juvenile vulgarities.   Poston was a teenager.   Manson varied his language depending upon whom he was talking to:

"Charlie talked to whoever he was talking to in the way that they would believe him. So if he was talking to hippies he'd talk one way. If he was talking to motor cycle guys he'd talk another way. He could just reflect whatever he draws out of people. Whatever he knows that they will agree with" [64]

Helter Skelter

In late 1968, the Beatles released a self-titled double album that came to be known as the White Album. This album seems to have flicked a switch in Manson's moody and capricious mind. He interpreted lyrics in the White Album songs as messages, sent across the Atlantic by the Beatles, that a war or revolution was imminent. One of the songs was "Helter Skelter". Manson interpreted "Helter Skelter" and other White Album tracks as signalling an uprising by

---

62. Interview with Sheriff Don Ward, 3 October 1969, courtesy LADA.
63. Leslie Van Houten, interviewed by Barbara Walters, ABC TV, January 1977, unedited version.
64. *Most Evil: Charles Manson,* Discovery Channel, 2006.

black people ("Blackie") against "Whitie". Specifically, according to testimony of Paul Watkins and others, Manson predicted that in summer 1969 there would be atrocious murders committed by black people who would come into the affluent Bel-Air and Beverley Hills districts and wipe out white people ("pigs" – a term coined by militant black political group, the Black Panthers, to describe white people). The blacks would cut bodies up and smear blood and write things on the walls in blood. These atrocious crimes would make Whitie mad. Manson said this would precipitate a retaliation by the whites who would shoot black people like crazy. But the end result would be a take-over of power by Blackie. But Blackie would not know what to do when he took over power. Manson had a plan for the Family to hide out the war underground in a bottomless pit in the desert, then arise upon Blackie's overthrow of Whitie, and then the Family would take over power from Blackie.

The Helter Skelter preaching started in earnest in early 1969. But by mid-summer, Blackie had not started the war. Charlie was becoming impatient. Time was becoming of the essence. Watkins would later testify: *"one day we was sitting around on acid and Charlie said that blackie never did anything on his own so somebody was going to have to show him how to start Helter Skelter"*. Manson declared he had to bring Helter Skelter down, the implication being he would have to start killing affluent white people and making it appear the crimes had been committed by black people.

At first blush, Helter Skelter sounds so bizarre that it could well be construed as a joke. Privately at least, Bruce Davis was sceptical. He would later tell a parole hearing he thought it was *"crazy"* and *"didn't make a lick of sense"*[65]. However, at another Parole hearing, Davis was not as dismissive:

> *"The fact that there was going to be a race war in a certain way connected itself to the Watts riots, to the riots in Chicago*

---

65. Parole hearing, 15 September 2008.

about the same time, the assassination of Martin Luther King, Bobby Kennedy, the race wars in Newark, New Jersey. There was just a lot of unrest. And so his proposal about a big race war was not a complete jump from nothing. I mean it had what felt like at least, some kind of basis" [66]

Tex Watson bought into Helter Skelter totally and testified at his own trial that it was talked about *"[E]very night and all day long . . . That's all that was talked about during this whole period of time"*.

Paul Watkins would also testify that he took Helter Skelter seriously. Brooks Poston would testify: *"[A]t first it seemed pretty far out to me but then after a while it started making more and more sense because . . . you could go out on the street and I could see people were up tight, and a lot of people were tense. . . . I never thought [the bottomless pit] really existed but I was going for it because it sounded like a good place to get away from everything"*.

To the extent there was ambivalence about Helter Skelter amongst the men, it was easy to let pass in exchange for the pleasant lifestyle on offer – drugs, sex, dune buggies and guns to play with and women to serve the men's whims. Davis would later explain to the Parole Board:

"Dep Comm. Alvord: *So what the Family gave you . . . was a significant amount of sex that you didn't have to work for readily available*
Davis: *That's right . . . That's why I was there"* [67]

And at another Parole hearing:

"Presiding Comm. Labahn: . . . when you were getting [Helter Skelter] from him did you then believe that by extension if you weren't the second to last man standing you'd

---

66. Parole hearing, 27 August 2015.
67. Parole hearing, 4 October 2012.

be one of the last guys standing or was it the other benefits
that were occurring to you at the time that kept you involved?
Davis: Well, the other benefits were the main thing for me"[68]

There was only a seemingly inconsequential price to pay for the benefits – go along with Helter Skelter.

As for the women, it will be seen they were all absolute disciples of Manson's Helter Skelter. In all of the contemporaneous material, including interviews with lawyers, Susan Atkins and Leslie Van Houten exclaimed their devotion to Charlie's revolution. The most emphatic indicator of Helter Skelter's spell over the girls was that Patricia Krenwinkel (Katie) wrote it in blood on a refrigerator door at one of the murder scenes. She also wrote other words on the walls – "arise" and "death to pigs" which came directly from Manson's Helter Skelter lexicon. And "WAR" was carved into the skin of a victim's stomach.

Leslie Van Houten would later recall that Helter Skelter *"was supposed to cleanse the whole world and I honestly believed that"*[69]. It has been said in a quasi-biography that Van Houten, and also Atkins and Krenwinkel, were so inculcated with Helter Skelter that later, in prison, they literally had to be de-programmed away from it[70]. The author, Professor Karlene Faith, was speaking from her personal experience as a researcher who worked with the three women at the behest of the governor of the California Institute for Women after their convictions. Academics and instructors were brought in to impart to the girls *"new perspectives on politics, culture, history, the arts, philosophy, economics, human relations, and gender issues"*. Faith's description of this work was a powerful illustration of how much the girls must have truly believed in Helter Skelter, and how massively detached from reality they had become:

"Some [of the teachers] engaged the women in debates that
shed critical light on some of the errors in Manson's thinking.

68. Parole hearing, 27 August 2015.
69. Interview with Barbara Walters, ABC TV, January 1977, unedited version.
70. Faith, *The Long Prison Journey of Leslie Van Houten*, pp.22, 23 and 75.

For example, Manson believed that killing white people and blaming the deaths on black people would cause an uprising in which blacks would gain dominion over whites. Their teacher pointed out the likely futility of a race war in the USA, given the numerical disadvantage of blacks against whites, and given the military force at the white government's disposal. More complicated was reckoning with the racism inherent in the idea of white people starting a race war on behalf of African Americans, the flaws in strategies based on the means justifying the end, and the sexism inherent to Manson's methods. Politically minded tutors placed Manson's thinking in context, bringing it from the realm of the remote revolution to the immediate challenges facing people in their day-to-day lives"[71]

Susan Atkins would later confirm this de-programming in a passage of her first book which was clearly referable to the work of Faith and others in late 1972:

". . . [Pat and Leslie] were revealing signs of easing into thought patterns and mannerisms of individuals, not cultish, family drones. Change was coming in them, ever so slowly . . . [O] ne night I even heard them discussing the possibility that 'helter skelter is not coming down after all'"[72]

This was a whole three years after the murders and arrests, and they were only just beginning to discuss the *"possibility"* that Helter Skelter actually might not happen. These matters arose independently of the criminal litigation in 1970/71 which suggests the women's reactions and words were genuine. It seems an understatement to say these women had been brainwashed by Manson.

---

71. Ibid, pp.22 to 23.

72. Atkins, S., with Slosser, R., *Child of Satan, Child of God*, Menelorelin Doray's Publishing, 1977, p.186.

Linda Kasabian would later testify that she believed in Helter Skelter and the Family would survive in a bottomless pit in the desert and *"it was always being mentioned everyday"*. Kasabian was a reliably truthful witness. Her testimony was another powerful indication of the intensity of Manson's Helter Skelter spell.

Outsiders were also exposed to Helter Skelter. Gregg Jakobson would later testify the White Album was Manson's *"scripture"*. And Dennis Wilson heard all about Helter Skelter from Manson, although Wilson struggled to comprehend it:

> *"Dennis wasn't all that given to recondite philosophical questions. He couldn't remember too clearly what Charlie read into [the White Album] but he could convey the general drift. 'Piggies' was about the cops. 'And, y'know, uptight straight people'.*
>
> *'Yeah, Dennis, I get that. But what is the <u>message</u>, man?'*
>
> *'Fuck if I know. Death to the Pigs. End of the world'"* [73]

It seems nobody who came into contact with Manson was immune from his Helter Skelter preaching. Even in a brief meeting with Stephanie Schram's sister on 7 August 1969, she was given the Helter Skelter treatment[74]. Two *Rolling Stone* reporters were also given an ear-full of it when they interviewed Charlie in early 1970[75]. Charlie even warned arresting police officers about it when arrested in October 1969 (discussed in more detail in a later chapter).

As to whether Manson himself genuinely believed what he preached, reasonable minds might differ. Paul Watkins would later testify Manson appeared serious about Helter Skelter. Gregg Jakobson testified that Manson *"firmly believed [Helter Skelter] was going to happen"*. Jakobson was a relatively mature and intelligent individual

---

73. Dalton, D., *If Christ Came Back as a Con Man*, Gadfly, October 1998.

74. Bugliosi, *Helter Skelter*, p. 368.

75. Dalton D., Felton D., "Year of the Fork, Night of the Hunter, *Rolling Stone*, no. 61, 25 June 1970. The interview took place in March 1970.

who was not a Family member. But caution is required. There is an inherent difficulty with people commenting, and witnesses testifying, about what is inside another person's mind[76]. And Manson, of all people, was someone whose head was hard to get into.

Prosecutor Bugliosi weighed in with his reflections about Manson's belief in Helter Skelter in an interview in 1976:

> *"I cannot conceive of [Manson] believing some of the things he preached about, such as the bottomless pit, the Family growing to 144,000 people, and himself becoming leader of the world. Oh, he was a megalomaniac and would've loved to become leader of the world, but I find it difficult to think he believed those mass murders would actually start a worldwide race war between blacks and whites. My guess is that he used Helter Skelter as a vehicle to work his followers into such a lather that they were going to kill for him. Whether he believed it, I have to guess no"* [77]

I shall return to the vexed question of Manson's true beliefs in due course. Whatever <u>he</u> may have believed, there was no doubt the Family members, especially those that would kill, intensely believed in the prophecy.

Transition to a War Footing

Whatever the extent of Manson's belief in Helter Skelter, one thing was certain – he loved war. He has always loved everything about it – guns, knives, death, fear, soldiers going to war. In most every public utterance he talks war.

One consequence of the impending war was that more money was needed to fund the weapons and other things such as dune buggies

---

76. It is generally inadmissible evidence, though there would be conceivable exceptional bases for its admission in this case.

77. *Penthouse* magazine, Vol. 7, No. 10, June 1976.

to facilitate the move to the desert. No-one had any legitimate employment and money raising was always going to involve some sort of criminal activity. Between January and August 1969, the Family accumulated a large cache of guns and knives. Plans were made for the Family to move to the desert to wait out Helter Skelter. Searching for the bottomless pit began.

There are numerous references to the Family's transition around this time to something akin to a war footing. Bruce Davis said at a Parole Hearing: *"[A]fter [spring 1969] the conversation had turned from peace and love to hatred and violence"*[78] and *". . . it was clear that a race war was on the agenda of the Family"*[79]. At another parole hearing, Davis said: *"[About spring 1969] . . . the scenario had changed to peace and love to Helter Skelter . . . we've got to be armed and there's going to be a race war, etcetera. And so I wanted to be like the rest of the guys and so I bought a pistol"*[sic][80].

Gregg Jakobson would later testify about a change in Manson himself:

> *". . . the change was like part of a pattern that began in the spring of '69 and became more and more agitated and radical until the last time I saw him . . . the only thing I can compare it to is I have seen cats that have been caught in cages, like bobcats and things . . . [T]he electricity was almost pouring out of him. His hair was on end. His eyes were wild. He was like an animal that moved just like an animal that was in a cage"*

Some Family members, such as Paul Watkins, disliked the growing bellicosity and departed. Later, as the violence unfolded, some of the girls such as Hoyt, Schram and Lutesinger left too. Immediately after the Hinman murder in late July 1969, long term member Ella Jo Bailey left[81].

---

78. Parole Hearing, 4 October 2012.
79. Ibid.
80. Parole hearing, 27 August 2015.
81. Atkins, *Child of Satan, Child of God*, p.130.

CHAPTER 2: THE BERNARD CROWE SHOOTING

"I could kill everyone without blinking an eye"

Charles Manson to Vincent Bugliosi, in
discussion about the Crowe shooting[82]

Drug Burn

By mid-1969, money was short for the desert move. One fund raising project involved a drug burn. On 1 July, Tex Watson and ex-girlfriend Rosina Kroner (aka Luella) went with a drug dealer named Bernard Crowe to score drugs, with Crowe putting up the $2,400 purchase price. Crowe gave the money to Watson to go into the apartment where the deal was supposed to take place. Crowe kept Rosina as security for Watson's return with the drugs. But instead of returning, Watson fled out the back door with the money into a car driven by Family member T.J. Walleman. The pair drove off to the Ranch leaving Crowe without money or drugs, but still holding Rosina.

Upon realising he had been burned, Crowe rang Spahn Ranch and told Manson he wanted his money back or he intended to visit violent retribution upon the Family, and also a presumably frightened

---

82. Bugliosi, *Helter Skelter,* p.497.

Rosina[83].   Manson placated Crowe and arranged to visit him to
sort things out.   This Manson did – armed with a gun.   Walleman
accompanied Manson.   There was a plan.   Manson would carry
the gun behind his back, secured in the back of his trousers.   On a
pre-arranged signal, Walleman was to pull the gun out from behind
Manson.   But Walleman didn't really want anything to do with killing
people.   He vacillated.   After some verbal jousting between Manson
and Crowe, Manson himself pulled the gun and said "*I came prepared*".
Manson shot Crowe in the stomach.   Crowe collapsed to the ground.
Manson and Walleman departed, assuming he was dead.   (As it
transpired, in fact Crowe was still alive and would later testify about
this incident at the first Tate/LaBianca trial).

Little else is known about Rosina.   It seems any lingering hopes of
a reconciliation with Watson had been dashed.   He would later write:

> "*The fact that I was badly 'burning' a woman I'd once loved
> never really sank in – it was for Charlie and for Helter
> Skelter – and besides, there was no right or wrong anyway,
> only what had to be*"[84]

Manson's Argument

This shooting was never the subject of police charges, much less a
trial.   Through various media, Manson has claimed the drug burn was
Watson's mess, and that he shot Crowe in order to help out Watson.
And, so the argument goes, the shooting can be explained by some
sort of honourable pact within the Family whereby there was nothing
Family members would not do for each other.   It sounds like a code of
honour from the wild west, or a pact between soldiers in a war.   It is a
recurring theme of Manson's rhetoric that his crimes were motivated
by his honourable desire to help out his brothers and sisters.   But what

---

83. It may have been Rosina who placed the call and conveyed Crowe's threat. In any event, there is no doubt the threat was conveyed.
84. Watson, *Will You Die For Me?*, p. 128.

is puzzling about this incident is why Manson figured that the way to help out Tex was to visit Crowe armed with a gun and a specific plan about using it. He has sought to explain this on the basis that Rosina's life was in danger and they might have to shoot to save her. However, at the risk of sounding naïve, why didn't Manson just give the money back? Manson says Watson had already spent the money on a dune buggy[85]. But this can't be right. Crowe's phone call was placed immediately he realised he had been burned. When Manson received the call, Watson had only just got back to the Ranch and was still showing off his newly acquired wealth[86]. It is difficult to believe Watson had time to buy a dune buggy. Manson has to be lying.

Furthermore, according to Vincent Bugliosi, Manson admitted the reason for shooting Crowe whilst "rapping" during the jury empanelment in the first Tate/LaBianca trial. Manson conceded to Bugliosi that he shot Crowe and then volunteered: *"[Crowe] was going to come up to Spahn Ranch and get all of us . . . [it] was kinda in self defense"*[87]. If Bugliosi's account of the conversation was true, as it probably was, then it was beyond doubt the reason for shooting Crowe was to pre-empt Crowe's threat to the Family whilst keeping the money, rather than some sort of honourable pact to help out brother Tex (nothing of which, incidentally, was said by Manson to Bugliosi), much less an act of chivalry to save Rosina. Although Tex would be a beneficiary of Manson's violence, Manson didn't do it for Tex at all. However, as will be seen, this did not prevent Manson from falsely advertising to Tex and the Family that he had taken action to protect them, and that they were in his debt.

---

85. Stimson, *Goodbye Helter Skelter*, p.126.
86. Watson, *Will You Die For Me?*, pp. 128 to 129. And Watson says nothing about buying a dune buggy.
87. Bugliosi, *Helter Skelter*, p.407.

CHAPTER 3: THE GARY HINMAN MURDER

"We had a friend over in Topanga Canyon . . . who had been kind to us in the last year. He had helped Mary with food and other things for her baby. His name was Gary Hinman. He was . . . a very gentle spirit, a kind man, who practiced transcendental meditation"

Susan Atkins[88]

"he's a pig, he's gotta go. He's just like society . . . so let's get rid of him. First, let's get his money"

Charles Manson and Bobby Beausoleil discuss their plans for Gary Hinman[89]

Hinman's Body is Found

On 31 July 1969, Los Angeles Sheriff's Office ("LASO") officers arrived at the home of Gary Hinman at Topanga Canyon. Hinman was 34 years old, a music teacher and a devout Buddhist. He was Caucasian. He was not a member of the Family, but he knew them and they had been on good terms.

The officers were responding to a call from Hinman's friends who had been unable to locate him for several days. Hinman was found dead

---

88. Atkins, *Child of Satan, Child of God*, p.119.
89. Danny DeCarlo's statement to police 19 November 1969, sourced from LADA.

on the floor of the living room. Near the body were Buddhist prayer beads known as "jizu". Stabbing and cutting wounds were obvious. The words "political piggy" had been scrawled in blood on a wall, together with a mark comprising a palm print and finger prints which resembled an animal's paw (I will refer to this as "the paw print"). Hinman's friends told the officers that Hinman's two vehicles, a 1965 Fiat car and a Volkswagen bus, were missing. The vehicles were logged as stolen.

Bobby Beausoleil

On 6 August, Bobby Beausoleil was found by police in possession of Hinman's Fiat. Beausoleil was a 21 year old travelling musician. Whether he was actually a member of the Manson Family is unclear, but he certainly associated with Manson. He told police he had acquired the Fiat from a coloured man. He also said he had found Hinman at his house with a cut across the left side of his face and Hinman claimed to have been jumped by Negros. Officers found a bloodied knife in the tyre well of the car. After running an ownership check on the Fiat, Beausoleil was arrested. Beausoleil's fingerprints were found at Hinman's place. Beausoleil was charged with Hinman's murder.

Manson and Atkins Are Charged

The police officers assigned to investigate the Hinman homicide were Sergeants Paul Whiteley and William Guenther. They spoke to Beausoleil's pregnant girlfriend, Katharine Lutesinger, who implicated Manson and 21 year old Susan Atkins. Both Manson and Atkins would be charged with murder.

Atkins initially told police that Hinman had been stabbed in a fight with coloured persons, and she had gone to his house to nurse him[90].

---

90. Davis, I., and LeBlanc, J., *Five to Die*, Thor Publishing, 1st Rev. Edn., 2009, p.162. I have been unable to source the initial police record of interview to verify this. However, Davis and LeBlanc's book is generally accurate and reliable and I have no reason to doubt the accuracy of their report.

Beausoleil's First Trial

On 12 November 1969, the trial of Beausoleil on one count of murder pursuant to section 187 of the California Penal Code ("the Code") commenced.

Deputy Medical Examiner Katsuyama testified that he conducted an autopsy on 1 August 1969. He estimated Hinman had been dead for between three and seven days. It can be safely assumed from Katsuyama's testimony, and other evidence, that Hinman died on Sunday 27 July 1969. Katsuyama found five lacerating or stab wounds, the likely fatal wound being a stab to the chest. There was another wound to the left side of the face extending from the jaw to the ear that was capable of causing death if allowed to bleed out.

Danny DeCarlo testified about a conversation with Beausoleil at the end of July 1969 in which Beausoleil said he had gone to Hinman's house to get money from him. Beausoleil told DeCarlo he had:

"pulled a gun on him and demanded that Gary give him the money he had. He was supposed to have $20,000. And Gary told him to get out of the house 'Take your gun and everybody else and get out'. So then Bobby hit him with a gun, punched him around . . . But Gary still wanted him out of the house . . . So Bobby called up a guy named Charley at the ranch . . . Charley and [Bruce Davis] went up to the house where Bobby was at . . . Charley had a long sword, hit him with the sword, cut his ear off. So he told Gary that, you know, 'You had better conform, or you had better do what you are told' along those words. So then he left. . . . and left Bobby up there again. So he stayed there, I guess, another six or seven hours with Gary, and then he called back Charley – up and said 'Gary isn't cooperating'. So Charley told him 'You know what to do'. So he stuck him with a knife . . . He didn't die right away. It took him awhile. After he was dead, they took the blood and put a

panther paw upon the wall with the words "Political Piggy"
or something along that line" [sic]

The *"panther paw"* was the mark of the militant black political group, the Black Panthers[91].

The jury began its deliberations on 24 November 1969. On 26 November, the jury foreman told Judge Shea an impasse had been reached. A mistrial was declared. Beausoleil remained in custody pending a new trial date.

Beausoleil's Second Trial

Beausoleil's new trial commenced in March 1970. I have been unable to obtain the transcript of this trial. What follows has been assembled from excerpts of available transcript and other sources. Nor have I been able to locate all of the relevant police records of interview.

Danny De Carlo testified for the prosecution again. He repeated his earlier evidence. He also testified that before Hinman's death he overheard a conversation between Manson and Beausoleil in which Hinman was referred to as a *"political pig"* who should die.

Digressing briefly, it is worth noting DeCarlo had given a more florid account of the conversation between Manson and Beausoleil when first interviewed by police back on 19 November 1969: ". . . *they talked about [Hinman] before, as being a Political Piggy. See, a political fuck up. 'Gary's fucked up in his head, he's a pig, he's gotta go. He's just like society, part of society, so let's get rid of him. First let's get his money"*[92]. I am inclined to believe DeCarlo's account of this conversation. DeCarlo was a rough and tumble bikie who loved guns and generally did the sorts of things that bikies do. He was into petty crime. I have read his testimony at the Hinman and Tate/LaBianca trials and, in my opinion, he was a generally truthful and reliable witness. If DeCarlo's

---

91. Some have expressed doubts about this. But it seems clear enough Beausoleil and Manson thought it was a mark of the Panthers, or would at least be seen that way.
92. Record of interview 19 November 1969, courtesy LADA.

account of the Manson/Beausoleil conversation was correct, then the Hinman homicide began to resemble Charlie's blueprint for Helter Skelter (as described by Paul Watkins and set out in the preceding chapter).

More evidence consistent with the Helter Skelter flavour of Hinman's murder would later come from the oral testimony of a number of witnesses (in other trials, notably the first Tate/LaBianca trial) to the effect that, by the beginning of July 1969, Manson was becoming increasingly uneasy about the failure of Blackie to start Helter Skelter. As highlighted in the preceding chapter, Paul Watkins would later testify that Charlie started saying he would have to bring Helter Skelter down on behalf of Blackie. It seems Charlie must have been saying this in Watkins' presence in June, for Watkins had departed the Family by the start of July. Tex Watson would later recall it was June when Charlie started talking about igniting Helter Skelter[93]. And there were even several false starts of Helter Skelter during June[94]. Dianne Lake would also later recall the talk about igniting Helter Skelter starting in June[95]. It can be inferred, safely in my view, that Charlie's plan to ignite Helter Skelter (on Blackie's behalf) was ready for implementation in June, and in any event well before Hinman's murder on 27 July.

That Hinman was a Helter Skelter killing also draws powerful support from the contemporaneous evidence, including Beausoleil's initial claims to police about the involvement of coloured or Negro persons, together with the paw print and the words "political piggy", and Atkins' initial report about the involvement of coloured persons, all of which appears to have been designed to implicate Blackie.

Furthermore, other evidence, which need not be set out here, tends to corroborate DeCarlo at least to the extent there can be confidence

---

93. Watson, *Will You Die For Me?*, p.123.
94. Ibid, pp.123 to 125.
95. Bugliosi, *Helter Skelter*, p.395.

that the plan to kill Hinman was well in train before anyone entered Hinman's house[96].

After DeCarlo, Family member Mary Brunner testified (in exchange for an immunity from prosecution) that she had seen Beausoleil stab Hinman to death.

The jury accepted Brunner's account. Beausoleil was convicted on 23 June 1970 and sentenced to death. An appeal was unsuccessful[97]. The death penalty was abolished while Beausoleil was on death row. He remains incarcerated at the time of writing.

Manson's Indictment and the Law

In the meantime, indictments for Hinman's murder had issued against Manson, Atkins and Bruce Davis. Manson and Davis pleaded not guilty. Atkins would eventually plead guilty.

Before looking at Manson's trial, which commenced in June 1971, it is instructive to consider some of the legal principles. It is difficult to make sense of these events, and ongoing debates, without having some familiarity with the applicable law.

Manson was indicted on two counts:

(i)   Murder of Hinman in violation of section 187 of the Code; and

(ii) Conspiracy to commit robbery and murder in violation of section 182.1 of the Code.

As to count (i), murder was defined by section 187 as the unlawful killing of a human being, with malice aforethought. Thus, the essential elements of murder were (a) unlawful killing and (b) malice (which must precede the act of killing). Malice is often referred to, and best understood as, the intent to kill[98].

96. I am indebted to two persons in particular for giving me help with this difficult question. These were people I met on www.themurdersofaugust1969.freeforums.net. I do not know their names. They went by the blogging pseudonyms of Starviego and SaintPat. Our discourse came to an end before I had the opportunity to fully develop certain matters, which was my misfortune.

97. *People v. Beausoleil* Cal. 2d Crim 22232, unpublished.

98. *People v Thomas* 41 Cal 2d 470;

If the jury is satisfied the defendant is guilty of murder, then it must decide whether the murder was of the first degree or the second degree. In a nutshell, first degree murder is the deliberate and premeditated killing of another human being. Deliberation and premeditation involve reflection upon the consequences. Second degree murder is, basically, anything that is not first degree murder. Second degree murder is often characterised as "spur of the moment" killing. The maximum penalty for first degree murder in California in 1971 was death by execution in the gas chamber at San Quentin penitentiary. This was a matter for the jury's determination. The judge had the power to set aside the death penalty if he considered the circumstances warranted a lesser punishment. Furthermore, a conviction in a capital case was automatically the subject of an appeal.

Count (ii) invoked both the law of conspiracy and the law of felony-murder. Conspiracy involved an <u>agreement</u> by two or more persons to commit a crime, followed by an <u>overt act</u> in furtherance of the objective/s of the agreement. Liability for the crime itself, even if only committed by one person, then devolved upon all parties to the <u>agreement</u>, irrespective of whether they physically committed the crime, or were even present at the scene.

The felony-murder rule ascribed malice aforethought (intent) to a felon who killed in the perpetration of an inherently dangerous felony[99]. A defendant need not have done the killing himself, nor even be present at the murder scene, to be guilty of felony-murder. He could be vicariously responsible for the actions of a co-felon:

> *". . . it is well established that if a homicide is committed by one of several confederates while engaged in perpetrating the crime of robbery in furtherance of a common purpose, the person or persons engaged with him in the perpetration of the robbery but who did not*

---

99. *People v Ford* 60 Cal. 2d 772; *People v Coefield* 37 Cal. 2d 865; *People v Washington* 62 Cal. 2d 777;

*actually do the killing, are as accountable to the law as
though their own hands had intentionally fired the fatal
shot or given the fatal blow . . ."*[100]

Conviction for felony-murder automatically attracted characterisation
as a first degree murder.

Manson's Trial

Manson's trial for the Hinman homicide commenced in June
1971. Manson sought leave (permission) to represent himself at
his trial (conduct his defence "in pro per"). The Court declined his
application.

The suggestion that someone could better conduct a court case
without a lawyer seems counter-intuitive. However, Manson and his
supporters have forever protested about the court's refusal to let him
represent himself.

Manson had sought to represent himself in the earlier Tate/
LaBianca trial. He had been allowed to do so briefly but proved so
inept that leave was withdrawn before the trial commenced. It is plain
from the transcripts of Manson's pre-trial motions in Tate/LaBianca
that he was unable to advance any sensible argument in support of the
various orders he sought and that he had no understanding whatsoever
about adducing evidence. Unrepresented persons are always at a
disadvantage in any court proceeding. I have conducted trials against
unrepresented persons. For the most part, Manson appears to have
been less capable than the unrepresented persons I have opposed.

Furthermore, as will become evident later in this chapter, it is clear
Manson has never understood even the most basic concepts of the law

---

100. *People v Ulsh* (1962) 211 Cal. App. 2d 258. Vicarious liability is often referred to as "joint
responsibility" or "dependent liability". Vicarious liability is a doctrine by which, in certain
circumstances, a person's liability for an action is assigned to another person. Employers are vicariously
liable for acts (or omissions) of their employees which cause injury to others. Aiders or abettors of
murder are vicariously liable for the actions of the murderers. Vicarious liability is not rooted in strict
legal theory. It represents a policy decision on the part of law makers to assign legal responsibility in
conformity with community expectations.

about murder (e.g. vicarious liability). If he could not understand the relatively simple parts of the law, it is inconceivable he could run his own case.

It might be added that it is hard see how Manson could have represented himself for the practical reason that he spent much of the Hinman and Tate/LaBianca murder trials confined in a detention cell nearby, but separate from, the court room. This was on account of his own misbehaviour in court. He was able to hear the proceedings, but it is hard to see how he could have conducted examinations of witnesses or made objections or submissions from the cell[101].

There has been argument about the denial of Manson's supposed constitutional right to represent himself. It is unnecessary to go into this. It is abundantly clear Manson would have been grossly and unfairly disadvantaged had he represented himself.

So the trial for the Hinman murder commenced with Manson being represented by one Irving Kanarek.

The prosecution adduced evidence from Mary Brunner that towards the end of July 1969 she went to Hinman's house with Beausoleil and Atkins. Beausoleil hit Hinman over the head with a gun. Manson and Davis then arrived. Manson had a sword. Manson and Hinman struggled in the living room. Atkins, Brunner and Beausoleil stayed at Hinman's house for two days and two nights. Hinman lay bleeding and sleeping. Atkins and Brunner were in the kitchen and heard a noise from the living room where they rushed to find Beausoleil with knife in hand and Hinman bleeding from his chest. Hinman went into a coma, then started breathing with a "*loud raspy breathing*". Beausoleil put a pillow over Hinman's head and asked Brunner to hold it. Brunner did so for about two minutes.

Ella Jo Bailey (aka Yeller, a Family member at the time of Hinman's death) testified she later saw Manson at the Ranch carrying a sword and he said:

---

101. In fairness to Manson, some of the misbehaviour was a response to the denial of pro per status. But not all of it was, and one gets the impression there would have been similar problems, leading to detention, even had he represented himself.

*". . . he and Bruce Davis had gone to Gary Hinman's house
. . . had words with Mr Hinman, and they had a heated
argument, and then it became necessary to quiet Hinman
down, and he stated that he used a sword and cut Gary
Hinman from his left ear down to his chin . . . and after that
he said that he had left Bobby to finish up . . . .*

*[Manson] said that all they had gained from going to
Gary's house were the two vehicles and around $27"*[102]

Marius John Arnesen (aka "Mark Arnesen") testified that Manson
had given him Hinman's Volkswagon bus. Manson told Arnesen that
if he ever got in a hassle over the registration of the bus that he should
say he got it from a Gary Hinman who was supposed to be a Black
Panther.

Al Springer, a member of the Straight Satans, testified that Manson
had tried to recruit him into the Family in August 1969. Manson had
explained how the Family got things:

*""Well we go up to the door and knock on the door of their
houses, and when they come to the door and open it up, . . .
we'll just do them in or stick them . . . Everything behind the
door is yours, then . . . for the taking . . . [Manson said he
had] whacked a guy's ear off; . . . a Hinman"*[103]

Sergeant Paul Whiteley testified that earlier in the trial, on 10
August 1971, whilst he was seated in court at the Bar table and the
attorneys were conferring with the judge, Manson said to him:

*"[S]ure I went to Hinman's house . . . and sliced his ear. I
don't deny that. I told Bobby how to stand up like a man.
He had a woman's thoughts. I told him what to do – no.*

102. *People v. Manson* [1977] 71 Cal. App. 3d 11, pp. 13 to 14.
103. Ibid, p. 15.

[Interruption] . . . Uh – I told him what to do. Hinman deserved to die. He was selling bad dope. He was greasy. "[104]

Another police officer, Clifford Blackburn, corroborated Whiteley and took it further, testifying Manson had also said:

"I told Bobby - to kill him. And I even showed him how to do it . . ." [105]

During argument about the admissibility of the above conversations, Manson testified:

". . . the conversation went something into the likeness of what [Whiteley] had said on the stand.
We were talking, uh, about my being at the Hinman house . . . And I told him that I had to go over there because my brother couldn't stand up. He was stuck in his mother's mind . . . and I had to cut him" [106].

The most plausible construction of this evidence was that Manson admitted he had (a) attacked Hinman (b) told Beausoleil to kill Hinman and (c) showed Beausoleil how to do it. Even if this is incorrect, Manson certainly placed himself at Hinman's house and in the thick of the action to the extent there could be no doubt he was a participant in the events, and thus vicariously liable (guilty) in respect of Hinman's murder. After the close of evidence, the jury began its deliberations on 21 October 1971. On 2 November, the jury returned a verdict of guilty against Manson.

In 1977, the appeal court had the following to say about the trial and Manson's appeal:

104. Ibid.
105. Ibid.
106. Ibid, footnote 7.

"Manson devotes 33 pages of his opening brief to the evaluation of the evidence with reference to . . . the Hinman [murder] as if this appeal were a [fresh trial], concludes that the evidence is close, and that the various errors complained of therefore were prejudicial and require reversal.

In our view, the major premise is erroneous. We do not agree that the evidence, viewed in the light most favourable to [Manson], indicates that [the] case was close. . . The totality of the evidence demonstrates that Hinman was killed in the course of a robbery. All of the participants in the robbery are therefore guilty of murder in the first degree . . . even though only one struck the fatal blow.

Manson was clearly an aider and abettor, if not the primary instigator of the robbery. By his own admissions he struck Hinman with a sword in aid of the robbery. . . . The evidence of Manson's guilt for the Hinman murder was more than substantial beyond a reasonable doubt"[107]

By this stage Manson's role in the killing of Hinman had been considered by a jury of 12, then the appeal court comprising three of the most eminent jurists in the state of California, and his guilt had been established beyond doubt. And it appears Manson agreed. Despite arguing on appeal the trial was *"close"*, he conceded, inconsistently, that the prosecution evidence *"appears overwhelming in favour of guilt"*[108].

It is difficult to conceive of how the case against Manson could become any stronger - but it did, by virtue of Davis, Beausoleil and Atkins all subsequently admitting their guilt and also implicating Manson. These admissions and statements were made in the context of either parole hearings or, in Atkins' case, her ultimate guilty plea

---

107. Ibid, p.25
108. Ibid, footnote 11.

followed by two books in which she expanded upon the circumstances of Manson's involvement in Hinman's murder.

Argument by Manson and Beausoleil – Hinman was a Drug Dealer

Manson and Beausoleil have put up various arguments over the years in mitigation of their crimes. In particular both men, and also Manson's most ardent supporter, George Stimson, have argued against the prosecution's case theory of a robbery-gone-wrong and in favour of an alternative theory postulating that the crime was related to a drug burn. The drug burn argument is developed this way:

- Beausoleil visited Hinman to seek a refund of money paid to Hinman for drugs that had been on-sold by Beausoleil to the Straight Satans and had turned out bad. The Satans had subsequently roughed up Beausoleil. He feared further retribution if he did not retrieve their money.
- Hinman wouldn't give Beausoleil any money. Beausoleil rang Manson who said "*You know what to do*". Beausoleil killed Hinman.

The drug burn motive assists Manson and Beausoleil in several ways:

(i) It mitigates Beausoleil's role by making it appear he had been roughed up and would be subject to further violence if Hinman did not give him money – Beausoleil makes himself a victim;

(ii) It commensurately shifts blame to the Satans, and particularly Satans' member Danny De Carlo, against whom both Manson and Beausoleil have major grudges because DeCarlo testified against them (in various trials); and

(iii) It further mitigates their guilt by making Hinman appear to have been a drug manufacturer and dealer. Thus, Hinman becomes less victim, more criminal.

The main thrust of the drug burn argument is that Hinman manufactured and dealt drugs. The best evidence for this (that I have seen) is that white powder residue was found by police on scales in a kitchen cupboard at Hinman's house. This powder could have been peyote, one of the raw ingedients of the drug known as mescaline. But the powder tested negative for narcotics. However, in fairness, it is questionable whether narcotic testing methods in 1969 were capable of detecting peyote. Therefore, the possibility remains that the powder was peyote. However, even if it was, it doesn't sound like commercial quantities were being produced. It sounds more like it was for personal consumption or possibly sharing or dealing on a very small scale. In the final analysis, despite several "ifs" and "buts", it was possible Hinman was manufacturing mescaline, but only in very small quantities, at the most for personal consumption or sharing, and this is the highest it can be put.

There are other difficulties with the drug burn claim.

First, there were lengthy Grand Jury proceedings in which every conceivable topic was explored up hill and down dale with each witness. There was detailed evidence about conversations, weapons, vehicles, fights, the layout of Hinman's house, and so on, but I have been unable to find anything relevant or significant about drugs or drug deals as now alleged by Manson and Beausoleil. Nor have I found any reference to drugs in any of the trials (bar Manson's comment to Whiteley), although as mentioned the transcript available to me is far from complete.

Second, the first utterance of a drug burn (that I've found) came more than two years after Hinman's death when Manson commented to Sergeant Whiteley that Hinman was "selling bad dope". The fact that it was not raised for a whole two years makes it sound unconvincing. It sounds more like a recent invention.

Third, none of the other participants in the crime seem to have ever had any knowledge about the drug burn. Brunner said nothing of it in her testimony to the Grand Jury in April 1970. Atkins mentioned nothing of any drug burn in her initial interview with Officers Whiteley and Guenther, nor in either of her books. And she did not know of any drug burn when pointedly questioned by Parole Board member Jauregui in 1985:

"Jauregui: *Did you ever hear Bobby Beausoleil ask Gary Hinman 'where's my $12,000'?*

Atkins: *No sir, not that I recall.*

Jauregui: *OK did you ever hear Beausoleil ask the victim 'Where's my dope that I gave you?'*

Atkins: *No sir.*

Jauregui: *Did you ever hear him say 'I'm in trouble. If you don't give me the money or the dope, I'm in a lot of trouble with this motorcycle gang'?*

Atkins: *No sir.*

Jauregui: *. . . I think you would have - if someone were saying, where's my $12,000, I think you would have remembered that, right?*

Atkins: *Yes sir.*

Jauregui: *Did you hear that conversation?*

Atkins: *No sir.*

Jauregui: *Did you at any time . . . think that Robert Beausoleil was there to collect money on a drug deal?*

Atkins: *No sir"*[109]

Beausoleil has argued that, if Brunner and Atkins have denied knowledge of the drug deal, it was only because he had not told them[110]. But then, in response to a sceptical Parole Commissioner's observation that *"I would think that somewhere during the time, they*

109. Parole hearing 31 December 1985, cited by District Attorney Sequeira in Beausoleil's Parole Hearing on 13 December 2010.
110. Advanced at his Parole Hearing in 1992, cited in Stimson, *Goodbye Helter Skelter,* p.138.

would have heard you say to [Hinman] 'I want that $1,000'", Beausoleil said:

> "*They did. This did occur when we arrived at the residence. But at the time that they asked to go along, they had no knowledge of what I was going there for . . . they eventually did become aware of what was happening.*"

However, if Brunner and Atkins "*eventually did become aware*", it would be expected they would eventually say so. But they've <u>never</u> said anything of the sort. They simply have never known of a bad drug deal at any time.

Fourth, it was unlikely the Satans would be relying upon Beausoleil to retrieve the money. By his appearance in photographs taken around this time, Beausoleil was a fresh faced 20-something stripling with none of the cred which might be expected of a criminal debt collector. By his own account, Beausoleil needed instructions about what to do, had never done anything like this before, this being completely out of any experience he'd had in his life and not knowing "*what the hell I was doing*"[111]. The Satans were not strangers to violence. It seems improbable they would delegate their debt recovery to the patently unsuited Beausoleil (even allowing that he might have created the problem in the first place).

Fifth, if Beausoleil was truly at Hinman's place to rectify his (personal) drug deal, why was Manson involved? There have been half-baked attempts to explain this on the basis that Manson feared for the safety of his girls. But why were <u>they</u> there? They hardly went anywhere without Charlie's imprimatur. And it would be inconsistent with what is known about Manson's relationship with the girls that he would involve himself to protect them. As will be seen in later chapters, Manson was, in fact, completely disloyal and uncaring about the girls.

---

111. Parole hearing 13 December 2010.

Sixth, when Straight Satan member Al Springer spoke to police in November 1969 (ostensibly about the Tate/LaBianca homicides) he spontaneously volunteered: *"Did you ever get a corpse with his ear cut off?"* Then in discussion about Manson's sword, Springer said he heard a guy called *"Henland, I believe it was"* had his ear cut off by that sword, and a guy named *"Bausley"* or *"Bousley"* killed him[112]. If Hinman's death was in connection with a Satans drug burn, it was unlikely a Satan would be volunteering this sort of information, or any information, about the affair to the law. (Admittedly, however, to play the devil's advocate, it is conceivable Springer was volunteering these matters to police so as to pre-empt police suspicion of the Satans' involvement. That is to say, he was seeking to implicate Manson in order to take the heat off the Satans.)

Seventh, if the visit to Hinman was truly to retrieve the Satans' money for fear of violent retribution, it would be expected the vehicles taken from Hinman would have been either given to the Satans or sold in order to provide cash to the Satans. And either way, it would be expected disposal of the vehicles would take place quick smart after Hinman's death on 27 July. So what did happen to Hinman's vehicles? As for the Fiat, Beausoleil was found by police sleeping in it on the side of a road on 6 August, some 10 days after killing Hinman. This was inconsistent with any (urgent) need to reimburse the Satans, or anybody for that matter. As for the Volkswagon bus, I have previously mentioned Arnesen's testimony that it was given to him by Manson. Arnesen was not a member of the Straight Satans. Nor was there any evidence he associated with the Satans. Arnesen told police that Manson *"asked [me] if [I] would like to have a car"*, which hardly sounds like a statement accompanying a pressing need to dispose of it to the Satans, or anybody. In summary, neither of the cars were used to reimburse the Straight Satans, urgently or at all.

---

112. Bugliosi, *Helter Skelter*, p.133.

In conclusion, the drug burn argument is beset with major problems. The strong probability is that it is a fabrication.

Conclusions on the Hinman Murder

I have given lengthy and somewhat anxious consideration to the available evidence about the Hinman crime. I consider, on the basis of the available evidence (not every painstaking detail of which I have set out) that it is impossible to be certain, or even very confident, about what exactly happened in the murder of Hinman, except that he was certainly robbed and killed by Beausoleil in a torturous, messy, long, brutal two day ordeal, and that Manson participated with a violent and ghastly sword attack on Hinman. Apart from that, the motive for the crime was not entirely clear.

Many of the circumstances favour the proposition this was a true Helter Skelter killing – white Gary was killed and it was made to look like Blackie did it so as to ignite Helter Skelter. On balance, though not without some reservations, I favour that scenario as the explanation of how the murder came about. I consider the evidence favours, on balance, the following findings:

1. By June 1969, Manson was becoming impatient about Blackie's failure to start Helter Skelter. As June wore on, Manson spoke increasingly of the need to ignite Helter Skelter on Blackie's behalf. Manson and Beausoleil cooked up a plan to kill Gary Hinman and make it look like the crime was committed by Blackie, which would incite white retaliation and the chain of events that would be Helter Skelter. And as Manson himself said at his trial, he even showed Beausoleil how to go about killing Hinman. They also planned to steal whatever money Hinman had.

2. Beausoleil and Manson both assaulted Hinman in his own home. Hinman claimed he had no money. Manson left. Hours went by. Beausoleil telephoned Manson and said *"Gary isn't cooperating"*. Manson merely said *"You know*

what to do". Beausoleil didn't have to ask Manson what he meant by that because it had been agreed and pre-planned that Hinman was to be killed. Beausoleil stabbed Hinman to death.

3. The words "political piggy" were scrawled in blood on the wall, together with the paw mark of the Black Panthers, so as to make it look like Blackie had murdered Hinman. Beausoleil told police he had acquired Hinman's Fiat from a coloured man and Hinman had been jumped by Negros, so as to implicate Blackie in the murder. Susan Atkins told police Hinman had been stabbed by coloured persons so as to implicate Blackie.

If this was a Helter Skelter murder, then there are important ramifications for Beausoleil and Manson. It would mean the crime was not just a robbery-gone-wrong. Nor was it related to a drug burn as both have sought to suggest. The implication is rather that this was a planned Helter Skelter execution from the outset. Yes, Hinman's money would be taken, but always the main intention of both Manson and Beausoleil was that Hinman would be murdered.

The Hinman murder has never been understood or written about in this way (to my knowledge). But this is comfortably explained by two factors:

(1) The prosecution never presented Helter Skelter at the Hinman trials. This was unsurprising for these reasons:

(a) the Hinman case was always a strong felony-murder case against both Beausoleil and Manson. Thus, it was unnecessary to go past the robbery-gone-wrong case theory and get into other possible motives, especially unusual ones such as Helter Skelter (particularly given motive is not an essential element of the crime of murder); and

(b) as will be seen, it was prosecutor Bugliosi who investigated and assembled the prosecution's case about the Helter Skelter motive in the later Tate/

LaBianca trial (June 1970 to April 1971). But Bugliosi did not prosecute any of the Hinman murder trials. It would be unusual, to say the least, for one prosecutor to tell another prosecutor how he should run his case, even allowing for the apparent connections between Tate/LaBianca and Hinman.

(2)   In a criminal trial, the defence is hardly likely to quarrel about the prosecution's suggested version of motive, only to substitute another version. It would be tantamount to saying: *"I didn't do it for the reason suggested by the prosecution, but I did do it for this reason"*. In other words, it would amount to a confession. Moreover, in the circumstances of this case, it has always suited Beausoleil and Manson to distance themselves from Helter Skelter because Helter Skelter was, by definition, cold-blooded and senseless execution of random individuals whereas the robbery-gone-wrong theory of the crime was, relatively, less sinister. I have also seen it suggested that life behind bars for both men may be less comfortable if other inmates associated them with the relatively strange Helter Skelter. This might be right, though impossible to verify.

In the result, neither prosecution nor defence at the Hinman trials spoke of Helter Skelter. It is therefore hardly surprising that Helter Skelter's relevance has always been obscured in the commentary about the Hinman murder.

It might be said against the Helter Skelter theory of the Hinman homicide that none of the other participants or Family witnesses (namely Davis, Atkins, Brunner or Bailey) have said anything consistent with it (to my knowledge). However, there are numerous difficulties with this. First, so far as concerned the females, generally speaking, they never asked "why?" and were never told "why" anything was done. It would be expected this Family rule would have been strictly enforced where the activity in question was serious crime. Therefore, the likelihood is they didn't really know why Hinman was to be killed. Secondly, it is questionable, to say the least, whether any of the other participants knew about the original suggestion of Hinman as a target. There was no evidence that any of them were in on the Manson/Beausoleil conversation about which DeCarlo testified. Davis has tended to disavow knowledge of the *"suggestion or planning"* of the crime[113]. Thirdly, as with Beausoleil and Manson, it has never suited any of these people to be associated with the cold-blooded execution style of murder represented by Helter Skelter. Fourthly, in any event, the contemporaneous evidence, including the paw print, the inscription and the initial statements to police, have considerably more probative weight than any later contradictory or out-of-court or unsworn statements (or absence thereof) by any of these people.

There was one problem with Charlie's system of having others do the dirty work of his crimes. Under the law of vicarious liability, as discussed, a defendant can be guilty of murder even if he was not present at a murder scene or did not inflict the fatal blow/s. But Charlie has clung stubbornly to the notion that one must be present at a murder scene or do the actual killing to be liable for murder. It seems this has always been a black spot in his understanding of the law. As late as August 1971, even after he had been convicted for Tate/LaBianca, he was still quizzing police officers about how he could be *"held responsible for something someone else did"* and about *"how many people could be held responsible for one murder"* [114].

---

113. Parole hearing, 28 January 2010.
114. *People v. Manson* [1977] 71 Cal. App. 3d 11, footnote 7.

CHAPTER 4: THE TATE AND LABIANCA MURDERS

"When you go to war against an enemy, you're going to war for God and country and you give your life for that cause . . . they were going out to fight the war"

Charles Manson to Dianne Sawyer[115]

". . . if these people in Hollywood have to go, so be it . . . In war, you know, sometimes killing is needed"

Sandra Good[116]

After Hinman

Events at the Ranch immediately after Hinman (27 July 1969) are difficult to piece together. Atkins would later write that Manson spent *"hours and hours, nights and nights . . . lecturing"* that Helter Skelter was coming down faster and faster and saying: *"We must survive. We have to kill or be killed"*[117].

It appears Beausoleil had left the Ranch in Hinman's Fiat on Tuesday 5 August (arrested 6 August). Manson was on the move too. His movements would later be traced through credit card records

---

115. *A Turning Point*, ABC TV, 1994.
116. *Charles Manson: The Man Who Killed the Sixties*, Channel 4, 2004.
117. Atkins, *Child of Satan, Child of God*, p.131.

of gasoline purchases, and a traffic violation record, as he motored around southern California between 3 and 8 August. Manson had left the Ranch on Sunday 3 August, probably around 7.00 am (gasoline purchase between 7.00 and 8.00 am). He told Family members he was going to Big Sur to recruit new members[118].

At about 4.00 am on Monday 4 August, Manson picked up 17 year old hitchhiker Stephanie Schram. The pair camped out that night[119].

On the evening of Tuesday 5 August, Manson and Schram drove to the Esalen Institute at Big Sur. Esalen was an alternative think-tank where philosophers, hippies and thinkers went to engage in mind expanding studies and courses. Leaving Schram in the van, Manson took his guitar in and played and rapped to Esalen patrons. Apparently the reception was cool, with people pretending they were asleep, complaining Manson was too heavy and finding his preaching incomprehensible [120]. He had been rejected.

On Wednesday 6 August, Manson and Schram purchased gasoline at San Luis Obispo and Chatsworth. The pair had dinner at the Ranch and spent that night together in the van (parked not far from the Ranch)[121]. It is tempting to think Manson would have learned about Beausoleil's arrest from the other Family members at dinner. However, Manson has apparently refuted this:

> "at this time no-one knew [Bobby] was already in jail. But shortly after I left, Bobby phoned the ranch and informed Linda that he had been picked up as a suspect for the murder of Gary Hinman"[122]

---

118. Bugliosi, *Helter Skelter*, p.366. Bugliosi also interviewed Manson's travel companion Stephanie Schram, but it was the credit cards that told most of the story of his movements.

119. Ibid, p.366.

120. Ibid, pp. 366 to 367.

121. Ibid, p.367.

122. Emmons, N., *Manson in His Own Words, as told to Nuel Emmons*, Grove Press, 1986, p.193. Despite the title of this publication, it has to be said the "*words*" don't sound much like Manson's words. They sound more like Emmons' translation and/or interpretation. There is something inherently unsatisfactory about a person coming along and saying, in effect, "*I can explain it for Charlie*" and then putting out a book purporting to be Charlie's own words. Manson himself has disavowed the contents of Emmons' book. All of that said, parts of the book have a ring of truth and parts are corroborated by evidence available elsewhere. I consider the quoted passage is likely correct.

On Thursday 7 August, Manson and Schram drove to her sister's flat in San Diego. En route, at 6.15 pm, they were pulled over for a mechanical violation and Manson was cited for having no valid driver's license. He was recorded as driving a Ford van, licence number K70683[123]. This licence number would later become an important link in the chain of proof against Manson. Upon arrival in San Diego, Manson warned Schram's sister that Helter Skelter was coming down[124]. That night, 7 August, Manson and Schram slept in the van on the side of the road[125]. They arrived back at the Ranch at about 2.00 pm on Friday 8 August. Manson now learned of Beausoleil's arrest. This was very bad news because of the risk that Beausoleil would implicate him in the Hinman killing.

Friday 8 August 1969

Manson must have perceived things were rapidly unravelling. Besides Beausoleil's arrest, there was the rejection of his musical aspirations. There were financial difficulties, and the rejection at Esalen. Charlie was also smarting from the loss of his right-hand man, Paul Watkins, who had joined up with prospector Paul Crockett. With the addition of these new pressures to Manson's already temperamental and violent make up, it is not hard to see that an explosive cocktail was brewing. Leslie Van Houten would later say Manson was shaky and quick tempered[126]. And still Blackie had not kicked off Helter Skelter.

Another consideration needs to be interposed. It has to be wondered whether Manson was influenced by the limited life span of his scripture, the White Album. It must have struck him that that album would be supplanted in the near future by the next Beatles album. The Beatles produced roughly one album per year, and each was eagerly anticipated. It would have been expected by mid-summer

---

123. Bugliosi, *Helter Skelter*, p.368.
124. Ibid.
125. Ibid.
126. Unedited version of interview with Barbara Walters, ABC TV, January 1977.

1969 that the next album was on the way. If the Beatles released a new album, with nothing susceptible to Charlie's apocalyptic interpretations, then the credibility of his Helter Skelter prophecy would be at risk. Manson had told his gormless disciples repeatedly that it was the Beatles who were conveying the message for war. They were telling it like it is, he beseeched them. But what if the Beatles started saying other things through a new album?

The precise state of apprehension during 1969 about the release of the next Beatles album is hard to nail down. News clippings from mid-1969 refer to the Beatles working on a new album. On 7 June 1969, John Lennon told the media in Toronto that *"the next album is due for release in July"*[127]. By Friday 8 August, the album that would be called *Abbey Road* was close to completion. On that very day, the group would walk across the zebra crossing outside Abbey Road studios in a photo shoot which would generate the iconic photo later used on the album cover[128]. Recording finished on 20 August and *Abbey Road* would be released in the USA on 1 October 1969[129]. Thus, whilst the White Album was extant as at 8 August, it was close to its use-by date. If Manson apprehended the next Beatles album might discredit Helter Skelter, then this could be added to the brew of anxieties working upon him on the evening of 8 August[130].

The final straw for Manson on Friday 8 August was when, late in the day or evening, he learned of the arrest of two of his closest followers, Sandra Good and Mary Brunner. They had been picked up for trying to purchase items at a Sears store with stolen credit cards.

---

127. Unidentified publication, dated 7 June 1969, in Barratt, C., *The Beatles in the News 1969,* Lulu Press Inc., 2015.

128. Lewisohn, M., *The Complete Beatles Recording Sessions,* Hamlyn Publishing Group limited, 1988, p.186.

129. Ibid., p.191.

130. We know *Abbey Road* did made its way into the Family's consciousness because some of its lyrics were painted on a door at the Ranch. The precise nature of Manson's reaction to the new album is not known. It would only be some 11 days or so between its release and his final arrest (12 October). During the first Tate/LaBianca trial Manson "rapped" with prosecutor Bugliosi about the Beatles calling for the revolution. This suggests that he was, by then at least, undeterred by the release of *Abbey Road,* or perhaps he found things in it consistent with the revolution, or perhaps he was just crapping on. The failure of prophecies of cult leaders will be considered in the final chapter of this book.

(Good and Brunner were recorded as driving the same Ford van, number K70683, driven by Charlie when booked the night before. This placed him back at the Ranch on 8 August.)   Charlie really erupted about the arrest of Good and Brunner[131]. He was having a bad day, a really bad day.

It is difficult to be much more precise about events on the evening of Friday 8 August. The most convincing account would later be given by Linda Kasabian who testified that everyone was sitting around and Charlie spoke. He talked about people being not together and they were off in their own minds. He announced to the group: *"now is the time for Helter Skelter"*. Blackie was incapable of starting it. So now Charlie would. (Well, sort of. Others would do it for him. He wouldn't be there, much less wield a weapon.)

It is hard to deduce much else from the other Family members. They were conditioned to never ask questions, and just do what Charlie said. None of the girls who would join 23 year old Tex Watson in Ranch hand Johnny Swartz' Ford later that night – Atkins (21 years old), Krenwinkel (21) and Kasabian (20) - knew where they were going. Whether they knew what was going to happen is open to debate. There were weapons in the car and Charlie had just proclaimed the time for Helter Skelter. It is hard to believe they had no idea what was in store. But when they got in the car, they certainly didn't know the destination. Tex Watson did. It was 10050 Cielo Drive in the Bel Air district of Los Angeles. Terry Melcher had lived there, and both Watson and Manson had visited the property. They also knew Melcher no longer lived there. But even if he wasn't there, most likely someone rich or famous would be. The old Ford, containing Watson, Atkins, Krenwinkel and Kasabian, pulled up outside 10050 Cielo at about 12.15 am on Saturday 9 August 1969.

10050 Cielo Drive on 8 August 1969

---

131. Emmons, N., *Manson in His Own Words*, pp.198 to 199.

On Friday 8 August, the residents at 10050 Cielo (hereafter "Cielo") would have been oblivious to the comings and goings at Spahn Ranch. The tenants in residence were film director Roman Polanski and his actor wife Sharon Tate. Polanski was overseas. Ms Tate was 26 years old and over eight months pregnant. Her acting career was on the up, and she was well liked in Hollywood circles. She had had supporting parts in several movies, including the moderately successful *Valley of the Dolls* in 1967. Friends Abigail Folger and Wojiciech "Voytek" Frykowski were staying at the house with Ms Tate. Folger, 25 years old, was heiress to the Folger coffee empire. She had worked as a social worker. Frykowski, 32 years old, was her partner. He referred to himself as a writer.

The occupants of Cielo were strangers to the Manson Family. There had been a brief encounter earlier in the year when Manson had turned up looking for Terry Melcher. Manson had spoken to Ms Tate's photographer, Sharokh Hatami, and she may have been in the vicinity of the conversation. Manson also spoke to the owner of the property Rudy Altobelli. Tex Watson had been to Cielo when Melcher lived there (Melcher left in January).

Friday 8 August was a busy day at Cielo. A small room was being painted as a nursery for the baby due shortly. The painter, Frank Guerrero, finished for the day at 1.30 pm. Ms Tate had two friends over to lunch, actor Joanna Pettet and singer/songwriter Barbara Lewis. They left at 3.30 pm. Winifred Chapman was the housekeeper and she finished work at 4.30 pm. She was due to return to work the following morning. Ms Tate asked if she would like to stay the night, but she declined and left for the day.

William Garretson, 19 years old, occupied a guest house a short distance from the main house. He was employed by Rudy Altobelli to look after the guest house and walk the dogs.

The gardener Tom Vargas started work at 4.30 pm. He signed a receipt for two blue trunks delivered to the property at 5.30 pm. As Vargas was finishing for the day, at 6.00 pm, he saw Garretson walking the dogs.

Between 6.00 and 6.30 pm, Ms Tate's younger sister, Deborah (13 years old), rang and asked if she could bring some friends over. Ms Tate asked if she wouldn't mind making it another time.

Between 7.30 and 8.00 pm, Dennis Hearst delivered a bicycle that Abigail Folger had purchased earlier in the day. Jay Sebring (Ms Tate's ex-boyfriend) answered the door.

About 9.00 pm, Garretson left to buy cigarettes and a TV dinner, returning around 10.00 pm. He saw lights on in the main house, and observed nothing out of the ordinary. At 11.45 pm, 18 year old Steven Parent arrived at the guest house to visit Garretson. Parent had a clock radio with him and plugged it in to demonstrate. Parent asked Garretson if he was interested in buying it, but Garretson declined. Parent accepted Garretson's offer of a beer, made a phone call, and then left.

Dead Bodies – The Tate Killings

The following morning, Saturday 9 August, Ms Chapman returned to work at Cielo and discovered an horrendous scene. Police were called and on arrival they saw four bodies in and around the house with stab, slash and gunshot wounds. They also found the body of a young man on the front seat of a Rambler motor vehicle.

Outside the house were the bodies of Abigail Folger and Voytek Frykowski. In the living room, connected by a rope looped over a roof rafter, were the bodies of Sharon Tate and Jay Sebring.

Ms Tate had been stabbed 16 times. It would be estimated that her unborn child passed away 15 to 20 minutes after the last fatal stab wound. The child had no actual wounds. Burn marks on Ms Tate's neck suggested she had been suspended by the rope. Jay Sebring, 35 years old, had seven penetrating stab wounds and one fatal gunshot wound.

Voytek Frykowski's body had 51 stab wounds, 13 scalp wounds inflicted with a blunt instrument and two gunshot wounds. Abigail Folger had been stabbed 28 times.

The body in the Rambler was Steven Parent. He had been shot four times. A clock radio was found in the car. It was set at 12.15.

William Garretson was alive and well in the guesthouse. He claimed he hadn't heard or seen anything. He was immediately arrested.

The word "PIG" was written in blood on the front door of the main residence. There was no evidence of ransacking or larceny. Jewellery and money were found on the victims and on the premises. In fact, about $70 had been taken from Folger's wallet. But police were not to know.

Telephone lines at the front of the property had been cut. A pair of spectacles was found in the house. Enquiries would reveal they did not belong to any of the victims. They were negative for fingerprints and blood. A Buck type knife was found wedged in the back of a sofa. Three pieces of black wood were also found which, when placed together, appeared to form the right side of a gun grip. Fingerprints were found on the front door and the door leading from Ms Tate's bedroom (rear of house) to the outside swimming pool.

After Tate – Saturday 9 August 1969

Not a great deal is known about events at the Ranch on Saturday 9 August. It seems to have been a relaxing day for most. Linda Kasabian slept most of the day. But Susan Atkins was buzzing. She tried to get some sleep but to no avail. She went to the trailer (caravan) where a television was situated, turned on the news, and crowed with excitement as news of the Tate slayings came on. She called Patricia Krenwinkel and others into the trailer where they all watched.

Manson was asleep and missed the news. Tex Watson slept late and was told by Atkins that the murders were on the news and *"we'd killed some really 'beautiful people"* [132].

After dinner, Manson called together Watson, Atkins, Krenwinkel, Kasabian, Van Houten and Steve Grogan (aka Clem). He told them last night had been too messy and tonight he was going to show them how to do it properly. Late in the evening, all seven bundled into Johnny Swartz' Ford. This time, everyone knew the agenda.

Leno and Rosemary LaBianca

In the early hours of Sunday 10 August 1969, Leno and Rosemary LaBianca were en route to their home at 3301 Waverley Drive in the Los Feliz district of Los Angeles (hereafter "Waverley") after a day trip to Lake Isabella. Leno was 41 years old. He was president of Gateway Markets, a wholesale food chain. Rosemary, 38 years old, was a business woman. She owned a dress shop and was a successful investor.

Just before 2.00 am, not far from home, the LaBiancas stopped at a newspaper stand operated by John Fokianos. They were regular customers. They were tired. They purchased the *Herald Examiner* and saw the headline about the Tate massacre. Rosemary was upset. Fokianos would later testify: *"She was in extreme shock when she heard about it . . . It was something that was new to her . . . [S]he was shaken up over it"*.

More Death

At about 8.30 pm, Sunday 10 August, Frank Struthers (16 year old son of Rosemary LaBianca) was returning from a vacation and arrived at Waverley. Struthers suspected something was wrong and called his sister, Suzanne, who arrived with her boyfriend, Joe Dorgan, at about

---

132. Watson, *Will You Die For Me?*, p. 145.

9.30 pm. Frank Struthers and Dorgan entered the house and came across Leno LaBianca's body in the living room.

Police were called and on arrival found Leno's head was covered with a pillow case. His hands were tied behind his back with a leather thong. A double tined kitchen fork was stuck in his abdomen and the word "WAR" was carved into the skin. An electrical cord was knotted around his neck. A coroner's examination found 13 stab wounds and 14 puncture wounds apparently made by the fork. A knife was found protruding from his neck.

Rosemary LaBianca's body was found in a bedroom. Her hands were tied with an electrical cord. Another cord was around her neck and a pillow case over her head. She had 41 stab wounds, 16 of which were post mortem. One wound which severed the spine was enough to have killed Mrs LaBianca.

It did not immediately appear that anything had been stolen. There was no sign of ransacking. Many items of value were found around the house. In fact, a collection of coins had been taken, but police were not to know.

The words "DEATH TO PIGS" were written in blood on a wall of the living room and "RISE" was written above a door. On the refrigerator door were the words "HEALTER SKELTER" [sic][133].

No fingerprints were found, even on the fork, which had clearly been wiped.

Investigation

The first suspect in the Tate killings was William Garretson. He remained in custody over the evening of 9/10 August. Therefore, if the Tate and LaBianca homicides were committed by the same person/s, then Garretson was almost certainly innocent. However, police did not immediately link the killings. Scientific tests established that despite Garretson's proximity to the killings, he was unlikely to

---

133. This was patently a misspelling of "Helter Skelter". I will refer to this inscription interchangeably as either "Helter Skelter" or "Healter Skelter".

have heard gunshots (or screaming). Eventually, Garretson passed a polygraph and he was released from custody.

On 16 August 1969, wholly by coincidence, police raided the Family at Spahn Ranch on charges relating to firearm possession, auto theft and handling stolen credit cards. Manson was found hiding under one of the Ranch buildings. To the relief of various Family members, nothing was mentioned about any murders. Then, due to a technicality, the charges were dropped. Manson and the other Family members were released and returned to the Ranch.

Meanwhile, police investigation of the murders was going nowhere. Various motives such as drug dealings or personal vendettas floated around. Roman Polanski was questioned, polygraphed and cleared of involvement. There was frenzied media coverage. But by the end of September 1969 there was no progress in the investigation.

By 10 October 1969, the Family members had mostly ensconced themselves at a different location known as Barker Ranch. On 10 and 12 October, they were again raided by police, this time on charges including grand theft auto and arson. Twenty four Family members, including Manson, Krenwinkel, Atkins and Van Houten, were arrested and taken into custody in Independence in Inyo County. Manson had sought to evade arrest by hiding in a cupboard. Arresting officer Jim Pursell would later recall Manson's ambitious request for release during the journey from Barker Ranch to Independence:

> *"On the way down he impressed upon us that his group was trying to find some place to be alone because the blacks were going to rise up and overwhelm the whites. There was going to be a bloodbath and he stressed that we in uniform, number one, were cops, number two, we were white, therefore we had two strikes against us immediately and he, he strongly recommended that we let them go, and we flee for our lives"*[134]

134. *Charles Manson: The Man Who Killed the 60's*, Channel 4, 2004.

Pursell also noticed the peculiar interaction between Manson and the others:

> *"At least twice Charlie made statements that would cause the others to say 'amen' two or three times in unison. Also a few times when the others would become involved in whispered, giggly conversations, Charlie would simply look at them and immediately they would fall silent. The amazing part of the stare was how obvious the results were without a word being spoken"*[135]

The local District Attorney at Independence was Frank Fowles. He would later recall that he took one of the Family members aside – *"I picked this one kid who seemed out of place with some of the rest of them. I decided to give her a break so that she wouldn't have a record following her around"*. Fowles told the girl she was moving with a rough crowd and she was too nice to get in over her head. *"She listened very respectfully"* and *"answered 'yes sir' and 'no sir', and thanked me most sincerely for letting her go"*[136]. The girl was Patricia Krenwinkel. She would later be arrested in Alabama. Her fingerprint would be found to match the print taken from the rear door leading to the pool of the Tate residence.

Cracks Begin to Emerge – Atkins and Van Houten

By early November 1969, Susan Atkins had been transferred from Independence to the Sybil Brand Institute for Women in Los Angeles on account of her involvement in the Hinman murder. At Sybil Brand, Atkins could not resist talking to fellow inmates about her other criminal achievements besides Hinman. On 6 November she opened up to inmate Virginia Graham about the Tate killings. Atkins

---

135. Quoted at Bugliosi, *Helter Skelter,* p.179.
136. Bishop, G., *Witness to Evil,* Dell Books, 1971, p.37.

told Graham she had stabbed Sharon Tate to death and she felt no remorse, indeed killing Ms Tate *"was quite a thrill"*. She also spoke enthusiastically about tasting the victims' blood: *"To taste death and yet give life, wow, what a trick"* and her love for the victims: *"You have to have a real love in your heart to do this for people"*.

On the same day as Atkins' revelations to Graham (6 November), Leslie Van Houten (still in custody in Independence) was interviewed by Lieutenant A.H. Burdick who wrote up the following report:

> *"I asked her if she had any knowledge of persons in her group who might possibly be involved in the Tate or LaBianca homicides. She indicated that there were some 'things' that caused her to believe someone from her group might be involved in the Tate homicide. I asked her to elaborate on the 'things' . . . she declined to indicate what she meant and stated that she wanted to think about it overnight . . . She did indicate that she might tell me the following day."*

When Burdick resumed the conversation the next day, Van Houten declined to say anything more[137].

On another day in November, precise date unclear, Atkins told Virginia Graham that the Family had a hit list of other celebrities they intended to murder including Elizabeth Taylor, Richard Burton, Tom Jones, Steve McQueen and Frank Sinatra.

Also in November, another inmate at Sybil Brand Institute, one Ronnie Howard (aka Veronica Hughes, Shelley Nadell), was the recipient of more admissions by Atkins. Howard would later testify:

- Atkins said *"I know something that would blow your mind"*. I replied *"Nothing would blow my mind"*. She said *"Oh yeah? Did you hear about the Tate murders?"*
- Atkins said that Tate pleaded for the life of her baby but Atkins had told Tate to *"Shut up you bitch, I have no mercy*

---

137. Bugliosi, *Helter Skelter*, p.121.

for you" and began to stab her in the chest. She then said that *"when you stab a person it's just like having a climax, the more you do it the better you like it".*

- Atkins said she felt thrilled and that everything in life, smoking, eating, stabbing, is one big sexual intercourse – in and out, in and out goes the knife.

Atkins also told Graham and Howard about Helter Skelter. Both women struggled to understand what it was about, but Howard got that *"you have to be killed to live"*[138].

On 26 November, Van Houten was interviewed by Sergeant Michael McGann. There were numerous admissions by Van Houten to the effect she knew more about the Tate murders than she was letting on, for example: *"Well, I have an idea that there were five people, but I don't know exactly who they were"*[139].

Charles "Tex" Watson is Arrested

Watson's movements after LaBianca are hard to pin down. It is known he was still at the Ranch on 30 August 1969, because he was involved in the murder of ranch hand Donald "Shorty" Shea on that day (although for reasons unknown he was never charged over that murder – see Appendix 2 for discussion). He was not rounded up with the others in the Barker Ranch raids between 10 and 12 October, which suggested he had left before 10 October. At some stage after 12 October, he returned to Barker Ranch only to be informed the Family had been arrested. Watson returned to Copeville and hooked up with his old girlfriend Jeanne Denise Mallett who would later recall:

"He was telling me about how the black people were in California . . . black panthers or something . . . they had enough ammunition and things to take over the City of Los

138. Ibid, p.140.

139. Ibid, p.210ff. Transcript of taped Interviews with Leslie Van Houten, 26 and 28 November 1969, Sergeant Michael McGann, at Sybil Brand Institute.

Angeles . . . and he felt they were going to start a revolution, but he was going to be safe because they were going to be in the desert and the ground was going to open up and they were going into a hole and live forever. I don't know whether you would call it religious belief or whatever . . . they were supposed to be in the same physical body as they were on earth or something like that"[140]

Finally, on 30 November 1969, Tex Watson was arrested in Copeville on a warrant issued in respect of his involvement in Tate/LaBianca. There would be a long extradition battle and he would not return to Los Angeles for trial until September 1970. At some point (date unclear), Watson's fingerprint was matched to the print found on the front door of the Tate residence.

Susan Atkins – Deal, Grand Jury, Indictments

By the start of December, Susan Atkins' admissions to her fellow inmates had come to the attention of police. On 4 December, Atkins agreed to be interviewed by prosecutor Bugliosi, and also to cutting a deal whereby the prosecution would not seek the death penalty against her, provided she testified truthfully to a Grand Jury.

On 5 December, Atkins testified before a Grand Jury and it went like this:

- On Friday 8 August 1969, Charlie told me to put on dark clothes and also a change of clothes and a knife. I got in the car with Katie (Krenwinkel) and Linda Kasabian and Tex was driving. It was late in the evening. Tex told us we were going to the house on the hill that used to belong to Terry Melcher. There was a rope and bolt cutters in the back of the car. Tex had a gun. We all had knives.

---

140. Deposition dated 24 November 1970.

- On the way Tex told us that the reason we were going there was to get all their money and kill whoever was there. We got there possibly around midnight. Tex climbed up a power pole and snipped two wires which led to the house.
- [After entering the grounds] Tex went out of sight. I heard Tex say: "*halt*". I heard a male voice say: "*please don't hurt me, I won't say anything*". Then I heard four gunshots.
- We walked towards the residence. Tex crawled in through a window and then let me in at the front door. Katie entered with me. Linda stayed outside.
- Frykowski was lying on a couch. He woke up and said: "*what time is it?*". Tex held a gun in front of his face and said: "*be quiet, don't move or you're dead*". Frykowski said: "*Well who are you and what are you doing here?*". Tex said: "*I'm the devil and I'm here to do the devil's business*".
- I checked out the rest of the house and told Tex there were three other people. Tex told me to tie up Frykowski and I loosely tied his hands. Tex then told me to get the others. Katie and I brought them into the room where we had Frykowski. Tex told the other three to lay down on their stomachs in front of the fireplace. Sharon Tate said something to the effect that she was pregnant. Jay Sebring said: "*Can't you see she's pregnant, let her sit down*". Tex shot him. Sebring fell in front of the fireplace. Sharon Tate and Abigail Folger screamed.
- Tex tied a rope around Sebring's neck and then around Tate's neck and Folger's neck and threw the rope over a high beam which made Tate and Folger stand up. I took $72 from Folger's wallet and put it in my pocket.
- Tex then viciously stabbed Sebring in the back many times. Someone asked: "*what are you going to do with us?*" Tex said: "*You are all going to die*". They began to plead for their lives.
- Tex ordered me to kill Frykowski. I went over to him and raised my hand but then hesitated. He jumped up and got

hold of my hair and pulled it very hard. I swung with the knife behind me and hit something three or four times but couldn't see what. He got away from me. He got to the door and Tex hit him over the head with the gun butt a couple of times. He was also stabbing Frykowski.

- Folger had got loose from the rope and was fighting Katie. I held Sharon Tate. She said: "*please let me go, all I want to do is have my baby*". I said: "*Woman I have no mercy for you*". I saw Tex stab Folger who said: "*I give up, take me*".

- Tex told me to kill Tate. I couldn't. I held her arms. Tex stabbed her in the heart area around the chest. She fell to the floor.

- We then went out the front door and saw Folger. Tex stabbed her three or four times. Frykowski was still moving and Tex kicked him in the head.

- We walked up to the gate. I went back to the house and got the towel I had used to tie Frykowski's hands and touched Tate's chest and then wrote "PIG" on the door with her blood.

- We got back to the Ranch about 2.00am. Charlie said: "*what are you doing home so early?*". Tex described to Charlie what we had done, there was a lot of panic and he said: "*Boy it sure was Helter Skelter*".

- When I learned who the four dead people were I said: "*it had served its purpose*". I said this had been done to instil fear into the establishment.

- The next night Charlie told me to get a change of clothes. He said we were going to go out and do the same thing we did last night. It was early evening. In the car was myself, Charlie, Clem, Katie, Leslie, Tex and Linda.

- We stopped outside a house. Charlie got out of the car then he came back and said: "*Tex, Katie, Leslie, go into the house, I have got the people tied up, they are very calm*". He said: "*Last night Tex let the people know they were going to be killed which caused panic*". Charlie said he reassured the people with smiles in a very quiet manner that they were not going to be harmed. He told Tex to "*paint a picture more gruesome than anybody had ever seen*"

- Charlie told them to hitchhike home. We drove off. Charlie had the woman's wallet and he told Linda to put it in the bathroom at a gas station.

- Charlie oftentimes used the words pig, pigs and Helter Skelter. He'd talk about Helter Skelter. We all talked about Helter Skelter. Helter Skelter was to be the last war on the face of the earth. It would be all the wars that have ever been fought built on top of the other, something that no man could conceive of in his imagination. You can't conceive of what it would be like to see every man judge himself and then take it out on every other man all over the face of the earth. And pig was a word used to describe today's establishment.

It is at once obvious that, contrary to what she had told her fellow inmates, Atkins was now denying she stabbed Sharon Tate. She would later be corroborated by Tex Watson who conceded in his memoir that he stabbed Tate. He pointedly absolved Atkins of responsibility[141]. Therefore, it seems likely Atkins never stabbed anyone except for some probably inconsequential blows to Frykowski's legs[142]. This was not exactly for want of trying, at least in Frykowski's case. Moreover, she was still highly culpable for having held Ms Tate while Tex stabbed.

It is worth noting Atkins had been interviewed by her lawyers, Richard Caballero and Paul Caruso, a few days before the Grand Jury testimony. I have read the record of that interview, the contents of which do not need to be set out. Suffice to say, save for some minor exceptions which will be considered in due course, the Grand Jury

---

141. Watson, *Will You Die For Me?*, p.143.

142. According to the autopsy report in respect of Frykowski, there were eight stab wounds to his left leg. Each wound was 1 to 1½ inches deep. None were fatal. Since the time of writing, I have seen a post on www.mansonblog.com entitled "Miss Scarlet in the Living Room With a Knife" in which the author forcefully argues that Atkins' blows to Frykowski were not as inconsequential as may have been previously thought.

testimony was a reproduction of what she had told the lawyers. This was significant. Clients usually tell the truth to their lawyers. The purpose of the client/lawyer privilege is to provide clients with an environment in which they can speak truthfully with their lawyers without fear of their words being used against them (a lawyer cannot be compelled to disclose his communications with his client). The relative formality of a legal interview also enhances the likelihood of a truthful accounting of events by the client. Clients do not always tell the truth to their lawyers, but they normally do. It follows that, all other things being equal, the interview, and the substantially similar Grand Jury testimony, were likely more reliably truthful versions of events than the versions given by Atkins to her fellow inmates.

On 8 December 1969, the Grand Jury returned the following indictments:

> Manson – 7 counts of murder, 1 count of conspiracy to commit murder
> Watson – 7 murder, 1 conspiracy
> Krenwinkel – 7 murder, 1 conspiracy
> Kasabian – 7 murder, 1 conspiracy
> Atkins – 7 murder, 1 conspiracy
> Van Houten – 2 murder, 1 conspiracy[143]

More Admissions by Susan Atkins

Atkins was now on a roller-coaster of admissions. On 13 December 1969, she wrote to a friend in Michigan, Jo Stevenson:

> *"Dear Jo,*
>
> *. . .*
>
> *As far as what is happening in court, I just got indited [sic] on 7 counts of murder and on one count of conspirisy [sic] to murder.*

---

143. Perhaps curiously, the prosecutor did not seek an indictment against Steven "Clem" Grogan. See Appendix 2 for further discussion.

You rember [sic] the Sharon Tate murder and LaBeicinca [sic] murder? Well because of my big mouth to a cell mate they just indited [sic] me. It seems to be nation wide news, so I don't want to say anything about it because of the censor."

In mid-December, precise date unclear, Atkins wrote to Ronnie Howard, referring to Manson as "M":

"I can see your side of this clearly. Nor am I mad at you. I am hurt in a way only I understand. I blame no one but myself for ever saying anything to anybody about it. My attorney is going to go insanity. Yes, I wanted the world to know M. It sure looks like they do now. There was a so called motive behind all this. It was to instil fear into the pigs and to bring on judgment day which is here now for all.

In the first place there are no strangers to me or M. In the word kill the only thing that dies is the ego. All ego must die anyway, it is written. Yes, it could have been your house, it could have been my father's house also. In killing someone phisally [sic] you are only releasing the soul. Life has no boundaries and death is only an illusion.

If you can believe in the second coming of Christ M is he who has come to save. Insanity is reality and not caring. When you truly love you do not care about anyone or anything you just love. M does not care, I know this to be the truth. Maybe this will help you to understand . . .

I did not admit to being in the 2nd house because I was not in the 2nd house. I went before the grand jury because my attorney said your testimony was enough to convict me and the all the others. He also said it was my only chance to save myself. Then I was out to save myself. I have gone through some changes since then. I am ceasing to be inside rather than seeming to be. I have been going through changes about feeling guilty about testifying and all that has happened. For

*me to say I am sorry is not enough for me. I have been dying
a little more every day. Giving up my useless thoughts. I
know now it has all been perfect.*

*Yes we are beyond pettie [sic] caring. Love is also beyond
limits. Those people died not out of hate or anything ugly. I am
not going to defend our beliefs. I am just telling it the way it is.*

*I am also content here. My attorney gives me money. He
just deposited $20 on my account. As I write to you I feel
more at ease inside. When I first heard you were the informer
I wanted to slit your throat. I snapped that I was the real
informer and it was my throat I wanted to cut . . .*

I hope now you understand a little more. If not ask."

It is doubtful Howard would have understood much more. But
she didn't bother asking for clarification.

On 17 December, Atkins wrote to one Kit Fletcher (also known as
Janet Owens):

"Dear Kit,
I just got your letter . . .
*Why did I do it? Or why did I open my big mouth to a cell
mate? To either one of those auestions [sic] I did what I did
because that is what I did . . . "*

Patricia Krenwinkel – Interview With Dr Brown

On 24 December 1969, Patricia Krenwinkel, having been arrested in
Alabama, was interviewed there by a psychiatrist, Dr Claude Brown.
Amongst other things, Krenwinkel implicated Manson. She told Dr
Brown that Manson had instructed her to go with Tex Watson on the
night of the Tate murders. Furthermore, she had gone to Alabama
"because she was afraid of Manson finding her and killing her", she was
not on drugs on the night of the Tate murders and she had feared
arrest for the murders but Charlie had said *"nobody could touch us"*.

Leslie Van Houten - Interview With Marvin Part

On 29 December 1969, Leslie Van Houten was interviewed by her attorney, Marvin Part. The interview was taped. Van Houten talked at some length about the Beatles and the Bible:

- *We read in the Bible, it said about the four-headed locusts. And it just described the Beatles so perfectly. We looked up Revelation in the New Testament, and in the Bible we read Revelations, and it talked about a four-headed locust that would have hair of woman and mouths of lions and faces of man and a shield of protective armour. And we thought it was like the guitars, because their album, when we would listen to it on acid, would say so much more.*

- *I believed the Beatles were the four-headed locust and a prophet. In and out of the White Album they've got parts of the Revelations in the Bible.*

- *We knew we were part of this Revolution – of the Revelations in the Bible. We knew we had a part in it. And so we read it and it talked about a hole in the desert or going to the Kingdom. We found out – we started looking into Death Valley, what's underneath Death Valley, and we found out there was the Armagosa River. And all kinds of things that just made us believe that there was a whole world underneath. And that what would happen is that about a couple thousand of the chosen people – white people – would go down into the center of the earth and stay there for about fifty years. And then we were going to come back up. And this was when we – the earth would be all black. And so it would be black just meaning that there would be no more white people, up on the earth. They would all be wiped out completely.*

- *We hadn't quite figured out yet how we were get to the centre of the earth. We were looking for the hole. That's why we needed more dune buggies. When we found it we could just walk down it and then we'd have to float down a river and we figured out it would take about two weeks to get to the center.*

- *And then once we got to the center we'd be tiny, and everything would be great big, magnified, like pearls. There'd be giant pearls, and we'd be just little tiny, about maybe five inches compared to everything else.*
- *The ones that usually talked about it the most were Charlie and myself, Gypsy (Catherine Share), Brenda (Nancy Pitman), Katie (Patricia Krenwinkel), Tex (Charles Watson), Clem (Steven Grogan), Snake (Dianne Lake) and Rachel (Ruth Ann Moorehouse). Sadie (Susan Atkins) talked about it sometimes but I don't know if she actually believed it or not. But the rest of us really believed it.*
- *We were going to buy the dune buggies and we were going to use the money given to us by Gary Hinman but he never gave us any money, so we stole them.*
- *Charlie is everything. And he said if you could give up your personality and your ego and be willing to die then you were already dead that the body didn't mean anything.*
- *After we knew what was going to come down we tried talking to black leaders and we saw that they were stalling. It was almost as if we had to make the first move for it to develop, to get bigger so that it would happen because the black man loves us so much that he would be our slave and do everything we said. He let us beat him and mistreat him for so many years that he almost doesn't want to do what he has to do, but he sees that he has to do it. And so it was up to us to start it and to just start killing people. Because it's going to be blood for blood. It would be that white man would kill white man. The Black man would sort of be there, too, helping him along. It's like white man is divided. Black man is more together. And so white man would kill white man for their beliefs and then black man would be there to sort of help them.*
- *The revolution would be started by killing, by doing a murder that had no sense behind it, and putting words that would make people scared because the more fearful people get, the*

more frantic it will get, and the faster it will happen.

- *On the night of the Tate murders, Charlie came into Katie and I as we were taking care of the babies and he said: 'Do you see why I believe that we have to kill?' We both said: 'Yes we see'. He said: 'Do you want to do it?' We said: 'No, but we know that it has to be done, so yes'.*

- *The next morning Katie told me they had murdered five people. The next night I wanted to go too because I wanted to be just like Katie. Charlie said to me: 'Are you crazy?' I said: 'Well yeah'. In other words it meant: 'Are you crazy enough to believe the way I believe that we have been sent out to start this in motion?' And he said: 'Are you crazy enough to be able to go out and kill someone for this? I said: 'Yeah'. He said: 'OK get two changes of clothes and get in the car'.*

- *We got to the (LaBiancas') house. Charlie went inside and came back to the car and said: 'I got everything OK. And they think it's a robbery. And just tell them everything is OK so that when they go don't make it so that they got to be tortured. Make it quick and easy'.*

- *They were going to go anyway sooner or later because when it came down they were going to get it. So we tried to make it easy.*

- *Tex stabbed the husband and then came in and helped Katie stab the woman. When I went into the bedroom Tex handed me the knife and said: 'OK get to it'. Stabbing her blew my mind. I lost control, I went completely nuts. It was hard to get through. It's not like cutting a piece of meat. It's much tougher. I had to use both hands and all my strength. The feeling was so weird I just kept doing it, I did it about 10 times I think.*

- *And we were going to make it look freaky to start this paranoia going. I went into the other room and I noticed things had been written on the wall "Pig" and "Rise" and "Helter Skelter" on the refrigerator. And that was used to let people know that the Beatles were the prophets, and they were telling it like it was and you just be ready you know, get it on. Do whatever you have to do for this whole thing to be over. And 'Pig' was the white business man who hated his neighbour, couldn't look at his neighbour with love, who was going to get it in the end. And then 'Rise' was for the black man saying that it was his turn to, you know, be leader after all that time'.*

- *I thought what I was doing was perfectly right. This paranoia had to be started to get the vibration going even stronger; and its just part of the plan. And I have no control over it.*

- *Question by Mr Part: Well, if Charlie's Jesus and you girls are angels and you are doing God's will and God's will is that the revolution start so that the coloured people can take over the earth, why do you think that everybody's in jail ? Answer by Van Houten: Oh I don't know. You know it would almost be for the publicity as silly as that sounds . . . we were trying to find out ways of letting the youth know, because the people that are going into the hole are going to be the young people. And we tried with our music, and nobody would put out our music and nothing worked. But now everyone is finding out. Like our music is finally coming out. And [Charlie] will be able to speak for himself at the court and – to show - it will be one of the movements towards starting [the revolution].*

Charles "Tex" Watson – Interview With Lawyer

In 1978, Charles "Tex" Watson would publish his memoir *Will You Die For Me?*[144]. Watson would later say his memoir was based on tapes of interviews with his lawyer which took place in December 1969[145]. On this basis, the memoir was an important, and probably reliable, primary source of information about Tate/LaBianca. It was based on a confidential legal interview. And it was reasonably contemporaneous[146].

144. Watson, C., as told to Chaplain Ray, *Will You Die For Me?*, Revell, a division of Baker Publishing Group, 1978, used by permission.
145. *Manson's Right-Hand Man Speaks Out*, apparently written in 2003 and revised in 2012.
146. Not all of the book could have been based upon the 1969 tapes, for some of it dealt with clearly

Watson wrote in his memoir that there were three *"basic"* motives for the murders. He said the *"most obvious"* was Helter Skelter. There was also the *"need for more cash"*. Watson then wrote that, *"beyond"* Helter Skelter and cash, there was a *"third, less important purpose"* being the so-called "brother Bobby" (or "copycat") motive[147]. The brother Bobby/copycat motive would later emerge as an explanation for the Tate/LaBianca murders to the effect they were intended as copies of the Hinman murder which would lead police to think Hinman's real killers were still at large, and therefore "brother" Bobby Beausoleil would be released.

It is at once obvious from the language of the passage that, as far as Watson was concerned, the principle motive was Helter Skelter and the least important was "brother Bobby/copycat". This was reinforced by the fact that only one sentence in the whole book was devoted to "brother Bobby/Copycat", whereas Helter Skelter got a whole Chapter entitled "Revolution/Revelation". Furthermore, the two chapters devoted to the Tate and LaBianca murders were entitled, respectively, "Helter Skelter 1" and "Helter Skelter 11". Furthermore, when later referring to the LaBiancas' house, Watson described it as the place where *"Helter Skelter would fall again"*[148]. Furthermore, when talking about the post Tate de-brief with Manson, Watson wrote that Manson asked *"[W]as it Helter Skelter?"* to which he, Watson, replied *"Yeah it sure was Helter Skelter"*[149]. For these reasons, and others which will be seen later, it follows that, as far as Watson knew, the murders were principally motivated by (or at least closely related to) Helter Skelter. Brother Bobby/copycat has the appearance of being an afterthought. I will return to brother Bobby/copycat in more detail in later chapters.

---

post-1969 events, such as Watson's trial in 1971. My interpretation of the memoir is that it was generally based on the 1969 tapes, with some augmentation to bring it up to date when published in 1978.

147. Watson, *Will You Die For Me?*, p. 135.

148. Ibid, p.147. This passage does not sound like something he said to his lawyer. It sounds more like a literary flourish. But whether he said it in 1969, or wrote it in 1978, does not alter its character. Either way, it emphasised Helter Skelter.

149. Ibid, p.144

As to the events of Friday 8 August 1969, Watson wrote that Manson called everyone together *"and his message was simple . . . 'Now is the time for Helter Skelter'"*[150]. There followed an apparently private conversation to this effect:

Manson: *I've got a favor I want you to do for me tonight . . . but it'll take a lot of nerve to do it.*

Watson: *You know I'll do anything you want*

Manson: *I took care of Bernard Crowe for you when it was really your mess. Now I want you to take care of something for me.*

Watson: *I'll do whatever you ask me.*

Manson: *What I want . . . I want you to go to that house where Melcher used to live — I want you to take a couple of the girls I'll send with you and go down there . . . and totally destroy everyone in that house, as gruesome as you can. Make it a real nice murder, just as bad as you've ever seen. And get all their money. Take some rope and good knives. Cut the telephone wires before you go in. Take the bolt cutters off of my dune buggie to do it. Don't use the automatic gate because it might be attached to an alarm system. Wear dark clothes, take a change of clothes with you and burn the clothes you do the killing in. I don't know who is living in the house or how many people you might find, but whoever and however many it is you are to kill all, mutilate them, pull out their eyes and hang them on the mirrors!', and write messages on the walls in their blood. Write things like HELTER SKELTER and RISE. Write something that will shock the world.*

Watson: *I can't remember all that.*

Manson: *It's okay, the girls will know what to write. Use knives whenever possible, not the gun. Borrow Johnny Swartz' Ford. We need money to get Mary [Brunner] out of jail,*

---

150. Ibid, p.134.

> *if you don't get enough money at the Melcher house, then*
> *go on to the house next door and then the house after that*
> *until you get six hundred dollars*[151]

Later, as the car started, Manson leaned in an open window and said to the girls *"Remember to leave a sign, something witchy"*[152].

It is immediately obvious from Watson's account that there was no specific disclosure by Manson of <u>why</u> he wanted the people at Melcher's former house killed. And Watson wouldn't dare ask "why?" because that was against Family rules. It could reasonably be inferred, therefore, that everything Watson said in his book about motive was his own theorisation (or assumption) about why the people at Cielo had to be killed. As will be seen, very little (in fact likely nothing) of what has been said by the participants in the murders could be characterised as direct first-hand knowledge of the reason for the murders. Quite simply, and curiously, none of them could really claim to know <u>why</u> they did what they did[153]. Unless and until Manson tells all, it is a matter of piecing together the most plausible inferences. Properly understood, this was exactly what Watson was doing when he spoke to his lawyers in 1969 (or published his book in 1978) and likewise Atkins and Van Houten when they spoke to their lawyers. It appears the most obvious inference to all of them from the circumstances, including the announcement *"Now is the time for Helter Skelter"* and in Watson's case the instruction *"[W]rite things like HELTER SKELTER and RISE"*, not to mention the intense Helter Skelter grooming of the preceding months, was that Helter Skelter was the motive for the murders.

Watson then described the Tate and LaBianca murders quite graphically. It is unnecessary to go into the detail of it all. Suffice to say, Watson's account did not differ substantially from the accounts

---

151. Ibid, pp. 136, 137 and 143. The sentence *"Write something that will shock the world"* appears on a later page and seems to be an amendment of, or addition to, the body of the passage. I will treat it as part of the overall instruction that Manson allegedly delivered.

152. Ibid, p.137.

153. Indeed, Linda Kasabian would later give evidence suggesting that the next day she was still perplexed about why the murders had been committed.

of Atkins (Grand Jury) and Van Houten.   He confessed to killing all of the seven victims at both houses, with active assistance from Krenwinkel, and some participation from Van Houten at Waverley although she showed none of Krenwinkel's "*enthusiasm*"[154].   Atkins was a willing participant at Cielo, but Watson emphasised she did not stab Ms Tate.   Watson also wrote that Krenwinkel scrawled "Healter Skelter" in blood on the LaBiancas' refrigerator door[155].

Another matter that was tolerably clear from Watson's account was that, of the victims, it was Frykowski who fought the longest and hardest.   (This could also be inferred from Atkins' Grand Jury evidence).   Watson's relentless stabbing of Frykowski has been cited in subsequent claims that Watson was unduly affected by ingestion of speed (the speed preservation theory previously mentioned).   But it seems more likely it was Frykowski's stubborn fight that provoked the relentless stabbing.   Frykowski wouldn't give up.   According to Atkins, even when the killers were leaving, Frykowski was still moving, which prompted a kick to the head by Watson to finish him off.   Watson didn't require excessive consumption of speed to do what he did.   But he did have to make sure he finished off the killing.   Charlie wouldn't have it any other way.

Another difficulty with the speed preservation theory is that it postulates, and largely depends upon, a static scenario in which the victim is essentially motionless and the stabber simply goes through a repetitive stabbing motion with his arm (George Stimson refers to the repetitive stabbing of an inanimate object – a chair arm[156]).   But the killing of Frykowski was anything but static.   The melee started in the lounge room (eight stabs by Atkins), moved to the door and then outside the house.   It was a wild fight and quite inconsistent with the preservation model that would be postulated by Dr Frank (unsuccessfully) at Watson's trial and by Stimson and others.

Finally, Watson touched upon a topic which has received little attention in the Manson literature - why the random murders did

---

154. Ibid, p. 150.
155. Ibid.
156. Stimson, *Goodbye Helter Skelter*, p. 246.

not continue after LaBianca[157].   Watson explained that on Sunday
10 August (after LaBianca) he received a message at the Ranch to
ring his mother. Watson asked Manson what he should do. Manson
said "*call her*".   But Watson decided against calling. He then lied to
Manson, saying he had called and learned from his parents that FBI
men had come to the Watson family home in Copeville, Texas, and
told of his involvement in murders in Los Angeles.   Watson wrote
that he hoped this would prompt Manson to activate the move to the
desert[158]. Later in his book, Watson reflected further:

> "*I wondered what would happen this next night and the
> night after that. . . . Charlie had made it clear that two
> nights would not be the end of it, that we would do more and
> more killing until either the blacks or the whites took matters
> into their own hands – and Helter Skelter would begin*"[159]

Manson Implicated by all Co-Defendants (except Kasabian)

By the end of 1969, each of the participants in the Tate/LaBianca
homicides (save for Manson and Kasabian) had directly, or effectively,
stated to various people that Manson was behind the murders.
Furthermore, all had spoken or written things consistent with Charlie's
Helter Skelter motivating the murders[160].   Little of this was known
by the prosecution. And whether, and in what circumstances, these
communications would emerge at the trial, or otherwise become
public, would be another matter.

---

157. There was another murder, that of Donald "Shorty" Shea, which will be dealt with in a following chapter. However, Shea's murder was not random. Shea was a ranch hand at Spahn Ranch and was well known to the Family.

158. Watson, *Will You Die For Me?*, pp. 14 to 15.

159. Ibid, p.151.

160. To recap, Watson had told his lawyer and Ms Mallett. Van Houten told her lawyer. Atkins told her lawyer, her fellow inmates and the Grand Jury. Krenwinkel wrote it on the refrigerator door at Waverley.

Figure 1 Bobby Beausoleil, 21 years old, convicted of
murdering Gary Hinman. (Getty images)

Figure 2 Vincent Bugliosi, prosecuted Manson, Atkins, Krenwinkel and Van Houten in first Tate/LaBianca trial and Charles "Tex" Watson in second Tate/LaBianca trial. (Getty images)

Figure 3 Roman Polanski and Sharon Tate. (Getty images)

Figure 4 10050 Cielo Drive, scene of the murders of Sharon Tate, Jay Sebring, Wojiciech ("Voytek") Frykowski, Abigail Folger and Steven Parent on 9 August 1969. (Getty images)

Figure 5 3301 Waverley Drive, Los Feliz, the home of Leno and Rosemary LaBianca, murdered 10 August 1969. (Getty images)

Wojiciech "Voytek" Frykowski. (Getty images)

Jay Sebring. (Getty images)

CHAPTER 5: TATE AND LABIANCA – ARRAIGNMENT, LAW, TRIAL

"No matter what happens, the girls will take the rap for it"[161]

Charles Manson

Arraignment and Legal Representation

Experienced and skilful trial lawyers are driven by the three "p's" – preparation, preparation and preparation. Regrettably, the defence lawyers in this case were driven by a different set of "p's" – publicity, publicity and publicity.

The first return date of the indictments was 10 December 1969 when Susan Atkins, Linda Kasabian and Leslie Van Houten were brought before Judge William Keene. None entered pleas, but all would eventually plead not guilty. Patricia Krenwinkel would soon be extradited from Alabama and plead not guilty. Tex Watson fought extradition from Texas and would ultimately be tried separately.

Also, on 10 December, Judge Keene made an order designed to curb the media frenzy which had enveloped the case. The terms of the order were, essentially, that no party (which included attorneys) was to release any information, statements or opinions pertaining to the case

---

161. Bugliosi, *Helter Skelter*, p.334.

for public dissemination. It will be seen that little regard was had to either the letter or the spirit of this order by the parties or attorneys.

On 11 December 1969, Manson was arraigned before Judge Keene and pleaded not guilty. Judge Keene appointed Paul Fitzgerald of the Public Defender's Office ("PDO") to represent Manson. Fitzgerald wasted no time breaching the previous day's publicity order. He told a Los Angeles *Times* reporter: "*There's no case against Manson and these defendants. All the prosecution has are two fingerprints and Vince Bugliosi*".

Apart from their professional relationship, Fitzgerald and Manson cultivated quite a friendship. Fitzgerald seems to have been infatuated and would later recall Manson as "*a very nice, very intelligent, very soft spoken, very quiet, very interesting man. He was a man that had a lot of cares, lot of interests, he was philosophical, he was thoughtful*"[162].

Fitzgerald had competition for Manson's attention. Between 11 December 1969 and 21 January 1970, Manson would receive 139 visits from attorneys (three to four per day). Regular visiting attorneys included Ira Reiner, Daye Shinn and Ronald Hughes[163].

Manson aspired to represent himself and would make the first of many requests for pro per status on 17 December 1969. On this occasion, Judge Keene declined Manson's request.

On 19 December, Leslie Van Houten, who had hitherto been represented by one Donald Barnett, asked Judge Keene for Barnett's removal. Judge Keene acceded and appointed Marvin Part to take Barnett's place. Prosecutor Bugliosi would later write:

"*Only later would we learn what was happening behind the scenes. Manson had set up his own communications network. Whenever he heard that an attorney for one of the girls had initiated a move on behalf of his client which could conceivably run counter to Manson's own defense, within days*

---

162. Unattributed and undated interview, sourced from www.mansonsbackporch.com.
163. Bugliosi, *Helter Skelter*, p. 260.

that attorney would be removed from the case. Barnett had wanted a psychiatrist to examine Leslie. Learning of this, Manson vetoed the idea, and when the psychiatrist appeared at Sybil Brand, Leslie refused to see him. Her request for Barnett's dismissal came immediately after. Manson's goal: to run the entire defense himself. In court as well as out, Charlie intended to retain complete control of the Family"[164]

On 24 December, Manson got his wish to represent himself. The PDO's retainer was terminated. It appears Manson was motivated by a genuine desire to represent himself rather than any discontent with Fitzgerald or the PDO.

Attorney Ron Hughes continued visiting Manson and ran errands and documents for him. It has been reported that Hughes had actually visited the Ranch before the murders and shared LSD with the Family[165]. Hughes was thought of, and referred to, as a hippie lawyer. He had never conducted a criminal trial himself.

Attorney Daye Shinn was also in regular contact with Manson although he would never be retained to act as Manson's attorney. Shinn's relationship with Manson deserves attention because it was pivotal to the wrongdoing which was to ensue. Amongst other things, although not being Manson's attorney, Shinn prepared documents for Manson on his office letter head during the period when Manson represented himself. Shinn's documents would later be described by Judge Keene as being *"throughout"* Manson's court file[166]. There was nothing necessarily wrong with this, but it bespoke the close relationship between Shinn and Manson. Shinn visited Manson 40 times between 11 December 1969 and 11 March 1970 (over three times per week) despite never acting for him. Also, during January at

---

164. Ibid, p.271. It will be recalled that Krenwinkel had been assessed by a psychiatrist, Dr Claude Brown, but that was in Alabama, prior to extradition to Los Angeles, and while away from Manson's control.

165. Davis, *Five to Die,* p.202.

166. Transcript of proceedings, 6 March 1970.

least, Shinn facilitated and sat in on visits to Manson in custody by other Family members and ex-members[167]. It was also reported that Shinn was acting as Manson's business agent, or *"business lawyer"*, and was attempting to negotiate the rights to sell Manson's story[168]. There was nothing particularly wrong, or sinister, with any of this <u>unless</u> Shinn accepted a retainer to represent one of the other defendants, in which case a serious conflict of interest would arise.

On 6 January 1970, attorney Marvin Part (for Van Houten) requested a court appointed psychiatrist examine his client. Part also advised Van Houten she should seek to be tried separately from Manson. Charlie was displeased and ordered Part's removal[169]. Charlie's orders were conveyed to Van Houten by Lynette Fromme: *"We think you ought to have another lawyer"*. Van Houten replied: *"I'll do anything Charlie wants me to do"*[170]. On 19 January, Van Houten formally requested that Ira Reiner be substituted for Part. Part said to Judge George Dell in chambers: *"This girl will do anything that Charles Manson or any member of this so-called Manson Family says . . . [she] has no will of her own left . . . Because of the hold that Charles Manson and the Family has over her, she doesn't care whether she is tried together and gets the gas chamber, she just wants to be with the Family"* and *"[she] is insane in a way that is almost science fiction"*[171]. According to Bugliosi, Part *"begged"* Judge Dell to listen to the tape of his interview with her[172]. Judge Dell decided against listening to the tape. Nor did he appoint a psychiatrist to examine Van Houten. On 6 February, Judge Dell granted Van Houten's request and Reiner replaced Part. With disarming candour, Reiner would later explain that he took the case on *"for the publicity"*[173].

---

167. Watkins, *My Life With Charles Manson,* pp.243 to 244.
168. Hendrickson, R., *Death to Pigs,* Tobann International Pictures, 2011, pp. 333 and 338.
169. Davis, *Five to Die,* p.201.
170. Bugliosi, *Helter Skelter,* p.290.
171. Ibid, p.291.
172. Ibid.
173. Bishop, *Witness to Evil,* p.76.

The seed of a problem was, I think, sewn by the court's failure to investigate Part's concerns. It was questionable whether Van Houten, Atkins or Krenwinkel were fit to plead (stand trial). This will be dealt with in more detail in a later chapter.

On 24 February 1970, Patricia Krenwinkel made her first appearance in court, having been extradited from Alabama. Krenwinkel asked that Paul Fitzgerald be appointed as her attorney. Fitzgerald told the court the PDO would represent Krenwinkel subject to any conflict of interest arising from having earlier represented Manson. This was an odd thing for Fitzgerald to say. He would have known, there and then, that there had to be a conflict, having earlier represented Manson. Irrespective of the declarations of Family unity, and the girls' desire to do whatever Manson said, the reality was their respective interests clashed. Objectively, Manson had an interest in putting the rap on the girls, and they had an interest in putting the rap on him. Therefore, having acted for Manson, the PDO and/or Fitzgerald would instantly place themselves in prima facie conflicts of interest if they now purported to act for Krenwinkel.

On 5 March, Manson met with Atkins at the Los Angeles County jail. Manson asked Atkins *"are you afraid of the gas chamber?"* She replied *"no I'm not afraid of it now"*[174]. Manson directed her to recant her Grand Jury testimony, fire her lawyer (Richard Caballero), stop talking to Bugliosi and drop her insanity defence. Caballero was promptly fired (the next day). Atkins also recanted her Grand Jury testimony, which resulted in losing her deal with the District Attorney's office.

On 6 March, Judge Keene withdrew permission for Manson to represent himself. The judge cited several instances of Manson bringing ridiculous applications to court and being unable to offer any evidence or argument in support. On my reading of the transcripts, it would be impossible to disagree with the judge.

---

174. Atkins, *Child of Satan, Child of God*, p.163.

On 11 March, Atkins came before Judge Keene and she asked that Daye Shinn be appointed as her lawyer. It can be surmised that this was ordered by Manson. It would later be revealed by Lynette Fromme that Shinn *"seemed willing to go along with the Family's plan to protect Charlie at all costs"*[175]. This statement would have alarming repercussions. It suggested, on its face, that the girls' interests would be sacrificed for Charlie. Judge Keene was aware of the relationship between Shinn and Manson, and raised with Atkins that there appeared to be a conflict of interest. Atkins said she didn't care. Judge Keene granted the substitution. Thus, Manson's chief lackey was now Atkins' attorney. This was a serious conflict of interest for Shinn.

It is appropriate to consider the role of Lynette Fromme at this point. She was the acknowledged mother-hen of the Manson flock. She was *"Charlie's number-one girl"*[176]. She was Charlie's chief line of communication and was de facto leader of the Family in his absence. I have previously mentioned that she was pimped to George Spahn. She was also pimped to Paul Fitzgerald during the trial[177]. Lyn Fromme and Paul Fitzgerald regularly met with Charlie to receive instructions about the conduct of the case[178]. And Lyn and Paul slept together. Paul Fitzgerald became a bona fide member of the Manson Family, or at the very least he became a client of Charlie the pimp.

On 19 March, the proceedings came back before Judge Keene. On this occasion, Manson's new (court appointed) attorney Charles Hollopeter sought orders for a severance of Manson's trial from the girls' trials and also sought the appointment of a psychiatrist to assess Manson. Presumably Hollopeter did this without Manson's approval because Charlie immediately spat the dummy and sought to have Hollopeter removed. After throwing a copy of the United States Constitution into a waste paper bin, Manson accepted the

175. Watson, *Will You Die For Me?*, p.164.

176. Watkins, *My Life With Charles Manson*, p.248.

177. Patricia Krenwinkel parole hearing 29 December 2016; see also Bravin J., *Squeaky: The Life and Times of Lynette Alice Fromme*, St. Martin's Press, 1997, p.113; Guinn, *Manson*, p.359.

178. Bravin, *Squeaky*, pp.113 to 115.

appointment of Ron Hughes in place of Hollopeter. Hughes' first two actions were to withdraw the motions for psychiatric examination and severance, just as Charlie wanted. In a later interview with *Rolling Stone* magazine, Manson would refer to Hollopeter as a "*mouse*" and pose this rhetorical, and rather immodest, question: "*How can a mouse represent a lion?*"[179].

It was obvious that a defence of diminished capacity (on psychiatric grounds) required at least investigation. The nature of this defence will be considered later in this chapter. The lawyers could not force the defendants to investigate or mount the defence. The girls were glued to Charlie, and whatever he wanted. It is not unheard of for clients to reject the advice of lawyers, but it would be rare that advice about such a fundamental matter as investigating and pleading a psychiatric defence in a criminal case would be rejected. The lawyers would, or should, have been troubled by this. They might have sought permission to cease acting for the defendants at this point, but they didn't.

There may have been a number of reasons for Manson's rejection of psychiatric defences for himself and the girls. For one thing, a psychiatrist might just say the girls had been brainwashed by him. And there was another good forensic reason for rejecting the psychiatric defence, of which Manson would have been aware. A psychiatric defence meant the girls would be interrogated by psychiatrists about the events, and they would talk without Charlie there to control things. This happened when Krenwinkel had been interviewed by Dr Brown in Alabama – she said things damaging to Charlie. Just as when Atkins had been separated out from Charlie in custody and had started talking indiscriminately to fellow inmates. Charlie was familiar enough with court cases to know the defendants could be cross-examined about things they said to the psychiatrists. Histories given to doctors are often manna from

179. Dalton D., Felton, D., "Year of the Fork, Night of the Hunter", *Rolling Stone*, no.61, 25 June 1970, p.35.

heaven for a cross-examiner. Charlie did not want the girls talking to anyone but himself[180].

On 22 March 1970, Ron Hughes foreshadowed to reporters that another attorney, Irving Kanarek, may take over as Manson's lawyer. Kanarek's appointment would not be confirmed until about 15 June when the trial commenced, although it appears Kanarek commenced acting earlier and Hughes probably hung around running errands.

In the meantime, the PDO had concluded that it, and its employee Paul Fitzgerald, would be in a conflict of interest if it assumed Patricia Krenwinkel's defence. This was undoubtedly correct. But Fitzgerald seems to have been determined to involve himself in the case. To get around the PDO's withdrawal, on about 24 March 1970, Fitzgerald resigned his employment and became Krenwinkel's private attorney.

The reaction to Fitzgerald's resignation was a mixture of incredulity and admiration. George Bishop would later write:

> "This is the stuff of heroes. From twenty-six thousand dollars a year to zero, overnight . . . According to Miss Bejou Nolan, an attorney and former co-worker of Fitzgerald's . . . [he] was motivated by a simple desire to see justice done. 'Paul is like that' she told me. 'he's an idealist'"[181]

Vincent Bugliosi would later write:

> ". . . Paul Fitzgerald resigned from the [PDO], after that office decided there was indeed a conflict of interest involved. Whether Fitzgerald's move was purely idealistic, or he hoped to make a name for himself in private practice by winning

---

180. In the penalty phase, the girls did obtain psychiatric evidence, but it was hastily cobbled together and, as will be seen, somewhat slap-dash. For example, one psychiatrist wrote a report for Van Houten without even examining her. Another examined Krenwinkel only briefly and, for the most part, relied upon Dr Brown's earlier report. It was also advanced in the context of the girls having already testified (in the penalty phase) that Manson was not involved in the murders, hence, one suspects, Manson's relaxation of the ban on psychiatric evidence.

181. Bishop, *Witness to Evil*, p.44.

an acquittal for his client, or both, the fact remained that
he gave up a $25,000 a year salary and a promising career
as a public defender to represent Patricia Krenwinkel with
virtually no pay"[182]

Neither Bishop, Bugliosi, nor presumably Miss Nolan, seem to have known about Lyn Fromme's services, the precise monetary value of which is unknown. Nor do Bishop or Bugliosi seem to have appreciated that, irrespective of what the PDO did, Fitzgerald remained in a serious conflict of interest, having earlier acted for Manson.

It is beyond question Fitzgerald wanted Krenwinkel's retainer for the publicity and self-promotion. As mentioned, it remained that Fitzgerald was in a conflict of interest. However, having resigned, his withdrawal could no longer be mandated by PDO. He was free to act, but he had to hope nobody noticed, or objected to, the continuing conflict of interest[183]. This he got away with. These machinations occurred at a time when acquittal still seemed possible and in any event the case would generate publicity for Fitzgerald that money could not buy. These temptations were great enough for Fitzgerald to take on the risks of (a) resigning his job and (b) running the gauntlet of the conflict of interest. This was quite a gamble on Fitzgerald's part but if it came off the rewards in terms of fame and career advancement would be priceless.

On 19 May 1970, Manson and Atkins were arraigned before Judge Dell in the separate proceeding in respect of the Hinman murder. In that proceeding, Manson had hitherto been represented by a court appointment by the name of Walton (Christian name unknown). Atkins was represented by Daye Shinn. Manson asked Judge Dell for Daye Shinn to be substituted as his attorney in place of Walton. Judge Dell immediately indicated his concern about Shinn placing

---

182. Bugliosi, *Helter Skelter*, pp.304 to 305.
183. This also applied to Shinn and Reiner.

himself in a conflict of interest by acting for both Atkins and Manson. Judge Dell declined to allow the appointment of Shinn to represent Manson. In the course of debate about the proposed substitution, Manson confirmed he wanted Shinn because Shinn obeyed him. This would have set off alarm bells in Judge Dell's mind. It was the final proof, if it be needed, that Shinn was in reality acting on Manson's instructions even though "on the record" he was Atkins' attorney.

Preparation of the Prosecution Case

Vincent Bugliosi would later write in respect of events in January 1970 that (i) the prosecution could not prove a motive against Manson and (ii) without Susan Atkins the prosecution had no case at all[184]. Bugliosi explained in his book the predicament he faced, saying evidence of motive would be "*extremely important – a jury wants to know why*" and it was "*doubly*" important in this case because the murders "*appeared completely senseless*" and Manson was not present when the murders took place[185].

In late January 1970, things started looking up for the prosecution. Straight Satans member Al Springer told Bugliosi he thought "*Helter Skelter*" must have been Charlie's "*pet words*" because he used them so much[186]. Springer also told Bugliosi that Manson had said: "*[W]e knocked off five of them just the other night*" and: "*[N]o matter what happens, the girls will take the rap for it*"[187].

In February, Bugliosi interviewed Gregg Jakobson (music producer, friend of Manson) who offered more evidence about Helter Skelter. Bugliosi's next port of call, also in February, was prospector Paul Crockett who had come across Manson in spring 1969 and

---

184. Bugliosi, *Helter Skelter*, pp.266, 285.

185. Ibid, p.293.

186. Ibid.

187. Ibid, p.334.   Springer was an interesting character, a tough bikie predisposed to criminal endeavours, but quite obsessive about cleanliness. He rejected Manson's overtures to join the Family because he thought conditions at the Ranch were filthy. Apparently he was comfortable with the usual sort of bikie crime, such as receiving stolen goods, as long as it was hygienic.

to whom Manson had related the Helter Skelter scenario[188].   It was through Crockett that ex-Family member Brooks Poston was found. Poston gave more evidence about Helter Skelter.   Then Paul Watkins corroborated Poston.   The evidence from Poston and Watkins about Manson's specific prediction of savage murders in the Bel Air district where rich "piggies" would be cut up and their blood used to smear things on the walls created a picture that would have seemed to Bugliosi remarkably similar to the Tate/LaBianca murder scenes.

The most important breakthrough was the interviewing of Linda Kasabian which commenced on 28 February 1970.   She had agreed to cooperate in exchange for an immunity from prosecution.   Not only did Kasabian offer evidence about Helter Skelter, she was also a direct witness to the murders of Parent, Folger and Frykowski.   Moreover, she seems to have come across well in conference.   This is not always a guarantee that a witness will do well in the witness box (on the stand), but it's a good start.   By the end of February the prosecution case was looking buoyant.   It would not have been lost on Bugliosi that Kasabian's evidence, if accepted by the jury, had the potential to make proof of motive superfluous to the prosecution's case.   It will be seen that, on her evidence, there was little or no room for Manson's innocence (motive or no motive).   It is no coincidence that from this point of Bugliosi's chronology of events in his book there was little or no rumination about motive.

In April, there were more breakthroughs.   It is necessary to back track a little.   In December 1969, a .22 Hi Standard Longhorn Revolver was found not far from Cielo.   It had a missing right grip, and the three pieces of gun grip found at Cielo fitted perfectly.   Tests matched it to the bullet fired into Jay Sebring.   There was no doubt it was the murder weapon.   On 15 April, shell casings were retrieved from Spahn Ranch which matched the gun.   Thus, the gun was linked to the Ranch, but not yet directly to Manson.   At about the same time (date unclear) Bugliosi interviewed Ranch manager, Ruby Pearl, who

188. Ibid, p.312.

also recognised the gun.   Pearl also identified the rope found at Cielo as similar to one Manson had, and the leather thong at Waverley as similar to thongs worn by Manson.   On the same day as the interview with Pearl, Bugliosi interviewed Ranch hand Randy Starr who identified the gun as one he had given to Manson.   The gun was now linked directly to Manson.

Also, in April, Patricia Krenwinkel refused to undertake a handwriting exemplar. This was a circumstance consistent with guilt. Then, on 25 May, Bugliosi came across a door which had been seized by police from the Ranch which bore the painted words "HELTER SKELTER IS COMING DOWN FAST"[189]. In June, more positives – Family member Dianne Lake was interviewed by Bugliosi and supplied evidence of admissions by Van Houten and Krenwinkel, the detail of which will be seen in due course.

Bugliosi would have been feeling confident about the prospects of conviction by this stage.   He would later write that when Paul Fitzgerald (for Krenwinkel) told the media at the start of the trial (15 June) that Helter Skelter was a *"truly preposterous theory"* he, Bugliosi, had a strong feeling that by the end of the case Fitzgerald wouldn't even argue against it[190]. Bugliosi's feeling proved right.

Fitzgerald's statement to the media was indeed puzzling.   He was supposed to be representing Krenwinkel.   But Helter Skelter was advanced by the prosecution as evidence of Manson's personal culpability – it was his prophecy.   Krenwinkel's interests clashed with Manson's interests to the extent that, objectively, they may as well have been regarded as opponents of each other. This was so, notwithstanding all the defendants expressed a desire to present a "united defence" and so on. Their expressions of unity were, legally, a superficiality about which the girls' lawyers ought not to have drawn any comfort.   It was illogical for Fitzgerald to concern himself with the case advanced personally against Manson. Fitzgerald was beginning to

---

189. Ibid, pp.390-391. This door had been in police custody since November 1969 but no-one had told Bugliosi about it.
190. Ibid, p.417.

sound as if he was in fact Manson's lawyer. It is safe to assume that by this stage, as well as having his own lawyer (Kanarek), Manson had Fitzgerald and Shinn well under his thumb. It appears Fitzgerald was totally at Manson's beck and call[191]. Fitzgerald was indeed in a unique position for a lawyer. He was, effectively, Manson's attorney and he was also Manson's client by virtue of the pimped services of Lyn Fromme.

Law – Proof

Different crimes have different elements. As we have seen, the essential elements of murder were (i) unlawful killing and (ii) malice (intent).

Proof of the elements of a crime is required beyond a reasonable doubt. In cases based on circumstantial evidence, this will usually be articulated for the jury in the following way:

> *You are not permitted to find a defendant guilty of any crime charged against him based on circumstantial evidence unless the proved circumstances are not only consistent with the theory that that defendant is guilty of the crime, but cannot be reconciled with any other rational conclusion . . .*

This was part of one of the directions given to the Manson jury. This sort of direction has been described as no more than a restatement of the basal proposition that the jury must be satisfied about guilt beyond a reasonable doubt[192].

Law – Conspiracy

We have already seen that conspiracy comprised an agreement between two or more persons, followed by an overt act committed

---

191. Bravin, *Squeaky*, p.115.

192. *Shepherd v R* (1990) 170 CLR 573, [1990] HCA 56; *Plomp v. R* (1963) 110 CLR 234, [1963] HCA 44, per Menzies J at paragraph 11; *The Queen v. Keenan* (2009) 236 CLR 126, [2009] HCA 1, per Kiefel J at paragraph 126.

for the purpose of accomplishing the object of the agreement[193].   It is instructive to go into a little more detail. The "<u>overt act</u>" is any act committed by <u>any</u> of the conspirators beyond the mere planning or agreement to commit the crime as long as it was in furtherance of the object of the conspiracy. For example, the overt act could be the act of driving to the scene of the proposed crime, or cutting telephone wires to prevent the victims calling for help.

In order for the defendant to be found a member of a conspiracy, the prosecution must prove the defendant had the intent to commit the crime which was the subject of the agreement. Therefore, if the alleged crime was murder, then the defendant must be proved to have had the intention of murdering people[194].

It is not necessary that the defendant know the precise details of the objective of the conspiracy. It suffices that there was a common understanding of the end to be achieved and an agreement to do whatever was necessary to achieve that end[195].

In summary, on conspiracy and as against Manson, the prosecution had to prove beyond doubt that:

1. Manson joined in an agreement which had the objective of murdering a person (or persons).
2. Manson himself had that specific intention.
3. One of the conspirators (even if not Manson) committed an overt act in furtherance of the objective of the conspiracy. This act had to be something in the nature of, for example, driving off with the intention of going to the site of the proposed murder.
4. The victims were killed unlawfully by one of the conspirators, even if not Manson himself.

---

193. Section 184 of the Code, and *People v. Cockrell* 63 Cal. App. 2d 779). The jury would ultimately also be instructed on felony murder and aid/abet murder, but the thrust of the prosecution's case was undoubtedly conspiracy.
194. *People v. Jones* 228 Cal. App. 2d 74.
195. *People v. Buckman* 186 Cal. App. 2d 38.

If the prosecution succeeded in proving the above matters, then Manson would be guilty of conspiracy to commit murder. Manson would then also become guilty of murder pursuant to the doctrine of vicarious liability previously discussed.

Law – Circumstantial Evidence

The prosecutor seeks to prove the elements of the offence by adducing evidence. There are two types of evidence – direct and circumstantial. Evidence is direct if it establishes a fact by itself, without having to infer anything. Eye-witness evidence is a common form of direct evidence. If a witness says: *"I saw A shoot B"*, and is believed, then the fact that A shot B is established. On the other hand, circumstantial evidence is evidence of a fact, or facts, from which inferences need to be drawn before anything is established. For example, a witness testifies: *"I saw B's body on the ground and I saw A running away with a gun"* or *"A told me he intended to shoot B"*. In both of these cases, inferences need to be drawn before A can be found to have shot B.

Some cases are wholly circumstantial. Some are part circumstantial and part direct. It is tempting to think circumstantial cases would always be weaker than direct cases. But this would be a mistake:

". . . circumstantial evidence is very often the best. It is evidence of surrounding circumstances which, by undesigned coincidence, is capable of proving a proposition with the accuracy of mathematics. It is no derogation of evidence to say that it is circumstantial"[196]

and:

"Sometimes circumstantial evidence constituting a 'chain of other facts sworn to by many witnesses of undoubted

---

196. *Taylor Weaver and Donovan* 21 Cr App R 20 at 21, per Hewart LCJ.

credibility' can actually be stronger than disputable positive eye witness evidence"[197]

A question that arises is: whilst the prosecutor has to prove the elements of the offence beyond doubt, does he also have to prove each individual circumstance beyond doubt? The answer is that it depends upon the nature of the case. In cases containing numerous circumstances, the general position is that no individual circumstance needs to be proved beyond doubt:

". . . the prosecution bears the onus of proving all the <u>elements</u> of the crime beyond reasonable doubt. That . . . does not mean that every fact – every piece of evidence – relied upon to prove an element by inference must itself be proved beyond reasonable doubt. Intent, for example, is . . . an element of every crime. It is something which . . . must be proved from inference. But the jury may quite properly draw the necessary inference having regard to the whole of the evidence, whether or not each individual piece of evidence relied upon is proved beyond reasonable doubt, provided they reach their <u>conclusion</u> upon the criminal standard of proof. Indeed, the probative force of a mass of evidence may be cumulative, making it pointless to consider the degree of probability of each item of evidence separately"[198] [emphasis added]

On the other hand, there will be cases in which there are few circumstances, or where one circumstance is indispensable to inferring guilt. In the latter case, the individual circumstance is said to be an indispensable link in the chain of proof. If the individual circumstance is that important, it may need to be proved beyond doubt[199]. It is

---

197. *De Gruchy v R* (2002) 211 CLR 85, per Kirby J at paragraph 48, citing *Commonwealth v Harman* 4 Pa St 269 at 272;

198. Ibid, per Dawson J at paragraph 6.

199. *Shepherd*, per McHugh J at page 593.

a matter for the jury to decide whether the circumstance attains that level of importance and requires that level of proof. Therefore, generally speaking, the fewer the circumstances, or the more important an individual circumstance, the better the proof needs to be of each circumstance, or of that individual circumstance.

The topic of a defendant's motive to commit a crime affords a good example of how circumstantial evidence works, and is apposite because it is the centre of attention of much of the literature about the Manson murders.

The direction on motive given to the jury in the first Tate/LaBianca trial was in the following terms:

> *13. Motive is not an element of the crimes charged and need not be shown. However, you may consider motive or lack of motive as a circumstance in this case. Presence of motive may tend to establish guilt. Absence of motive may tend to establish innocence. You will therefore give its presence or absence, as the case may be, the weight to which you find it to be entitled.*

Motive is but one circumstance. It is not an essential element of the crime of murder. That being so, it is not, generally speaking, something that has to be proved:

> *"The law does not require impossibilities. The law recognizes that the cause of the killing is sometimes so hidden in the mind and breast of the party who killed, that it cannot be fathomed, and as it does not require impossibilities, it does not require the jury to find it"*[200]

The criminal law is generally concerned with the question of whether the defendant committed the crime, not <u>why</u>. Motive may be

---

200. *Pointer v. United States* [1894] USSC 38; 151 US 396 at p.413.

a clue to the question of whether the defendant committed the crime, occasionally a significant one, but never more than a clue.

Motive tends to only have importance in close cases. The presence of motive is a circumstance that may help the prosecution in a close contest. Absence of motive may help the defence in a close case. In a strong prosecution case, motive rarely comes into it. Likewise, in a weak prosecution case, motive cannot fill in gaps or act as a makeweight for the prosecution. In the result, motive is rarely a decisive, or turning, point in a criminal trial. It certainly wasn't in any of the trials considered in this book.

Law – Defences - Insanity

If the prosecution fails to prove the essential elements of the crime, then the defendant will be acquitted. Alternatively, there are various defences which, if made out by the defendant, will result in acquittal. One such defence is that of diminished responsibility on the grounds of psychiatric illness. The onus of proof is upon the defendant. The defendant must prove that he was, more probably than not, insane under the so-called *M'Naghten Rules*. They provide that if the defendant can prove (1) he did not believe it was wrong to commit the alleged offence and (2) he believed that society did not consider it wrong, then he will be found legally insane, resulting in acquittal. The nub of the defence is that the inability to distinguish between right and wrong means the defendant cannot have formed the intention to do wrong.

As we have seen, many lawyers who came into contact with Manson and the female defendants considered they should investigate and consider pleading insanity. Proof of insanity would require examinations, reports and testimony by expert psychiatrists. It is by no means clear that an insanity defence would have been successful, but it at least required investigation. Manson refused to investigate or plead insanity and also prevented the girls from going down that path.

Commencement of Trial

The trial of Manson, Atkins, Krenwinkel and Van Houten commenced on 15 June 1970 before Judge Charles H. Older and a jury yet to be empanelled ("the first Tate/LaBianca trial" - there would later be a separate trial for Watson and two re-trials for Van Houten).

The line-up of defence lawyers on the record was:
- Irving Kanarek (for Manson).
- Paul Fitzgerald (for Krenwinkel).
- Daye Shinn (for Atkins).
- Ira Reiner (for Van Houten).

Fitzgerald, Shinn and Reiner were all in conflicts of interest because they had either acted for Manson or been in his confidence. And it is a safe assumption that at least two of these attorneys, namely Fitzgerald and Shinn, were acting in adherence to the plan to protect Charlie at all costs, as expressed by Lyn Fromme. The trouble was that this, of itself, generated a new set of conflicts of interest. Although the girls expressed their instructions as being to do whatever Charlie said, the reality remained, as foreshadowed, that their interests clashed with Charlie's interests. If Fitzgerald and Shinn were now going to proceed in accordance with Charlie's plan to save himself, then they would have to act against the interests of their own clients, the girls. This was a serious, indeed sinister, conflict. It was beginning to look, sound and smell like a conspiracy to pervert the course of justice. It would later transmogrify, potentially, into a conspiracy to commit perjury. The conspiracy would reward Fitzgerald and Shinn by enabling them to stay in the "trial of the century" and get the career defining publicity they craved. The reward for Manson would be acquittal, or a reduced sentence. There would be no reward for the girls, just the gas chamber. It is a testament to Manson's powers of manipulation and persuasion that he was able to bring about this terrible state of affairs.

Jury Empanelment

The jury is the sole arbiter of the facts. The jury comprises 12 persons. The judge directs the jury as to the elements of the offence in question, so the jury can convert its factual findings into a determination of whether the defendant is guilty or not guilty.

Before evidence can be received, a jury has to be selected and empanelled. The parties are given an opportunity to question prospective jurors.

There were several strange happenings during the empanelment. One was a portent of things to come. Paul Fitzgerald asked one of the prospective jurors: *"Have you or any member of your family ever been the unfortunate victim of a homicide?"*. This question was asked twice before someone nudged Fitzgerald and informed him the person would not be much use on the jury if he'd already been a homicide victim[201].

On 24 June, during Fitzgerald's questioning of jurors, Krenwinkel interrupted and asked aloud that Fitzgerald be dismissed because he wasn't doing as she asked. She said: *"he is to be my voice, which he is not"*. Later outside court, according to Bugliosi, Fitzgerald had tears in his eyes and Bugliosi tried to console him. Fitzgerald said: *"they're savages, ingrates. [T]heir only allegiance is to Manson"*[202]. Fitzgerald was feeling the heat. It would have been looking like his gamble was backfiring, which would leave him without a regular job and without his high profile gig. The only way to keep the gig would be to follow Charlie's orders to the letter and become Charlie's mouthpiece, irrespective of what that entailed for Krenwinkel.

During Kanarek's interrogation, Manson himself requested permission to question the prospective jurors. This was refused. In a typical hissy-fit, Manson immediately instructed Kanarek to refrain from asking any more questions. Kanarek obeyed.

---

201. Bugliosi, *Helter Skelter,* p.404.
202. Ibid, p.408.

Ira Reiner (for Van Houten) asked this question: *"If the evidence proves Leslie Van Houten 'not guilty', would you render that verdict even though she herself expresses a desire to be found guilty?"*. This unusual question tended to confirm the defendants' plan for the girls to take the rap. It also suggested Reiner was keen to separate out Van Houten's defence from the other defendants. This would not have pleased Charlie. It was not in his interests. Manson ordered that Reiner was to be removed as Van Houten's attorney. He instructed Shinn to arrange for Ron Hughes to be substituted for Reiner[203]. And so, on 17 July 1970 with the jury still being empanelled, Reiner was replaced by Hughes. It can safely be assumed Hughes agreed to the grand plan to protect Charlie. Thus, he was in the same conflict as Fitzgerald and Shinn, acting for and against his own client.

Observer George Bishop later spoke to Ira Reiner who said he had initially been hired *"because they thought I would go along with the general defense . . . I found that I couldn't do it. I had to put on the best defense I knew how"*[204]. Bishop asked him why he hadn't pulled out earlier. Reiner replied: *"Two reasons. First, the court wouldn't let me, and second, I just might have got her off. The key to her case is separating it from the others . . . But [Van Houten] wouldn't [agree to separation]; she wouldn't give herself that chance"*. Bishop asked *"why?"* and Reiner replied: *"I don't know. I really don't know. Charlie tells her to do it, and she does it"*. Bishop asked if it could be because Manson wanted the girls represented by lawyers who he could order around and Hughes was one such lawyer. Reiner said: *"I'm still bound by the court's gag order, I can't answer that"*[205].

Fitzgerald and Reiner later told the Los Angeles *Times* that all of the defence attorneys had been instructed to remain silent and not interrogate any prospective jurors[206]. Reiner had disobeyed the order,

---

203. Sanders, E., *The Family,* Penguin Books Inc., 1989, pp.402 to 403.
204. Bishop, *Witness to Evil,* p.76.
205. Ibid, p.77.
206. Bugliosi, *Helter Skelter,* p.408.

and been removed.   Kanarek, Fitzgerald and Shinn obeyed, and stayed in.

Thus, the final line up of defence lawyers was in place:
- Irving Kanarek for Manson
- Paul Fitzgerald for Krenwinkel
- Daye Shinn for Atkins
- Ron Hughes for Van Houten

This line up represented a very unsatisfactory state of affairs. Each of the girls' attorneys was in fact a Manson crony. On the record, Fitzgerald, Shinn and Hughes acted for the girls, but in reality they were acting for Charlie and against the girls. To pretend to act for someone on trial for her life, and in fact be acting against that person, was hideous. As will be seen, Fitzgerald would be active in harming the interests of his own client (Krenwinkel) by way of cross-examinations he chose to conduct, objections he took and submissions he made.   Hughes would do the same but he was so inexperienced that he may have been genuinely unaware of the problem.   Shinn couldn't care less. Life was comfortable for him because he was being paid from the proceeds of a quickie tell-all paperback book containing Atkins' confessions[207].

Empanelment of the jury took five weeks and finished on 21 July 1970.   Pursuant to an earlier order by Judge Older, the jury would be sequestered at the Ambassador Hotel. Sequestration is rare. Judge Older stated the purpose of the sequestration was *"to protect [the jurors] from harassment and to prevent their being exposed to trial publicity"*.

The *Rolling Stone* Interviews

On another front, on 25 June 1970, while the jury empanelment was still underway, an article was published in *Rolling Stone* magazine entitled "Year of the Fork, Night of the Hunter".   The story was written by David Dalton and David Felton. Manson had agreed to

---

207. Schiller, L., *The Killing of Sharon Tate*, New American Library, 1969. The publication of this book was a whole other story. It was one of many side-shows which accompanied the trial.

be interviewed in breach of Judge Keene's publicity order. He gave the reporters an expose of Helter Skelter. This was at a time when the prosecution was seeking to promote Helter Skelter as Manson's motive, and the defence attorneys were keenly denouncing it. It would be expected Manson would renounce any knowledge of it. But it seems he couldn't help himself:

Interviewer: Can you explain the meaning of Revelations, Chapter 9?

Manson: *What do you think it means? It's the battle of Armageddon. It's the end of the world. It was the Beatles' 'Revolution 9' that turned me on to it. It predicts the overthrow of the Establishment. The pit will be opened, and that's when it will all come down. A third of all mankind will die. The only people who escape will be those who have the seal of God on their foreheads. You know that part, 'They will seek death but they will not find it.'*

Interviewer: How do you know that these things are coming about?

Manson: *I'm just telling you what my awareness sees. I look into the future like an Indian on a trail. I know what my senses tell me. I can just see it coming, and when it comes I will just say, 'Hi there!' [He says it like a used-car salesman greeting the Apocalypse from a TV screen in some empty room.]*

Interviewer: Why do you think that this revolution predicted in 'Revolution 9' will be violent? Why will it be racial?

Manson: *Have you heard of the Muslims? Have you heard of the Black Panthers? Englishmen, do you remember cutting off the heads of praying Muslims with the cross sewn onto your battledress? Can you imagine it?*

Well, imagination is the same as memory. You and all Western Man killed and mutilated them and now they are reincarnated and they are going to repay you. The soul in the white man is lying down. They were praying, kneeling

in the temple. They did not want war. And the white man
came in the name of Christ and killed them all.

Interviewer: Can you explain the prophecies you found in the Beatles'
double album? [Charlie starts drawing some lines on the
back of a sheet of white paper, three vertical lines and one
horizontal line. In the bottom area he writes the word SUB.]

Manson: OK. Give me the names of four songs on the album.
[We choose 'Piggies', 'Helter Skelter', 'Blackbird', and he
adds 'Rocky Raccoon'. Charlie writes down the titles at
the top of each vertical section. Under 'Helter Skelter'
he draws a zigzag line, under 'Blackbird' two strokes,
somehow indicating bird sounds. Very strange.]
This bottom part is the subconscious. At the end of each
song there is a little tag piece on it, a couple of notes. Or
like in 'Piggies' there's 'oink, oink, oink' Just these couple of
sounds. And all these sounds are repeated in 'Revolution
9'. Like in 'Revolution 9', all these pieces are fitted
together and they predict the violent overthrow of the
white man. Like you'll hear 'oink, oink', and then right
after that, machine gun fire. [He sprays the room with
imaginary slugs.] AK-AK-AK-AK-AK-AK!

Interviewer: Do you really think the Beatles intended to mean that?

Manson: I think it's a subconscious thing. I don't know whether
they did or not. But it's there. It's an association in the
subconscious. This music is bringing on the revolution, the
unorganized overthrow of the Establishment. The Beatles
know in the sense that the subconscious knows"[208]

The journalists also spoke to Steve "Clem" Grogan:

*"Now it's Clem's turn. Clem really is on his own trip, or at
least, he's much further advanced than the others.*

---

208. Dalton D., Felton, D., "Year of the Fork, Night of the Hunter", *Rolling Stone*, no.61, 25 June 1970, p.36

'I was in jail with a bunch of Panthers,' he says, 'and they'd tell me it was coming down. They had this chant, 'Look out, whitey, we're coming to get you.'

'They have this plan, and they will take over because the white man's karma is almost used up. If you read Revelations, Chapter 9, it's there. They are going to open up the bottomless pit, and the only people that will escape are the people that go to the desert. There won't be very many who make it — 144,000, that's all.'"[209]

Bugliosi should have been pleased with this development. The article made it potentially untenable for Manson or Grogan to testify in rebuttal of Helter Skelter.

There were also some downers for the prosecution in the *Rolling Stone* article. Bugliosi's co-prosecutor Aaron Stovitz had agreed to be interviewed. Incredibly, Stovitz said two things adverse to the prosecution's case. First, at a time when Bugliosi was cementing the Helter Skelter motive, and in the very same article in which Manson was admitting as much, Stovitz gratuitously offered up his own different view of motive. He came up with the "brother Bobby/copycat motive", which would later be picked up and run with by the defendants. As far as I can tell, this was the very first public airing, by anyone, of the brother Bobby/copycat motive:

"Now — this is only a supposition on my part, I don't have any proof to support it — I suppose he, meaning Manson, said to himself, 'How am I going to help my friend Beausoleil out? By showing that the actual murderer of Hinman is still at large. So I know that Melcher used to live in this house on Cielo Drive'.

Go out there, Watson, with these girls and commit robbery and kill anyone that you see there.

209. Ibid., p.47.

> *Don't forget to leave – and this is very important because*
> *in the Hinman case they wrote POLITICAL PIGGIES in*
> *blood. He said – 'Don't forget to leave a sign'.*
> *So after the killings were all over, Susan Atkins goes back*
> *and writes the word PIG on the door"*[210]

Stovitz got one thing right - there was no proof to support what he said. In fact, as will be seen, brother Bobby/copycat was nonsense. Stovitz would later concede Bugliosi was right to go with Helter Skelter[211]. The next thing Stovitz said was even worse. He told *Rolling Stone* that the prosecution case on LaBianca was weak:

> *"On La Bianca, I'll rap with you on the level, our case is not*
> *that strong. There are no fingerprints, no one saw them"*[212]

Bugliosi must have been apoplectic about this. Here was a person from his office – his co-prosecutor no less - bad mouthing the prosecution's case. And getting it wrong. The LaBianca case was strong. True it had no fingerprints and no witnesses to the actual slayings. But it had just about everything else. It had direct evidence about the forging of the agreement to kill (Kasabian's evidence about a conversation outside of Waverley, the detail of which will be seen in due course). There was also evidence of admissions by Krenwinkel and Van Houten. And there were the words "Helter Skelter", "rise", "death to pigs" and "WAR" around the house, linking Manson's scripture to the house.

Stovitz was clearly in breach of Judge Keene's publicity order by agreeing to the interview with *Rolling Stone*. He was cited for contempt of court. District Attorney Evelle Younger told Stovitz *"no more interviews"*[213].

---

210. Ibid, p.28.
211. Davis, *Five to Die*, p.206.
212. Dalton D., Felton, D., "Year of the Fork, Night of the Hunter", *Rolling Stone*, no.61, 25 June 1970, p.29.
213. Bugliosi, *Helter Skelter*, p.452.

CHAPTER 6: TATE AND LABIANCA – GUILT PHASE OF TRIAL

"The courtroom was just a follow-up of the crimes. Charlie was conducting the courtroom. He was telling us what to say, you know, when to stand up, when to carve the x, when to shave our heads. Every day it was like a new agenda on what we should do for the day"
Leslie Van Houten to Barbara Walters[214]

"I have covered almost 50 of the most famous trials in American history and without doubt the Tate-LaBianca trial was the weirdest, wildest and craziest experience I have ever witnessed"
Bill Lignante, ABC TV courtroom artist[215]

Their Day in Court

The guilt phase of the trial, as the name suggests, is the part of the trial in which the jury determines whether the defendants are guilty as charged.

---

214. ABC TV, January 1977.
215. Quoted in Davis, *Five to Die*, p.194.

The taking of evidence commenced on 24 July 1970. Manson arrived at court for the big day with his forehead decorated with an "X" and with a press release about the "X" in case anyone missed its significance:

> *"I am not allowed to be a man in your society. I am considered inadequate and incompetant [sic] to speak or defend myself in your court. You have created the monster. I am not of you, from you, nor do I condone your wars or your unjust attitudes towards things, animals and people that you won't try to understand. I haved [sic] Xed myself from your world. I stand in the opposite to what you do and what you have done in the past. You have never given me the constitution you speak of. The words you have used to trick the people are not mine. I do not accept what you call justice. The lie you live in is falling and I am not a part of it. You use the word God to make money.*
>
> *You! Look at what you have done and what you are doing. You make fun of God and have murdered the world in the name of Jesus Christ. I stand with my X with my love, with my god and by myself. My faith in me is stronger than all your armies, governments, gas chambers or anything you may want to do to me. I know what I have done and your courtroom is mans (sic) game. Love is my judge. I have my own constitution; its (sic) inside me.*
>
> *No man or lawyer is speaking for me. I speak for myself. I am not allowed to speak with words so I have spoken with the mark I will be wearing on my forehead. Many U.S. citizens are marked and don't know it. You won't let them come from under your foot. But God is moving. Moving, and I am a witness.*
>
> *I have tried to stand on the constitution but I am not afforded the rights another citizen may enjoy. I am forced to contend with communicating to the mass without words.*

I feel no man can represent another man because each man is different and has his own world, his own kingdom, his own reality. It is impossible to communicate one reality through another into another reality"[216]

To make sense of Manson's statement, media and observers made bee-lines for the nearest mental health professionals. Psychologist Nathaniel Branden was asked his opinion of Manson's statement:

"The staggering irrelevance of his statement in the context of the legal charges confronting him, and its projection of vacant grandiosity, immediately suggests a diagnosis of paranoid psychosis or pre-psychosis. This is the obvious diagnosis and it may be the correct one. Having never examined the author I am not in a position to say"[217]

The following day, the other defendants would arrive in court similarly decorated with "X"ed foreheads. This was a bad move. As the appeal court would later say: *"This behaviour had some tendency to show the affinity between the [defendants] as well as the asserted leadership of Manson"*[218]. Leadership was a more important circumstance to prove against Manson than, for example, motive. Nothing much worked in the prosecution case without proof of leadership. If Manson wasn't the leader, then the Helter Skelter prophecy meant little or nothing[219]. Manson's stunt had given the prosecution a significant leg-up. The association of Manson with his followers, and the circumstance of his leadership, had the effect of linking Manson to the murder scenes. That his disciples were at the scenes was probably

---

216. Bishop, *Witness to Evil*, pp.88 to 89.

217. Cited in Bishop, *Witness to Evil*, pp. 89-90.

218. *People v. Manson & Ors.* [1976] 61 Cal. App. 3d 102 at p. 157.

219. Bugliosi would later write: *"Domination. Unless we could prove this . . . we'd never obtain a conviction against Manson"*, *Helter Skelter*, p.287.

the most decisive of a number of links which would be proved against Manson. It had not been proved yet, but it soon would be.

With Charlie's hoop-lah out of the way, proceedings began in the usual way with Bugliosi's opening argument. It is unnecessary to set out the opening. The opening and closing arguments of the lawyers are not evidence in the case. Too many of the commentaries on the Manson trials look to the lawyers' arguments as quick fixes to understanding the cases. Accordingly, the arguments are conflated with the evidence. For example, reference is often made to the Helter Skelter motive as if Bugliosi was the one testifying about it, and as if he had come up with it. This is incorrect. The Helter Skelter prophecy came from the large number of persons (at least 32 of whom I am aware, 10 of whom testified on oath about it[220]) who represented or heard things consistent with Helter Skelter being the central plank of Manson's manifesto. It was never Bugliosi's theory, or Bugliosi's evidence.

During Bugliosi's opening, a pattern of misbehaviour by the defendants started to develop. Manson smiled inappropriately, and the girls sniggered, whispered and looked at him. This was noticed by juror William Zamora[221]. It was probably noticed by the judge and other jurors.

Prosecution Case

The first witness was Paul Tate, father of Sharon, who testified to identifying her at the mortuary. The last time he had seen his daughter

---

220. The 10 witnesses who testified during the first and second Tate/LaBianca trials were: Richard Caballero, Danny DeCarlo, Juan Flynn, Barbara Hoyt, Gregg Jakobson, Linda Kasabian, Dianne Lake, Brooks Poston, Paul Watkins, Charles Watson. The 22 other persons were: Susan Atkins, Paul Crockett, Dr Coburn, David Dalton, Bruce Davis, Karlene Faith (plus other teachers at California Institute for Women), David Felton, Virginia Graham, Steven Grogan, Dr Grosvenor-Bailey, Ronnie Howard, Patricia Krenwinkel, Jeanne Denise Mallett, Charles Manson, James Pursell, Stephanie Schram's sister (Christian name unknown), Catherine Share, Al Springer, Dr Suarez, Dr Tweed, Leslie Van Houten, Dennis Wilson.

221. Zamora, W., *Blood Family*, Zebra Books Kensington Publishing Corp., 1976, first published as *Trial By Your Peers*, 1973, p.57.

was 20 July 1969 when they had watched the moon landing together. Mr Tate also identified Folger, Frykowski and Sebring.

The next witness was Steven Parent's father, Wilfred, who cried when testifying about identifying his son at the mortuary.

Then followed the cleaner of the Tate residence, Winifred Chapman. She testified that on Friday 8 August she had washed the front door where Tex Watson's fingerprint was later found. This generated an inference that Watson was at the premises after Ms Chapman had finished her day's work (i.e. after 4.30 pm). Likewise, Ms Chapman had washed the rear door from Ms Tate's bedroom to the pool on Tuesday 5 August. It was on this door that Krenwinkel's print had been found. This placed Krenwinkel at the house after 5 August.

After the close of evidence on the first day (24 July 1970), Manson attempted to bribe one of the court officers, Sergeant William Maupin. Maupin submitted the following report:

> *". . . Manson stated to [me] it would be worth $100,000 to be set free. . . . Inmate Manson commented additionally that money meant nothing to him, that several people had contacted him regarding large sums of money. Inmate Manson also stated that an officer would only receive a six month sentence if caught releasing an inmate without authority"*[222]

There was a primitive logic about Charlie's proposal – six months in prison in exchange for $100,000 – a fortune in 1969. But Sergeant Maupin thought better of it. Charlie's first attempt at corrupting the trial had failed. But he wasn't a quitter, as events would show.

Linda Kasabian commenced her evidence on 27 July 1970. Her evidence deserves detailed consideration for at least two reasons: (i) it

---

222. Bugliosi, *Helter Skelter,* p.419.

was the only direct evidence of guilt in the prosecution case; and (ii) it was without doubt the cornerstone of the jury's decision.

Kasabian's evidence was punctuated by heckling and sniggering by all of the defendants and also a threat by Manson about which Sergeant Gutierrez would later give this evidence: ". . . *[Manson looked at Kasabian and] took his right index finger from right to left and made a motion across the bottom [of] his chin from right to left*"[223]. This was a circumstance consistent with consciousness of guilt on Manson's part. Bugliosi must have thought it was his lucky day. It is rare in litigation that a party serves up such an unexpected bonus to the opposition.

Manson's next trick, again during Kasabian's evidence, was to hold up a newspaper headline which read "MANSON GUILTY, NIXON DECLARES". He pointed it in the direction of the jury. President Richard Nixon had indeed waded into the case by referring to Manson's guilt in a public statement. This was later corrected by saying he had mistakenly omitted the word "*allegedly*" from the statement. After a lengthy examination of the jury, Judge Older was satisfied no juror had been influenced and so Kasabian's evidence was able to resume.

Kasabian's evidence can be summarised in point form:

- *I moved to Spahn Ranch and joined the Family on 4 July 1969. That night I made love to Charles "Tex" Watson. I told him about a friend Charles Melton who had inherited money. As soon as I mentioned money, Tex started going on this trip and telling me that it wasn't my money, that it was everybody's money and it was just there to take, and there was no right or wrong, it was just their's. Tex kept saying "but there's no wrong" and he just kept going on and on. And I accepted the fact that there was no danger [in taking the money].*

- *When I first met Charles Manson ("Charlie") he felt my legs. Before I made love to Charlie for the first time, he told me I had a father hang-up which impressed me because I had no father and I hated my stepfather.*

---

223. *People v. Manson & Ors.* [1976] 61 Cal. App. 3d 123, p. 156.

- *Charlie used to say to us that "everything was right, nothing was wrong", and "no sense makes sense".*
- *When there were male visitors to the Ranch we were told by Charlie to make love to them to try to get them to join the Family, and if they wouldn't join don't make love to them.*
- *I was told "never ask why, we never question Charlie, we know that what he is doing is right", I was afraid, Charlie was a heavy dude. I felt he was the Messiah, the second coming of Christ, a God-man. I never saw or heard anyone say "no" to Charlie. We always wanted to do anything and everything for him. He was head of the Family.*
- *I remember an incident with a shy young girl, about 16 years old. She was in the middle of the room. Charlie took her clothes off and started making love to her. She was pushing him away. She bit him on the shoulder. He hit her in the face and she fell back. He then told Bobby Beausoleil to make love to her and he told everyone to touch her and make love to her and everybody did.*
- *I loved Charlie when I first met him because he generated love and truth.*
- *The term Helter Skelter was explained to me by Charlie as a revolution where black and white people will kill each other. Blackie would start Helter Skelter. Charlie thought the Beatles were sending him messages. Blackie was much more aware than Whitie, and Blackie was really together. Helter Skelter was written on a jug at the Ranch and on a door.*
- *The term "karma" referred to "what you have to do to pay for it". The philosophy of Manson and other Family members was that the blacks have been under the whites, like picking up the garbage left by the whites, and Karma is coming. That is, it is going to be the reverse – whites are going to pick up the garbage left behind by the blacks. The karma is already happening and the blacks are going to start Helter Skelter.*
- *On the afternoon that Charlie returned from Big Sur, he was talking about people not being together and being off in their*

own minds. He said: "Now is the time for Helter Skelter". In the evening, Charlie told me to get a change of clothing, a knife and my driver's license. Charlie told me to go with Tex and do whatever he said. I went over to the car and Katie and Sadie were sitting inside. Tex was standing over by the driver's side and he was talking to Charlie. Tex got in the car and we started to drive off and Charlie called us and told us to stop. He came to my side of the car, stuck his head in and told us to "leave a sign, you girls know what I mean, something witchy".

- Tex then drove off. I did not know where we were going. I did not ask because I had been told by Charlie and others never to ask questions. I had the idea we were going on a creepy-crawl mission. A creepy-crawl mission is when you creep and crawl into people's houses and take things. I held the three knives and one gun which Tex asked me to discard in the event we were stopped.

- We stopped outside a house on top of a hill. We got out and proceeded with Tex carrying some rope. We climbed over a fence into the property and a car approached towards a gate opening onto the street. As it stopped, Tex leaped forward with gun in hand. The driver said "Please don't hurt me, I won't say anything". Tex shot him. I saw the driver slump over. Tex turned off the car's ignition.

- We then proceeded to the house. Tex ordered me to go to the back and look for open doors or windows. I did, but found none and returned to the front of the house. I saw Tex cut a flyscreen. Tex then told me to return to the car to stand lookout, which I did.

- Within a few minutes I heard screams and the words "No, please, no" coming from the house. I ran towards the house. I saw a man exiting the house with blood on his face. We looked into each other's eyes. I said "Oh God I am so sorry. Please make it stop". The man fell to the ground. Sadie came out and I said "Sadie please make it stop". She replied "It is too late". *The man got up. Tex then stabbed and clubbed him. Then in the background I saw Katie with a knife in her hand chasing a woman. I ran back to the car.*

- *Eventually Katie, Sadie and Tex returned to the car. They had blood on their clothes. Tex got behind the wheel. The others got in and we left. I noticed we no longer had one of the knives and that a portion of the grip of the gun was broken. It had been intact earlier that night. We changed clothes during the journey. Katie and Sadie complained that their heads hurt from having their hair pulled. Katie said her hand hurt because when she stabbed there were bones in the way and she couldn't get the knife all the way through and it took too much energy. Katie also said that one of the girls in the house was crying for her mother and for God.*

- *After having driven for some blocks, we stopped at a house with a hose in front of it. Tex told Sadie and Katie to wash the blood off themselves. I heard a woman's voice coming out of the house. She said "who's there?" or "who is that? what are you doing?". Tex told her we were getting a drink of water. The woman got hysterical and said "my husband is a policeman" or something like that. Her husband came out and said "Is that your car?" We told him "no, we're walking". We walked to the car. The man followed us. We got in and the man put his hand in the car and reached for the keys of the ignition, but Tex blocked him and we drove off fast.*

- *We drove for 10 or 15 minutes, then Tex stopped the car and the bloodied clothes were thrown out of the car and later I threw out the knives while the car was in motion. The knives were between five and a half and six and a half inches long.*

- *When we got back, Charlie was outside waiting for us. Tex told Charlie about the killings, and told him that he had said "I'm the devil and I'm here to do the devil's work". Tex said that there was a lot of panic and it was real messy and bodies were all over the place but they were all dead. Charlie asked* us if we felt any remorse and we all said "no". He directed us not to talk to anyone at the Ranch and to get some sleep.

- I did not ask Tex why the murders were committed. But he showed me some money he said he had taken from the victims and I said "Wow you killed these people for money". Later that day [Saturday 9 August] Sadie told me to come and watch the TV news. I found out the names of the victims.

- After dinner, I was with Katie and Leslie Van Houten. Charlie told us to get a change of clothes and me to get my driver's license. We then met at the bunkhouse with Charlie, Sadie, Tex and Steve Grogan ("Clem"). Charlie told us we were going out again and that the previous night's killings were too messy and this time he was going to show us how to do it. He said that we needed better weapons, last night's weapons were not effective, not good enough. I knew we were going out to kill. I went because I was afraid to say no. As we got in the car, Charlie gave me a leather thong and he was wearing one around his neck.

- We stopped in front of a house and Charlie got out and told me to drive around the block, which I did. When I got back, Charlie was standing where I had left him and he got back in the car. Charlie said he looked inside the house and saw pictures of children on the wall, but he said that later on we shouldn't let children stop us for the sake of the children of the future.

- Charlie continued giving me instructions. I don't know the district or the areas but we came to one point I couldn't drive any more so he took over. Then I took over again.

- After driving east on Sunset Boulevarde there was a small white sports car in front with a man driving. Charlie told me to follow it and pull up beside it at the next stop light. Charlie was going to kill the man. So I pulled up beside the sports car at the next red stop light. Charlie proceeded to get out of our car but the light turned green and the sports car drove off.

- We drove to an A-framed house but Charlie decided the houses were too close together.

- *At about 2.00 am I was driving and Charlie directed me to stop in front of a house on Waverley Drive in the Loz Feliz area. I recognised the house as that of Harold True. I said "Charlie you're not going into that house are you?" Charlie said "No, I'm going next door". He got out and left. We stayed in the car. A few minutes later, after we smoked about ¾ of a Pall Mall cigarette, Charlie returned and called Leslie, Katie and Tex out of the car and they were standing sort of to the side, to the back of the car on the passenger side, and I heard him say something about there was two people in the house and that he had tied them up. I think he said a man and a woman, but I am not sure and he told them not to be afraid, that he wasn't going to hurt them and he told them not to create fear and panic in them like the night before and not to let them know that they were going to kill them. Then he told them to hitchhike back to the Ranch.*

- *After the others got out, Manson got back in the car and handed me a wallet, saying that he wanted it disposed of so that it would be found by a black person who would use the credit cards. He expressed hope that the blacks would be blamed for the crime. Leaving Tex, Katie and Leslie there, we then departed. We stopped at a gas station and Charlie told me to hide the wallet in the ladies' restrooms in the toilet tank. I hid the wallet in a rest room.*

- *[After going to the beach and driving around for a while] I took over the driving. Charlie asked us (Clem, Sadie, me) if we knew anybody at the beach and we said "No". Then he looked at me and said "What about that man you and Sandy met? Isn't he a Piggy?" I said "Yes he's an actor". He asked me if the man would let me in and I said yes. Charlie said "OK I want you to kill him". I said "Charlie, I am not you, I cannot kill anybody". I remember having a knife in my hand and I said "With this?" and he showed me how to do it [by motioning across the throat a slitting action]. Charlie said*

"As soon as you enter the house, as soon as you see him slit his throat right away" and he told Clem to shoot him. And he said that "if anything goes wrong don't do it".

- *Sandra Good and I had met the actor while hitchhiking and gone to his apartment and I had had sexual intercourse with him.*
- *Charlie asked me to show him the apartment where the man lived so I took him there. Clem and Sadie stayed in the car and Charlie and I went inside and upstairs. I pointed at a door which was different to the man's door. We returned to the car. Charlie gave Clem a gun. He instructed Sadie and Clem to wait around the corner while I knocked on the door. Charlie then drove off and told us to hitchhike home.*
- *I knocked on the door which I knew wasn't the door and a man said "who is it?" I said "Linda". He sort of opened the door and peeked out and I said "Oh excuse me, wrong door" and that was it. I knocked on the wrong door because I didn't want to kill anybody.*
- *Clem and Sadie were singing the Beatles' song about piggies, and knives and forks, and eating your bacon.*

Judge Older said this about Linda Kasabian:

"She appears to be perfectly lucid and articulate. I find no evidence of aberration of any kind insofar as her ability to recall, to relate. In all aspects she has been remarkably articulate and responsive"

The appeal court obviously agreed:

"In 18 days of examination Kasabian testified clearly and comprehensibly. Her descriptions were not unclear and her demeanour was candid"[224]

---

224. *People v. Manson & Ors.* [1976] 61 Cal. App. 3d 102, at p.138.

As will be seen, much of Kasabian's evidence was independently corroborated. Moreover, with the emergence of the records of legal interviews, we now know that Kasabian also gained substantial corroboration from Atkins, Van Houten and Watson. This is unusual. Normally, in contested litigation, it can be expected the witnesses in the opposing camps will dispute many matters. Often there is furious disagreement. But in this case, there seems to have been furious consensus (give or take some minor matters) between the opposing camps. This was indeed a curious piece of litigation in that the female defendants did not substantially (or at all) disagree with the prosecution's star witness (Kasabian) and they did not contest fitness to plead and they did not put up any special defences (e.g. insanity), and yet they all pleaded not guilty. In retrospect, Leslie Van Houten's comments to Marvin Part to the effect the murders and the trial were all for the publicity were accurate in the sense that there certainly wasn't much genuine factual or legal dispute between the parties at the trial. I have struggled to identify what was actually in issue between the parties in respect of the substantive events[225,226]. One is tempted to surmise the trial was indeed merely some sort of publicity vehicle for the revolution.

It has to be concluded that what Kasabian said in evidence about Tate/LaBianca was as close to the truth of what happened (outside the respective houses) as there ever will be. There were, to be sure, inconsistencies and discrepancies from time to time in her 18 days of evidence but I have been unable to detect any more than the usual sorts of minor discrepancies that might be expected in such an evidentiary marathon, and certainly nothing to cast serious doubt

---

225. Correspondingly, and unsurprisingly, the later appeals would be dominated not by arguments about the actual events, but rather by the question of whether the defendants could get a fair trial in light of the adverse publicity they received (plus other matters about the conduct of the trial as opposed to the jury's resolution of the substantive issues).

226. In fairness to the defendants, they were perfectly entitled to agree in substance with the prosecution's case, but still plead not guilty and put the prosecution to proof, which is what they did. But there was an oddity about the way the defendants so aggressively huffed and puffed and blustered their way through the trials and yet never said much, or anything, directly antagonistic to the prosecution's substantive case.

upon her account. If her evidence was any more internally consistent than it in fact was, then there might be questions about it being so pristine that it was rehearsed or coached.

Apart from a few minor blows, there was no effective cross-examination of Kasabian. Paul Fitzgerald (for Krenwinkel) clearly had an interest in discrediting Kasabian, because her evidence implicated Krenwinkel. But his cross-examination was notable for having more to do with Manson than Krenwinkel. For example, he put to Kasabian that Manson never forced anyone into doing anything, and never prohibited people from leaving the Ranch. In short, Fitzgerald gave the appearance of acting for Manson and against Krenwinkel.

Daye Shinn (for Atkins) was out of his depth. The following series of exchanges summed up Shinn's cross-examination. It started with this:

Q. *Do you recall what Mr Bugliosi said to you the first meeting?*
A. *Well, he has always stressed for me to tell the truth.*
Q. *Besides the truth I'm talking about.*

There was no response by Kasabian to Shinn's last utterance, because it wasn't a question. Shinn, apparently with his back to the witness and looking over his shoulder at Judge Older, asked the judge: "*Did she answer the question your Honor?*"[227]. Before Judge Older could answer, Kasabian said: "*I was waiting for you. I thought you were busy*". Then:

Q. *You can answer the question, I'm sorry.*
A. *I have no questions to [answer].*

Kasabian was right. There was no question. Shinn then turned again to Judge Older: "*I did not get the last answer your Honor*". Judge

227. Bishop, *Witness to Evil*, p.194.

Older: "*I would suggest you put the question to her again Mr Shinn*".
Shinn: "*I forgot the question*".

Kanarek (for Manson) came close to scoring some points, but he was way too long winded. He cross-examined Kasabian for no less than seven days. The essence of skilful cross-examination is identifying when a point has been made against a witness, and then stopping. It is all about knowing when to stop. Bishop would later write that, before being directed by Judge Older to wind up his cross-examination, Kanarek had "*succeeded in accomplishing one of his most cherished goals: [Kasabian's] theft of $5,000* [from Charles Melton] *. . . was finally brought out before the jury. It's emergence brought out the best and worst about [Kanarek's] tactics. He got the information out . . . then proceeded to worry it to death. Having paraded before the jury the potentially damning information that she was a thief, he proceeded to turn her . . . into a badgered witness, a near-martyr to his seemingly inexhaustible capacity for formulating different approaches to the same question*"[228].

Furthermore, many of Kanarek's questions were unhelpful, for example: "*Compare your idea of time, Mrs Kasabian, before you first took, let us say, LSD, compare that meaning of time, whatever it was in your mind, to the meaning of time between let us say, the first time you took LSD and the date of your arrest*".

The incompetence of some of the other cross-examination of Kasabian was extreme. Most of Ronald Hughes' cross-examination was just plain weird:

> Q. *Let's take a situation, Mrs Kasabian, where A talks to B, B comes and tells C what his interpretation of A's conversation was with him. Now C turns around and tells someone else what B said about A and B's conversation. Is it not a fact that all C heard was what B told him?*
> *[Objection – sustained]*

---

228. Bishop, *Witness to Evil*, p.226.

Q. *[despite the successful objection, Hughes now carries on as if there had been no objection]*
In fact he never really talked to A did he?
[Objection — sustained]

Q. *Mrs Kasabian do you follow the truth you see or the truth you hear?*

A. *Both.*

Q. *What is truth to you?*

A. *The reality, the actual reality.*

Q. *Do you judge others from your reality or from the reality you feel in somebody else's mind? [this question, implying different realities - a favourite Charlie theme, sounds like it was scripted by Manson]*
[Objection — sustained]

Q. *Mrs Kasabian, do you cry for the mutilated children in Biafra?*
[Objection — sustained]

Q. *. . . are you in such a state of mind now Mrs Kasabian that you could sit on a rock for the rest of your life?*
[Objection — sustained]

Q. *Would you again let public opinion crucify the truth?*
[Objection - sustained]

Q. *Christ said: 'To enter the kingdom of heaven you must be as a child'. Is that right?*

A. *Excuse me?*
[Objection — sustained]

Q. *Are you going to send [your son] to war when he is eighteen?*
[Objection - sustained]

Q. *What type of Yoga do you practice?*
[Objection — sustained]

Q. *What kind of Yoga do you practice?*
[Objection — sustained]

Q. *Do you know of a form of Yoga that deals with mysticism?*
[Objection — sustained]

Q. *Do you know a form of Yoga that deals with werewolves?*
[Objection — sustained]

Q. *Devils?*
   [Objection - sustained]
Q. *Monsters?*
   [Objection – sustained]
Q. *Is the purpose of Yoga to have your mind leave your body through
   the third eye . . . and travel effortlessly through space?*
   [Objection - sustained]
Q. *Have you ever left your body through the third eye?*
   [Objection – sustained]

During Kasabian's evidence, Bugliosi sought to tender a photograph to which objection was taken by Hughes on the ground that it had not been disclosed to the defence. Bugliosi told the judge: "*For the record, I just saw it for the first time a few minutes ago myself*". The response by Hughes: "*That is a lot of shit Mr Bugliosi*". Judge Older sentenced Hughes to one night in custody for contempt of court. The response by Hughes: a clenched fist salute of the militant left and their war cry "*Right on*"[229]. It is understandable that things happen in the heat of the moment which are later regretted. But Hughes had no basis for alleging impropriety by Bugliosi. He seems to have immersed himself in the puerile bellicosity of his client and the other defendants. This sort of anger is usually a sign that a lawyer has insufficient professional detachment and is allowing personal feelings to dominate his conduct. He was beginning to sound like a mere mouthpiece for the defendants, something which was, and still is, forbidden by the rules governing the professional conduct of lawyers.

Following Kasabian, Mr Timothy Ireland gave evidence. He was at premises about three quarters of a mile away from the Tate residence. He testified that at about 12.40 am on Saturday 9 August 1969 he heard a male voice coming from the direction of the Tate residence scream: "*Oh God no, please don't, don't, don't, please don't*". This corroborated Kasabian's evidence about screams. (Kasabian was,

---

229. Bishop, *Witness to Evil*, pp. 141 to 142.

in law, an accomplice of the defendants. The general rule is that the testimony of an accomplice should be viewed by the jury with distrust unless independently corroborated. This is not an absolute prohibition on uncorroborated testimony, but it does mean that the more corroboration the better.)

The next witness was Mr Rudolf Weber who lived about two miles from the Tate house, but on a different street. He testified that at about 1.00 am he got out of bed and found four people, one male and three female in his property. He said *"what the hell do you think you're doing?"*. The male *"seemed very pleasant"* and *"said in a youthful voice 'we're just taking a drink of water'"*. They walked down the street to an unfamiliar car. Weber noticed the license plate was GYY435, later identified as Johnny Swartz' Ford. Weber walked to the car and reached in towards the ignition key. Watson had already started the car and they sped away - more corroboration of Kasabian. This was indeed a peculiar incident. It occurred barely minutes after committing five vicious and senseless murders. Watson would later write in his memoir: *"For some reason it never occurred to any of us to try to kill [Mr Weber] – he didn't live on Cielo Drive"*[230]. Lucky Mr Weber.

Los Angeles County Coroner Thomas Noguchi testified he had conducted the autopsy of Sharon Tate and supervised the autopsies of the other victims from Cielo. He testified that many of the stab wounds on each of the victims had penetrated bones. This corroborated Kasabian's evidence of Krenwinkel complaining about striking bones when stabbing. Noguchi also testified that many of the wounds were five inches deep, which tended to corroborate Kasabian's evidence that the knives were five and a half to six and a half inches long. Noguchi also testified that he found rope burns on Tate's face and neck consistent with hanging. He considered she had not died from hanging, but she had been suspended briefly during the agonal stage – the dying process.

---

230. Watson, *Will You Die For Me?*, p. 144.

The evidence then turned to the LaBiancas. Frank Struthers testified about the discovery of Leno's body. Ruth Sivick was a business partner of Rosemary. Sivick had dropped in on Saturday 9 August to feed the dogs and opened the refrigerator door to take the dog food out. (Police found no prints on the door handle, suggesting it had been wiped). Sivick had left the house at about 6.00 pm.

John Fokianos (news vendor) testified about Rosemary LaBianca being upset by the Tate headlines. The last Fokianos saw of them was as they headed away. Apart from the killers, Fokianos was the last person to see the LaBiancas alive.

Los Angeles County Deputy Coroner, Dr David Katsuyama, testified about the autopsies conducted on Mr and Mrs LaBianca. After Katsuyama's evidence, Susan Atkins complained of illness. After delays and medical attention, Judge Older resumed the trial, apparently forming the view she was acting. Aaron Stovitz was asked by a reporter what he thought of Atkins' complaints and he replied: *"It was a performance worthy of Sarah Bernhardt"*. The next day Stovitz was summoned to District Attorney Younger's office and told he was off the case for having breached the earlier instruction prohibiting interviews. Stovitz was replaced by Steven Kay and Donald Musich.

Police Sergeants Jerome Boen and Harold Dolan testified that fingerprints found at the Tate residence were the prints of Watson (front door) and Krenwinkel (rear door). No prints were found at the LaBiancas' house, even on the fork protruding from Mr LaBianca's abdomen.

Paul Fitzgerald blundered in his cross-examination of Sergeant Dolan. Kanarek had earlier, cleverly but improperly, managed to plant the seed of a suspicion that police had found Kasabian's fingerprints inside both the Tate and LaBianca homes. Although the jury was admonished by Judge Older to disregard the remark by Kanarek that had brought this about, there was little doubt the seed had been planted, and that it was troublesome for the prosecution. The other attorneys should have left it at that. But Fitzgerald charged in and repaired things for the prosecution:

> "Q. *Now did you have occasion to compare the latent fingerprints obtained at the Tate residence and the latent fingerprints obtained at the LaBianca residence against an exemplar of one Linda Kasabian? Yes sir I did.*
> Q. *What was the result of that comparison?*
> A. *Linda Kasabian's prints were not found at either scene.*

This would not be the last unwise cross-examination by Fitzgerald.

Eleven year old Steven Weiss testified about finding the .22 Hi Standard revolver – the murder weapon as it turned out – in his backyard.

Sergeant William Lee of LAPD's Firearms Unit identified the bullet retrieved from Sebring's body as having been fired by the gun found by Steven Weiss. On microscopic examination, shell casings that Lee had test fired from the gun had been left with marks identical with those on shell casings found by police at Spahn Ranch. Thus, the gun that had been fired into Sebring had also been fired at Spahn Ranch.

Family member T.J. Walleman testified the gun looked like the gun he had seen Manson fire at Bernard Crowe. This was the first evidence heard by the jury which linked the gun to Manson[231].

Edward Lomax, marketing manager for the gun's manufacturer, Hi Standard, testified the gun model was uncommon.

Danny DeCarlo testified that Manson's favourite gun was a Hi Standard .22 caliber Buntline and the gun found by Steven Weiss was similar to Manson's gun. DeCarlo also testified that the rope found at Cielo appeared to be Manson's rope and he had seen Manson wearing a leather thong similar to the one found at Waverley.

DeCarlo also testified that Manson said he wanted the blacks to go to war with the white establishment (the pigs). Manson talked about

---

231. Ranch hand Randy Starr had been due to testify to giving that very gun to Manson, but Starr had passed away from natural causes before being able to testify. Walleman was a reluctant witness, whose membership of the Family was intermittent.

Helter Skelter many times, and when the blacks and whites were finally against each other we'd just sit on top of the mountain and watch them shoot each other. Manson used the word "pigs" to describe the white collar workers, people who work from 8 to 5 daily, and said they ought to have their throats cut and be hung up by their feet.

Kanarek did land some blows in cross-examination of DeCarlo. In particular, DeCarlo had previously testified at the Beausoleil trials that he was "*smashed*" on alcohol 99% of the time at Spahn Ranch. Kanarek put to DeCarlo he was so smashed that on many occasions he had to be carried to bed, to which DeCarlo replied: "*I made it a few times myself*". Kanarek stopped there. The other defence attorneys should also have left it there. However, Fitzgerald asked DeCarlo to define the difference between "*drunk*" and "*smashed*". DeCarlo said "*drunk*" was when he was totally out of it "*on the ground*", whereas "*smashed*" was "*just when I'm walking around loaded*". Kanarek's cross-examination had been undone.

Fitzgerald also made it plain through his cross-examination of DeCarlo that he was acting for Manson and against his own client Krenwinkel. DeCarlo's testimony was almost wholly to do with Manson, and did not touch Krenwinkel (if anything it helped her). It would be expected Fitzgerald would desist from cross-examining DeCarlo, or at least cross-examine him in a non-confrontational way with a view to extracting concessions consistent with Krenwinkel's best interests. However, Fitzgerald attacked DeCarlo from the outset by accusing him of being a "*professional prosecution witness*". Most of the cross examination was pro-Charlie and it follows, as night follows day, anti-Krenwinkel. Furthermore, during DeCarlo's earlier direct evidence, Fitzgerald had vigorously joined in objections to testimony which was adduced ostensibly, if not solely, against Manson. For example, he objected to evidence about Manson ordering people around at the Ranch, in particular ordering the girls to take their clothes off. These objections could only be interpreted as being in Manson's interests and against Krenwinkel's interests. Hughes and Shinn objected and cross-examined in the same vein.

Ruby Pearl, stable manager at the Spahn Ranch, gave evidence linking the gun, rope and thongs to Manson. The links between Manson and the murder scenes were now rapidly accumulating. In addition to his disciples being at the murder scenes, there was now his gun, rope and thong. Furthermore, the evidence of Kasabian and DeCarlo about Helter Skelter connected Manson's *"scripture"* to, at least, the LaBiancas' refrigerator door. The connections could now be listed as follows:

1. Disciples.
2. Gun.
3. Rope.
4. Thong.
5. Scripture.

Barbara Hoyt testified about Manson's prophecies of Helter Skelter. She said that Manson spoke frequently between April and September 1969 of Helter Skelter *"coming down fast"*, the blacks would rise up against whites and everyone would die for us (the Family) and that he *"would like to show the Blacks how to do it"*. Hoyt testified that on the evening of Friday 8 August, Atkins had asked her to bring three sets of dark clothing to the front of the Ranch, but when she got there Manson told her they had already gone – more incrimination of Manson.

Hoyt also testified about being ordered by Manson to perform oral sex on Juan Flynn:

> *"Bugliosi:*   *What did Mr Manson tell you to do with Juan Flynn?*
> *Hoyt:*   *That oral whatchamacallit.*
> *Bugliosi:* *Orally copulate?*
> *Hoyt:*   *Yes . . .*
> *Bugliosi:* *Did you want to do it?*
> *Hoyt:*   *No"*

Cross-examination by Kanarek backfired:

> *Kanarek:*   *. . . Miss Hoyt did you orally copulate anyone else?*
> *Hoyt:*   *Yes, for the same reason.*

Kanarek: What was that?
Hoyt: I was afraid not to"

Sheriff's Officer Donald Dunlop testified about finding Manson hiding under a building at the raid on Spahn Ranch on 16 August 1969. This was a circumstance consistent with consciousness of guilt on Manson's part. Once again, Fitzgerald took up Manson's cause, suggesting to Dunlop in cross-examination he had roughed up Manson by pulling him out by the hair.

Juan Flynn, Ranch hand at the Spahn Ranch, testified he had heard Manson saying: "*Well, I have come down to it, and the only way to get going is to show the black man and the pigs is to go down there and kill a whole bunch of these fuckin' pigs*" [sic] and the word "*karma*" was a reference to the black people taking over. Flynn identified the gun which had fired the bullet into Sebring as the same gun used by Manson to fire shots in his direction at the Ranch. He also identified the rope. Flynn also testified that one night in early August he had been watching television in the trailer when Susan Atkins came in dressed in black. Flynn asked: "*where are you going?*". Atkins replied: "*we're going to get some fucking pigs*". Flynn looked out the window and saw Atkins, Manson, Grogan, Kasabian, Watson and Krenwinkel in Johnny Swartz' Ford. Manson was in the driver's seat.

Fitzgerald's cross-examination again gave the impression he was only acting for Manson. For example, he put to Flynn that he didn't like Manson (of no relevance to Krenwinkel).

Kanarek cross-examined Flynn to suggest he was testifying merely to bring publicity to himself to assist with his ambition of becoming an actor. Flynn's retort: "*It's not the kind of publicity I want, you big catfish*".

Charlie Turns the Trial Into a Circus

While Flynn was on the stand, Manson disrupted proceedings by starting to sing: "*The old gray mare ain't what she used to be . . . she is a judge now"*. Upon being ordered to stop, Manson replied: *"Stop from what? Why don't you stop doing what you're doing? You are a woman"*. Manson was removed from court. On his return, Manson resumed ranting: *"I'd like everyone to know I am not represented in this trial. I do not have an attorney. I am not allowed to speak for myself"*. He was removed from court again. Then Atkins, Krenwinkel and Van Houten shouted in unison: *"the judge is a woman, the judge is a woman"*. They were also removed. As they left, Van Houten said: *"The judge is a joke"*. Atkins said: *"Your wife's in the front row, telling you what to do"*.

At the beginning of the next day's proceedings, the girls chanted *"Hail Caesar"* and extended their right arms in a Nazi salute. Manson stood up and said: *"Your Honor, may I suggest that the court continue to try itself, as it has been doing a very poor job of showing the public any justice. You've only shown your force and power"*. On being ordered to sit down, Manson started singing: *"That old black magic has me in its spell . . ."*. He then said: *"I'd like to go back to my room and relax, you can handle your own matters, now Your Honor if you would allow me to maintain a voice I could bring to you the thought that I have done what I'm told"*. Upon being ordered to stop, Manson replied: *"You have been ordering me forever, all my life you have ordered me to cease to live. You bring me in here and charge me with murder and you say I have rights and hold up rights in front of me but you give me none"*. Turning to the gallery he continued: *"Look at yourselves. Where are you going? You're going to destruction, that's where you're going. It's your judgment day, not mine"*. Atkins, Van Houten and Krenwinkel parroted the last line. If there was any doubt Manson was orchestrating things, that doubt was now erased. For their troubles, all four defendants were removed from the court.

After the defendants' performance, the evidence went from bad to worse for Manson. A tape recording of a police interview was played in which Flynn had said:

"Then [Charlie] was looking at me real funny. . . and then he grabbed me by the hair . . . and put a knife to my throat

[and said] 'Don't you know I'm the one who is doing all the killings?'"

Flynn also testified about having received threats from Family members. (The argument about the admissibility of these threats prompted a comment from Paul Fitzgerald that he too had received threats.)

On Monday 5 October 1970, Sergeant Paul Whiteley had finished giving evidence when an exchange developed between Manson and Judge Older:

> "Manson: *May I examine him Your Honor?*
> Judge: *No you may not.*
> Manson: *You are going to use this courtroom to kill me? . . . I am going to fight for my life one way or another. You should let me do it with words.*
> Judge: *If you don't stop, I will have to have you removed.*
> Manson: *I will have you removed if you don't stop. I have a little system of my own.*
> Judge: *Call your next witness.*
> (Bugliosi: *Sergeant Gutierrez)*
> Manson: *Do you think I'm kidding?"*

Manson then leaped over the bar table and landed only a few feet from the bench. Before he could move further, he was pounced upon by the court officers. As he continued to struggle, he yelled: "*In the name of Christian justice, someone should cut your head off*". Manson was removed from court again. If there was any doubt Manson was a violent man, that doubt had now been erased.

Beside Manson's attempted attack, there was another in-court incident in which Susan Atkins would knock over an exhibit board. The day-to-day arrangements of this court case were not such as most lawyers in other common law jurisdictions would be familiar with. For the most part, the four defendants sat, unrestrained and unconfined, with their attorneys at or near the bar table. The relatively relaxed atmosphere facilitated two problems. First, the in-court violence, which would not have happened had the defendants been appropriately secured. Secondly, the relaxed arrangements surely helped Manson with his game plan of keeping control of the girls. His control depended on physical proximity and the power of his personality. If the defendants had been appropriately secured and, as a general rule, separated during the trial there would have been (i) no violence in court and (ii) an amelioration of Manson's control over the girls, both of which would have been beneficial.

The relaxed arrangements contributed to the circus atmosphere that prevailed. Celebrities such as Sal Mineo, Truman Capote and Peter Falk dropped in to watch. And star gazers dropped in to watch the stars. There were many running side shows to the trial. One side show stunt was a rumour that the defence intended to call the Beatles to testify. This had to be a publicity stunt. There would be nothing useful the Beatles could add which was in the defendants' interests. Even if they said they were transmitting messages to Charlie, such evidence would merely tend to confirm the prosecution's contention that Helter Skelter was a motive for, or at least related to, the murders.

Writer and in-court observer, Ed Sanders, also joined in the circus. He claims to have exchanged notes through one of the lawyers (presumably defence) with Manson (in the detention cell) wherein Manson admitted he visited Cielo after the murders[232]. Exchange of notes between a defendant and a member of the gallery would be an exceedingly rare occurrence. And for a defence lawyer to turn over a potentially incriminating note to a gallery member (Sanders) was bizarre. It is not known whether Sanders realised that, by reading the note, he made himself a compellable witness against Manson, or even potentially liable for unlawfully concealing evidence (assuming the note was not turned over to the police). The note might have been an important piece of evidence against Manson. If it was not turned

---

232. Sanders, *The Family,* p.424.

over to the prosecuting authorities, the relatives of the victims would be entitled to feel aggrieved.

The carnival atmosphere surrounding the trial was grotesque. It was very much Charlie's circus. The magazine and newspaper articles of the time give the impression Manson was using the trial as his performance space.

Circus Over, Evidence Resumes

The next witness was Virginia Graham who recounted Atkins' revelations at Sybil Brand Institute, previously set out. Ronnie Howard also testified about Atkins' revelations. Another inmate Roseanne Walker testified about hearing a news broadcast about the murders and Atkins saying: *"That ain't the way it went down"*.

Gregg Jakobson, music producer, was the next witness to give evidence about discussions with Manson about Helter Skelter and Revelations 9 in the Bible. Manson told Jakobson there was no right or wrong and there was nothing wrong with killing. Manson didn't believe in death, he had died long ago and it was just a physical change that took place at the end – the essence of life went on. Manson told Jakobson he wanted to start the Helter Skelter revolution. Manson felt the Beatles were singing directly to him and he believed Revelations 9 was reflected in the Beatles' song "Revolution 9". The bottomless pit in Revelations 9 would be a refuge for the Family when the black/white Armageddon descended. The *"four angels"* were the Beatles who were leaders and prophets. And the Beatles were the smoke locusts who came out of the bottomless pit. The line that *"Their faces were as the faces of men"* yet *"they had hair as the hair of women"* was a reference to the Beatles and their long hair. The issue of fire and brimstone from their mouths was the power of their music. And referring to Verse 15 of Revelations 9 which reads *"And the four angels were loosed, which were prepared for an hour, and a day, and a month, and a year, for to slay the third part of men"*, Manson said the third of men were the people who would die in Helter Skelter – one third of mankind – the white race.

Kanarek spent a lot of time cross-examining Jakobson, but got nowhere. Fitzgerald also cross-examined Jakobson, again giving the appearance he was acting for Manson. Shinn did too, and so did Hughes. In fact Hughes took it even further than the others, asking questions which invited an inference that Family members were not foreclosed from having their own thoughts. This cross-examination could only have been part of Charlie's plan for the girls to take the rap.

Rudy Altobelli testified about Manson's visit to Cielo in March 1969. Altobelli was able to identify Manson (who had been seeking out Terry Melcher). Thus Manson was now linked to the house.

Fitzgerald again cross-examined as if acting for Manson. His questions, and the answers he elicited, emphasised the unity and loving bonds within the group. This was a theme that Fitzgerald would run with in subsequent interviews about the case, even many years later:

> "... one must understand that there was an incredible unity there ... there was an incredible love there. They, these female defendants ... and the rest of the outside members, female members, of the Manson Family loved him with an incredible power that I have never seen the likes of in my entire life"[233]

It is difficult to see how Fitzgerald thought the promotion of this at the trial was beneficial to his client, Krenwinkel. The only thing I can come up with is that he felt cornered by the circumstances of (i) the plan to protect Charlie and (ii) the near impossibility of Krenwinkel's defence. And in recognition of the hopelessness of his position he set about actively promoting Manson's innocence and the spellbinding love between Manson and the girls in the hope the jury might at least take pity on Krenwinkel in sentencing. In other words, he saw Manson's defence as the key to his client's survival. It seems an odd-ball way

---

233. Collage of Fitzgerald interviews on YouTube, unattributed, undated, sourced from www.mansonsbackporch.com.

to approach the defence of Krenwinkel. And fraught with the risk of conflict of interest already discussed.

It was significant that witnesses such as Jakobson and Altobelli were only offered up as witnesses against Manson. Despite this, the girls' attorneys cross-examined them extensively. There was no absolute prohibition on the girls' counsel cross-examining witnesses who did not testify against their own clients. This happens, though it is not commonplace. But in the circumstances that had developed in this case, it is plain that all counsel were in fact following Charlie's instructions. There was no other reason for the constant and lengthy cross-examinations and objections by the girls' counsel. It was not as if the girls' counsel could have misunderstood the ambit of the evidence of these witnesses, for it was explicitly stated by Bugliosi and Judge Older that it was only being offered against Manson.

Charles Koenig, an employee of the Standard Oil Company, testified about finding the wallet of Rosemary LaBianca in a toilet at a Sylmar service station. More corroboration of Kasabian.

Harold True testified about living next door to the LaBianca house, but before the LaBiancas had taken up residence. True said Manson had visited him several times, having met Manson in March 1967. Thus, there was a link of sorts between Manson and the LaBianca house. It was now open to the jury to infer from the evidence of Altobelli and True that Manson had connections with each of the murder venues. The list of links was now:

1. Disciples.
2. Gun.
3. Rope.
4. Thong.
5. Scripture.
6. Houses.

Police Sergeant William McKellar testified about arresting Krenwinkel in Mobile, Alabama, in December 1969. He had observed her in a car and she was wearing a hat and covered her face on both sides. On stopping the car, she gave her name as Patricia Montgomery but the officer recognised her as a wanted person. The jury was entitled to regard this as evidence consistent with Krenwinkel's guilt. In fact, each of the female defendants had supplied police with false names, a circumstance consistent with the guilt of each[234].

Paul Watkins testified that Manson told him Helter Skelter would start in summer 1969 and Manson talked *"constantly"* about it. Watkins testified to the matters set out earlier including black people committing atrocious murders of white people and scrawling on walls in the victims' blood.

Brooks Poston corroborated Watkins and also testified about life in the Family:

- When Charlie was around, things would be like when a school teacher comes into class. I felt he was Jesus Christ.
- In late 1968 Manson started saying *"The shit's coming down"*, and he said the revolution, the Black-White war was happening.
- On New Year's Eve, Manson said *"Are you hep to what the Beatles are saying?"*, and the Beatles were telling it like it is and they were programming the people to Helter Skelter.
- The Family played the White Album constantly. Manson said the Beatles were talking to him through the White Album. Manson talked about the lyrics in "Helter Skelter", "Blackbird" and "Piggies". "Blackbird" was telling the black man to revolt, now was the time. "Piggies" was telling the black man to rise up and put a stop to whitie.
- "Revolution 9" was talking about Helter Skelter and this time you better get ready because it is going to happen. And Revelations 9 in the Bible was also a reference to Helter Skelter. He said the Beatles were the four headed locust in Revelations 9.
- Helter Skelter amounted to blackie rising up and completing Whitie's karma and he is going to do this

---

234. *People v. Manson & Ors.* [1976] 61 Cal. App. 3d 123, at p. 149.

by coming out of the ghetto and going into some rich piggy homes in the Bel Air and Hollywood districts and committing atrocious murders and smearing blood on the walls and writing "pig" on the walls and this was designed to get Whitie angry so he would run into the ghetto after Blackie because of the viciousness of the murders.

• We were supposed to be in a hole in the desert and the group was supposed to grow to 144,000 people and when the revolution was over and Blackie had cleaned up Whitie's mess then Charlie and the Family would come out of the hole and Blackie would turn everything over to Charlie and Charlie would scratch him on his fuzzy head and kick him in the ass and tell him to pick cotton. The 144,000 was the 12 tribes of Israel from the Bible. Ultimately, Blackie would turn over power to Charlie.

Dianne Lake testified for the prosecution that in summer 1969 Manson stated Family members had to be willing to kill pigs to help start Helter Skelter. Lake also testified that Krenwinkel had admitted dragging Abigail Folger from the bedroom to the living room. Lake also testified Van Houten had admitted stabbing a dead body. Lake also said Van Houten had stated that at first she didn't want to do it, but later it was fun.

The prosecution's case closed on Monday 16 November 1970. Before turning to the defence case, there are some points which are best to make at this juncture. They are (i) the role of Judge Older and (ii) the state of the prosecution's case.

Judge Older

The impartiality and patience of Judge Older was, with respect, mightily impressive. However, it is hard to escape the suspicion that he tried to help the struggling defence up by the boot straps. There were rulings toward the end of the prosecution case that could only be construed as judicial assistance to the defence. First, the prosecution sought to tender evidence of Krenwinkel's refusal to give a handwriting sample. Her refusal was clearly admissible against her. Despite agreeing it was admissible, the judge offered her another opportunity to give a sample. There was no requirement in law for this offer. It was generous to Krenwinkel[235]. Secondly, a note pad was found outside court with Krenwinkel's name on it and the words "*healter skelter*" written three times. This was admissible against Krenwinkel, but the judge disallowed it.

Sometimes, judicial assistance occurs when the struggling party is handicapped by the incompetence, or absence, of legal representation. Sometimes, it is sub-conscious. Either consciously or subconsciously, Judge Older drifted towards helping the defendants. Far from ongoing claims of an unfair trial by followers of Manson, if there was any unfairness on Judge Older's part, it was minimal and, if anything, it worked in favour of the defendants. There was a separate unfairness operating behind the scenes which was Charlie's plan, facilitated by the lawyers, for the girls to take the rap, but Judge Older could do nothing about that.

State of Prosecution's Case Against Manson

The prosecution's case against Manson was looking very strong. Every witness came through cross-examination unscathed. There was, to some extent, a peculiarity about the prosecution's case in this trial. Most of the witnesses were people who were not professional witnesses or career criminals. In many trials, the prosecution has to rely upon informants or people of dubious backgrounds. Criminal trials are often crim v. crim. But here the prosecution witnesses were for the most part people with backgrounds devoid of criminality. And they gave their evidence in the way people inexperienced in the ways of criminals or court cases often do – sincerely and believably.

---

235. As it transpired, on advice from Fitzgerald, she rejected the judge's offer. This was bad advice, for various reasons. It is not known whether Fitzgerald's advice was a deliberate pursuit of the plan for Krenwinkel to take the rap, or simply a mistake.

The most important witness was undoubtedly Linda Kasabian. Lengthy and unsuccessful cross-examination often enhances a witness's evidence, and this was probably the case with Kasabian. This raises a question as to whether Kasabian's evidence by itself, and assuming of course she was sufficiently corroborated and accepted as a reliable witness, was enough to convict Manson (with or without proof of any motive). A convenient starting point is a submission that Bugliosi would later make to the jury: *"Linda's testimony about these two nights of murder . . . without anything else, all by itself, I think convinced you that these defendants committed these murders, just her testimony alone"*. In my opinion, this submission was correct. Kasabian's evidence was sufficient.

It might be wondered why the prosecution would even bother to press proof of Helter Skelter if it was unnecessary to prove motive. There may have been several reasons. Some were obvious:

(i)   as mentioned, Helter Skelter was not only relevant to the issue of motive. The *"scripture"* served another forensic purpose as a link between Manson and the murders. The linkage was two-fold:

(a)   as would later be identified by the appeal court, the murders bore a remarkable similarity to the scripture; and

(b)   the words of the scripture were written at the murder scenes.

(ii)   Helter Skelter also served another forensic purpose as corroboration of Kasabian[236].

(iii)   even if not advanced as evidence of motive, it would seem unreal to run the case without reference to Helter Skelter because it was self-evidently such a central part of the fabric of the group and life at the Ranch. It would be impossible to avoid.

(iv)   given the strength of the Helter Skelter evidence (9 witnesses at the first Tate/LaBianca trial, all apparently

---

236. *People v. Negra* (1929) 208 Cal.64 at p. 69; *People v. Alcalde* (1944) 24 Cal. 2d 177; *People v. Wilt* (1916) 173 Cal. 477.

credible, and Manson potentially foreclosed by the *Rolling Stone* interview from rebutting it) and its intense personal incrimination of Manson, it would make little sense to leave it out. It might have been a different matter had the evidence about it been equivocal.

(v)   Helter Skelter was evidence of cold-blooded calculated premeditated planning of murder, which would be relevant to the question of what penalty should be imposed if the defendants were found guilty. It was powerful evidence for a finding of first degree murder (death penalty). It intensely and personally incriminated Manson. Arguably, it transformed him from being a reasonable candidate for the death penalty into being an absolute certainty for it.

(vi) the prosecution could never be sure of the extent to which the jury accepted all of the other evidence which incriminated Manson. There would have been confidence, but no guarantees. For this reason alone, Helter Skelter had to stay in the prosecution case for all of its forensic purposes (including motive).

In summary, Kasabian's evidence, if believed, was sufficient to convict Manson. There was no doubt Helter Skelter was everything the prosecution said it was – motive, corroboration, intensely incriminating etc – but it ended up being unnecessary to prove it <u>as a motive</u> because those other matters rendered proof of motive an unnecessary part of the prosecution's case. One way to test this is to take stock of the circumstances proved against Manson before coming to, and irrespective of, motive. These circumstances included:

1. The connection between Manson and the murder scenes by virtue of his <u>disciples</u> being there.
2. The <u>gun</u> connection.
3. The <u>rope</u> connection.
4. The <u>thong</u> connection.
5. The <u>house</u> connection.
6. The throat slitting gesture.

7. The cupboard hiding.
8. Atkins telling Flynn: *"we're going to get some fucking pigs"* and then seeing Atkins in the Ford with Manson in the driver's seat.
9. The admission to Flynn: *"I'm the one that's doing the killing"*.

It would be absurd if the jury received and accepted all of that evidence against Manson but then hesitated to convict because it couldn't be satisfied why he had done it.

Defendants' Case

After a two day break, the proceedings resumed on Thursday 19 November 1970. It was time for the defendants' case. To the surprise of many, the defendants announced they were resting their case. This has been widely misreported as an announcement that they were not putting on a defence. In fact, it only meant they would not be calling any oral evidence. This was not, of itself, such an unusual move, especially given no special defence (e.g. insanity – imposing an evidentiary onus) had been pleaded. And it did not diminish the other elements of the defence, including the cross examinations already conducted, exhibits tendered and making of submissions in the usual ways.

What happened next <u>was</u> unusual and surprising: Krenwinkel announced in open Court that she and her *"sisters"* actually would like to testify *"and put on our defense"*. Obviously there was dissension in the defendants' ranks. The lawyers for the women advised Judge Older they opposed their clients going into the witness box (stand). The women insisted on their right to testify. Judge Older questioned them about their knowledge of the risks of giving evidence. The lawyers informed the judge that the women's evidence would be self-incriminating and amounted to a *"judicial confession"*[237]. It was clear enough the women were proposing to take the rap for Charlie. The

---

237. *People v. Manson & Ors.* [1976] 61 Cal. App. 3d 123, p.160.

lawyers informed Judge Older they were not prepared to call their clients into the witness box and they were not prepared to ask any questions.

To some extent, it is pointless speculating about the lawyers' motives for declining to participate in the female defendants' testimony. They certainly made a song and dance about not wanting to join in their clients' virtual guilty pleas. It is not clear to me what the lawyers were thinking. It seems to me a defendant has an inviolable right to testify in her defence if she so desires, even where such testimony is known in advance to be self-incriminating and tantamount to a plea of guilty. This was what was ultimately held by Judge Older, and endorsed by the appeal court in this case.

Having read several hundred pages of transcript dealing with this impasse, it is hard to get to the bottom of it. Observer George Bishop was unimpressed by what he thought was the insincerity of the defence lawyers. He would later write that *"in the light of five trial months during which it appeared frequently that all four defense counsel were representing only Charles Manson"* that their protests were *"a nauseating display of for-the-record self-righteousness"*[238]. Judge Older made comments to the same effect during the interminably long exchanges between all of the parties.

I am inclined to agree with Bishop, although it is hard to take it further. It is clear from the transcript there had been disagreement between the defendants and their lawyers brewing for some time before 20 November. The girls wanted to take the rap for Charlie. The lawyers opposed this course. Their opposition was somewhat mysterious given most everything else they did in the case conformed with Charlie's plan to incriminate the girls[239].

---

238. Bishop, *Witness to Evil*, p.309.

239. Bishop's contention that it was done *"for-the-record"* was one possible explanation of the mystery. Another possible explanation was that the attorneys didn't want their prized gig being brought to an abrupt halt by their clients' (virtual) guilty pleas. There were other possible explanations however further speculation is undesirable.

At any rate, on 20 November, there followed this sequence of events:

- Judge Older offered to the defendants they could testify to the jury in narrative form (i.e. not in the usual question and answer format) provided they agreed to give a preview of their evidence in the absence of the jury so that any inadmissible statements could be excised prior to going to the jury. The women refused this offer, and insisted on testifying to the jury without preview. However, Manson accepted the judge's offer and proceeded to deliver a narrative in the absence of the jury. He spoke for at least one hour, and his narrative will be considered in due course.
- After he had finished his narrative, Manson was asked by Judge Older if he wished to testify to the jury. Manson declined the offer.
- It has been reported by various sources, reliably I think (although not in the transcript) that, on returning to his seat, Manson addressed himself to the women and told them they did not have to testify "*now*".
- Judge Older then (generously) offered to the women that, if they wished, they could testify to the jury <u>without</u> preview. They declined.

This sequence of events has been widely misreported, and according to Bishop was widely misunderstood even by those in court at the time[240]. However, it is clear from the transcript the women were offered the right to testify to the jury and they declined (doubtless as a result of Manson's comment that they did not have to testify). There would later be claims the women were unjustly foreclosed from giving evidence and there are complaints by Manson supporters to this day to the same effect. These claims are false. There was no doubt it was the women's choice (albeit under Manson's say-so).

---

240. Bishop, *Witness to Evil*, p.311.

As for Manson's narrative, because it was given in the absence of the jury, it was not evidence in the case. It comprised Charlie-speak gibberish about how the world had wronged him. It was irrelevant to the point of being an annoying distraction from the real issues in the case. He did make a few comments about the evidence against him, for example he said the gun was available for use by anyone at the Ranch. But he said nothing which particularly assisted him or rebutted the cumulative effect of the evidence against him. He rambled on for over an hour. It would be hard to find in the annals of jurisprudence an instance of one person using so many words to say so little.

The speech also demonstrated what a tenuous grip on reality Manson had. And it was monstrously disingenuous. Manson glorified himself and sought to evoke sympathy as someone from another world who was the victim of *"your world"*, and someone who showed young homeless boys and girls *"the best I could what I would do as a father"*, but omitted to mention he bashed and pimped them. He also omitted the shocking plan in train to consign his co-defendants to the gas chamber in order to get himself an acquittal.

Some, even Bugliosi, have conceded there was an impressive theatricality about Manson's narrative. It has certainly been portrayed dramatically in movies about the case. It may have been impressive in form, but in substance it was completely vacuous. The record of it left me with only one impression: if this was the best he could say for himself, then his guilt for the crimes charged was beyond all doubt.

Closing Arguments

After the defendants tendered their exhibits, the Court was recessed until 30 November 1970 for the parties to present closing submissions.

On 30 November, another surprise unfolded. Ron Hughes was nowhere to be found. By 3 December, Hughes was still missing and Judge Older appointed a new lawyer Maxwell Keith to represent Van

Houten, over her objection[241]. Van Houten asserted that she could better represent herself than newly appointed counsel. She stood up and announced to Judge Older: "*I have nothing to do with Ronald Hughes's disappearance, I'm beginning to wonder what you did with him*". Judge Older told Van Houten to sit down. She replied: "*You stand up*". Then in an exchange between Manson and Judge Older, Manson said: "*Hey you look at me when I'm talking to you*".

Closing argument by the prosecution commenced on 21 December 1970. As mentioned, Bugliosi submitted that Kasabian's evidence alone established the defendants' guilt. Bugliosi's submissions were forceful and skilful. But it is unnecessary to set them out. Suffice to say, by my reckoning, only about one eighth (12%) of these submissions dealt with Helter Skelter, which tends to confirm the diminution of its importance (as a motive).

On the other hand, the defendants' submissions require some attention – partly because they were so bad (except for Maxwell Keith) and partly because they offered up more proof that Fitzgerald and Shinn were acting in furtherance of the plan to save Charlie.

Fitzgerald went first. Fitzgerald's closing submissions on behalf of Krenwinkel were atrocious, featuring a number of simple errors such as:

- Asking the jury to bring in a conviction against his client (subsequently corrected to acquittal).
- All at Cielo had been stabbed to death (Sebring and Parent had been shot).
- Sharon Tate-Polanski was "Mary Polanski".
- Manson was accompanied by two girls when he went up the LaBiancas' driveway (only evidence – from Kasabian – was that Manson was unaccompanied).

Fitzgerald argued Krenwinkel's fingerprint was found at a place in the house (rear doorway to pool area) which was not where the bulk of the killing went on. Also, because the fingerprint was undated, the jury could not be satisfied that it was placed there on the night

---

241. Hughes was later found dead, his death being deemed accidental.

of the murders. To some extent, I sympathise with Fitzgerald. Most attorneys would be familiar with the predicament of not knowing what can be said in submissions. The problem was, however, that he ended up highlighting the damning fact that his client's print was found at the house. Fitzgerald told the jury that he didn't intend to rebut every prosecution witness because it would take until 1974 to do so. This only drew attention to the strength of the prosecution case. What the jury <u>did</u> need to hear was rebuttal.

In addition, there were bizarre submissions such as:

- *"a .22 caliber pistol [was] a classically inefficient way to kill somebody"*;
- *"[I]t . . . does not make sense to hang anybody"*;
- Bodies left inside and outside the house showed poor planning;

In conformity with the master plan to save Charlie, Fitzgerald spoke at length in Manson's defence. He said little about his own client Krenwinkel. He argued that if Manson had truly wanted to send her out to kill, he would have armed her with a machine gun, or better still sent men. He also submitted the girls were bright, intuitive, perceptive and *"they had the benefit of the same training and education that we have"*. These statements could only be construed as submissions for Manson, and against his own client.

As for Daye Shinn's submissions, George Bishop summed it up this way:

"Daye Shinn argued for approximately one hour and a half. He was on too long"[242]

Irving Kanarek's submissions went for an incredible eight days. At one point, lost for something to say, he started talking about the French Revolution and then moved on to reciting chunks of the Bible. At the end of day two, Judge Older told Kanarek he was putting the jury to

---

242. Bishop, *Witness to Evil*, p.323.

sleep. On day five, the jury sent a note to Judge Older requesting No Doz tablets. At one point Manson could be heard yelling from the detention room: "*Why don't you sit down Irving? You're just making things worse*". Amongst many ambitious submissions, Kanarek argued that Kasabian could have stopped the carnage at Tate by saying: "*Hey there, what's going on? stop it*" and she could have saved Frykowski's life by rendering medical assistance. As one of the prosecutors quipped, even Dr Christian Barnard couldn't have saved Frykowski.

The best defence submissions came from Van Houten's new attorney Maxwell Keith who set about putting the rap on Manson. For the first time, a lawyer was doing what a lawyer should do – representing his client, rather than joining in the plan to protect Manson. Bishop would later write: "*A strange thing happened in Department 104 at ten o'clock on the morning of January 11, 1971; a defense attorney began making sense*"[243]. The Family plan to protect Charlie had obviously not eluded Bishop: "*It soon became clear that Keith, alone among the defense attorneys, was defending his client, not Charles Manson, and that he was attempting to shift the blame for the murders onto the Family leader's shoulders*"[244].

Jury Deliberations and Verdict

On the afternoon of Friday 15 January 1971, after receiving directions from Judge Older, the jury retired to commence deliberations.

Paul Fitzgerald was interviewed by NBC news. He was asked if he had watched the jury during submissions. He had, and he was full of praise:

> "*I'm amazed. This jury's been locked up, sequestered for seven months now. Obviously this has to be a very boring, trying sort of situation for them. But they're very attentive,*

---

243. Bishop, *Witness to Evil*, p.327.
244. Ibid., 328.

sit forward in their chairs. They listen raptly. Many of them take notes. I'm very, very impressed. They're a very conscientious and earnest jury"[245]

Sounds like a recipe for a fair adjudication. The jury's deliberations commenced the following day, Saturday 16 January. Sunday was taken off and the jury resumed on Monday 18 January.

According to juror William Zamora, who later wrote about the trial, the first issue was whether Linda Kasabian was truthful. The jurors all agreed she was[246]. It is difficult to decipher what happened next in the jury room. Disagreement arose about the extent of Van Houten's culpability. Debate about this consumed several days. Ultimately, agreement was reached that she was guilty of murder in the first degree[247].

It gradually becomes evident from Zamora's account that the jury believed every prosecution witness. The jury was given a record player to play the White Album, which Zamora considered "*monotonous*" and "*boring*". An afternoon was devoted to the issue of Manson's leadership. Ultimately they considered there was "*no question*" Manson was the leader and he was guilty[248].

On Monday 25 January, the jury returned the following verdicts:

Manson – 7 counts of murder, 1 count of conspiracy to commit murder - GUILTY

Krenwinkel – 7 murder, 1 conspiracy - GUILTY

Atkins – 7 murder, 1 conspiracy - GUILTY

Van Houten – 2 murder, 1 conspiracy – GUILTY

Paul Fitzgerald was again interviewed. He now claimed the jury had been "*hostile and antagonistic*"[249].

---

245. NBC News Archives, date unspecified, presumably shortly after 15 January 1971.
246. Zamora, *Blood Family*, p.395.
247. Ibid, p.403.
248. Ibid, p.404.
249. Bugliosi, *Helter Skelter*, p.540.

CHAPTER 7: TATE AND LABIANCA – PENALTY PHASE OF THE TRIAL

"I think it would be quite obvious that a whole lot of things that I said then were . . . deliberate lies"

Patricia Krenwinkel[250]

Post Verdict

The penalty phase of the trial was scheduled to commence on Thursday 28 January 1971. On Tuesday 26 January, the Los Angeles *Times* ran an interview with Manson's mother under the headline *"MOTHER TELLS LIFE OF MANSON AS A BOY"*. Those expecting a tale of impoverishment were disappointed. Mum pointed the finger at young Charlie: he was loved by all, everything was handed to him, he was conceited and too lazy and hopeless to hold down a job, and he never had to take a fall: *"[H]e was a spoiled and pampered child"*.

The Penalty Phase

The trial now entered the penalty phase in which the jury's task was to determine the appropriate penalties for the defendants. The principal

---

250. Patricia Krenwinkel parole hearing, 17 July 1978.

issue was whether the murders were of the first degree (death penalty) or the second degree.

The prosecution called two witnesses. First was a police officer, Thomas Drynan, who testified that in 1966 he had arrested Atkins and she had been carrying a gun and stated if she had the chance she would have used it. This tended to prove Atkins had a mind of her own to kill. The second witness was Bernard Crowe, having survived the shooting back on 1 July 1969. The shooting was proof of Manson's capacity for killing.

The defendants called a number of witnesses. The parents of Krewinkel and Van Houten testified their daughters had conventional upbringings. They also testified to their continuing love for their daughters.

Manson's parole officer Samuel Barrett was called although his evidence mostly confirmed parole should have been revoked by mid-1969. By that time, Manson had been charged with a litany of offences including rape, grand theft auto and narcotics possession. It beggars belief that Manson was still a free man when the killing spree occurred.

The next witness, Lynette Fromme, was called to the stand by Fitzgerald. The purpose of adducing evidence from Fromme was to exculpate Manson by rebutting that he was the leader of the group. This evidence would, in turn, harm Krenwinkel because it made her appear less the blind minion. Thus, Fitzgerald was now positively adducing evidence against his own client.

Fromme was asked whether Manson was the leader of the Family and her reply was *"No, we were riding on the wind"*. She said Charlie was in fact a follower. Fromme testified she had never heard Charlie use the words "Helter Skelter". But then she talked about him predicting a black-white race war. She said that black people are coming to the top, as it should be.

The next witness was Nancy Pitman who gave evidence in terms similar to Fromme – Charlie was not the leader, he was a follower. But then in cross-examination she testified she would die for Charlie.

The next witness was Sandra Good who testified Charlie could see every thought we had. He had "*magical powers*". He breathed on a dead bird and it came back to life. Good believed Charlie's voice could shatter the court building if he wanted. Notwithstanding these powers, Good maintained Charlie did not dominate anyone. Good said the babies were the leaders and wherever they went we followed them. And Charlie agreed with everyone and had no opinions.

Fitzgerald continued acting against his own client by setting out to prove through Good that Charlie was not dictatorial and, by implication, his own client Krenwinkel was to blame for her actions. The transcript of Good's testimony is torturous reading. It was hocus-pocus psycho babble. Judge Older's patience was incredible. But he finally interrupted the questioning with this warning to Fitzgerald:

"*This girl's personal naïve infantile philosophy has nothing to do with this case*"

Fitzgerald asked Good about Krenwinkel's activities within the Family and this was Good's gushing answer:

"*Ohhhhhh, she was always giving – taking care – bringing somebody coffee. I used to have pictures of her bending over, you know, flowing, and handing someone a cup of coffee. She's always laughing.*"

It was doubtful Krenwinkel's victims would have agreed with this glowing testimonial. The only flowing they experienced at her hands was their own blood.

Sandra Good has appeared in a number of television interviews. In 2004, she claimed the establishment: "*didn't want to face the fact that their products, their children, children of the system would do this, they didn't want to know the reasons . . . even though during the trials the . . . female defendants were willing and capable of saying why they killed the people that they killed. Each woman had her reason for doing what they did . . . . they didn't want to hear it"*[251]. It is impossible to accept this statement. Charlie had ordered the three female defendants not to testify. And, as will be seen, when they did testify to the jury in the penalty phase they chose to lie. Thus, the girls <u>were</u> given a hearing about their reasons for *"doing what they did"* and Charlie ordained that, one way or another, they were not to tell.

Good also spat out this piece of venom:

> *"When I met Charlie what impressed me most that I did not see in my own culture growing up was this strong sense of brotherhood, loyalty, honour and brotherhood, and that immediately struck a chord within me . . .a man's no better than his word type thing . . . Sticking together, word being good, it's like a war, like a soldier reality. In other words, if these people in Hollywood have to go, so be it. That made sense to me. And that made sense to all of us. In war, you know sometimes killing is needed"*[252]

Catherine Share ("Gypsy") was the next witness. She said she loved Manson and she would die for him. Her evidence drew this comment from Judge Older:

> *"It is inconceivable that this witness in any way is helping the defendant [sic]. Again I will say I am not judging; it is up to you gentlemen to decide. It seems to me that all they are doing is removing any possible doubt from the jury's mind on the issues of this case . . . this is merely cumulative, repetitive, rambling, incoherent, irrelevant."*

Then on her second day of giving evidence, in re-direct examination, Share came up with some incredible evidence.

---

251. *Charles Manson: The Man Who Killed the 60's*, Channel 4, 2004.
252. Ibid.

She claimed Linda Kasabian had masterminded Tate/LaBianca. She also testified Kasabian had come up with the copycat idea of committing murders which were similar to the Hinman murder and that, with Beausoleil in custody, police would figure Hinman's real killer must still be at large (as discussed, this theory having been the brain-child of co-prosecutor Stovitz). Share also said Kasabian had been in love with Beausoleil. Share claimed Manson knew nothing about any of this (which was a twist on Stovitz' original version which implicated Manson in the plan). Thus, if Share was accepted, Manson would be exculpated, at least from the Tate killings. I shall refer to Share's version of events as "Copycat".

Share's evidence was unconvincing for a number of reasons. First, it only came out in her re-direct examination. Generally, the evidence of a witness is divided into three phases. The first phase is called direct examination in which the witness is questioned by the attorney who calls the witness to the stand. In a question and answer format, the witness sets out what she has to say about the subject events. It is expected the whole of the witness's evidence will be brought out in her direct examination. Then the opposing attorney is given an opportunity to cross-examine the witness. After cross-examination, the attorney who called the witness is given an opportunity to re-interrogate the witness to clarify anything requiring clarification. This is called re-direct examination and is limited to matters arising from cross-examination. It is not an occasion for testifying about matters that should have been brought up earlier in direct examination. In conformity with this general pattern, Share was questioned in direct examination by the attorney who called her to the stand (Kanarek). She said nothing about Copycat. She was then cross-examined by Bugliosi. Still nothing about Copycat. Then, only in re-direct by Kanarek, Share came out with Copycat. If Copycat was genuine, it would have been expected to be the subject of testimony in direct examination, or even cross-examination. That it only came out in re-direct tended to expose it as a fabrication.

Share also testified that Kasabian had murdered Hinman. Zamora noticed Share was teary while testifying and kept looking at the female defendants and whispering and eventually said: *"I don't know why I'm doing this"*[253].

The major problem with Share's evidence was that Manson (the love of her life) had been languishing in jail on the Tate/LaBianca indictment for 18 months, and indeed by this time had endured the guilt phase of the trial, and all the while Share had mentioned nothing about Copycat to anyone. She had kept to herself the most vital piece of information in the defence of her beloved Charlie. Share's evidence was patently ridiculous, and was predictably decimated by Bugliosi's cross-examination.

Share has since publicly stated Copycat was *"concocted"*[254]. And further:

> *"I was held up a note by one of the girls on the outside 'this is what you say' and I read it over and over again and I memorised it and I was told exactly what to say . . . I didn't have a choice. Charlie was also looking at the same time making sure I said every word"*[255]

Share has also confirmed Helter Skelter:

> *"People killing each other. Riots. Blacks against whites. It was the mother of all wars that he was talking about where everyone would just start killing everybody else. I had to believe in him. I had to because I didn't want to be left behind to die with the rest in the burning cities. I wanted to be one that survived and so everyone there was just wanting to be part of this great thing that was happening"*[256]

---

253. Zamora, *Blood Family,* p.426.
254. *Most Evil: Charles Manson,* Discovery Channel, 2006.
255. Interviewed on *Hard Copy,* 1997.
256. *Most Evil: Charles Manson,* Discovery Channel, 2006.

Next came the female defendants. It is anybody's guess why the women would now be giving evidence, having not done so in the guilt phase of the trial. It can be assumed that at all times they were eager to get into the witness box and exculpate Charlie. For some reason known only to himself, Charlie had previously decided they were not to testify in the guilt phase. But he decided that now, the penalty phase, would be the right time. It is trite to say Manson was a capricious individual. It is impossible to know what the thinking was. It may be Charlie in fact recognised the jury might not believe Copycat and realised it could backfire if he played his hand in the guilt phase, because the story potentially made it appear even more that he was orchestrating things. It is conceivable he still clung to the hope of acquittal in the guilt phase, and he may have decided it was best to defer Copycat for deployment only if the case had to progress to a penalty phase, by which time he had nothing to lose. This is possible, albeit of course speculative.

Nor is it known what advice, if any, Shinn and Fitzgerald delivered to Atkins and Krenwinkel at this point. It is not known why they did not repeat their previous protests and refuse to engage in questioning their clients[257]. The transcript evinces a sense of capitulation by Shinn and Fitzgerald. Keith's position was distinguishable for reasons which will be seen shortly.

Atkins was the first of the defendants to testify. Her testimony was a roller coaster of lies and false confessions to killing Hinman and Tate, and Charlie not knowing anything. The following passage was delivered with true Hollywood melodrama. It would be amusing, were it not for the real life horror that underpinned it:

> *"This whole thing, what I am in this courtroom for, what Patricia and Leslie and Charles Manson are in this*

---

257. In fairness to Fitzgerald, the available transcript appears incomplete. I have reason to suspect there may have been an exchange between Judge Older and Fitzgerald which revealed he (correctly) advised Krenwinkel against testifying. But I do not have the transcript.

courtroom for, what Bobby Beausoleil is on death row for, he
is on death row for me.

This whole thing started when I killed Gary Hinman
because he was going to hurt my love. And I just did it. I
saw it had to be done and I did it.

And I tried to tell you all the truth for so long.

When I went to the Grand Jury, I lied, and I knew I lied,
and I told Mr Caballero I lied.

And he told me: It is too late now Baby.

And I was put incommunicado. I couldn't talk to anybody.

I have tried and tried and tried to tell you all the truth,
and now you all know.

. . . Can't you all see it? I couldn't take anything I couldn't
give, and I couldn't give you anything that I couldn't take"

In later years, Atkins would devote her energies, including the bulk of her second book, to explaining that in fact the above was false, and that her Grand Jury evidence was the truth. In any event, after the violin refrain had finished on the above passage, Atkins said the following about remorse:

- Question: Did you have any emotional feeling towards the victims? Answer: I didn't know any of them, so how could I feel any emotion.

- Question: Did you consider they were mercy killings? Answer: No as a matter of fact I told Sharon Tate I didn't have any mercy for her. The reason for the Tate killings was that I believed it right to get my brother [Bobby] out of jail. I did what I did because I did it.

- Question: How could it be right to kill somebody? Answer: How could it not be right when it is done for love?

- Question: Did you ever feel any remorse? Answer: Remorse? For doing what was right to me?

- Question: Did you ever feel sorry? Answer: Sorry for doing what was right to me? I have no guilt in me.

The following was the gist of the cross examination of Atkins:

- Question: Even though living with Charlie between July and October 1969 you hadn't got around to telling him about killing Gary Hinman or Tate/LaBianca? Answer: That's right.
- Question: Why? Answer: Because he never asked. It was two days ago (February 1971) that I first told anyone that Linda Kasabian masterminded the murders.
- Question: Between 9 August 1969 and February 1971, how come you never told anyone that Linda was behind these murders? Answer: Because I didn't. It's that simple.
- Question: Did you tell anyone in the Family that you committed all these murders? Answer: No.
- Question: If you told outsiders like Ronnie Howard and Virginia Graham, how come you didn't tell members of your own Family? Answer: Nothing needed to be said.
- Question: Just one of those things, seven dead bodies? Answer: No big thing.
- Question: So killing seven people is just business as usual, no big deal, is that right? Answer: It wasn't at the time. It was just there to do. They didn't even look like people. I didn't relate to Sharon Tate as being anything but a store mannequin.
- Question: You have never heard a store mannequin talk have you? Answer: No sir but she sounded like an IBM machine, she kept begging and pleading and I got sick of listening to her so I stabbed her. And the more she screamed, the more I stabbed her. I said *"Look bitch, I have no mercy for you"*.

As already discussed, the likelihood was that she did not stab Tate. Her testimony was purely grandstanding to impress Charlie. Atkins would later concede:

> *"[the penalty phase] was a chaotic, dragged-out affair in which we did all we could to throw everything into confusion*

> *by changing our stories all around and trying to prove Charlie innocent"*[258]

and:

> *". . . my testimony and the testimony of my co-defendants was a joke"*[259]

Atkins' former lawyer, Richard Caballero, also testified in the penalty phase. He revealed Atkins told him Manson wanted to start Helter Skelter because it wasn't happening quickly enough, and that was why all the murders were committed.

Patricia Krenwinkel was next in the witness box. She trotted out the Copycat motive and said the following about remorse:

- Question: What did you feel after you stabbed [Abigail Folger]? Answer: Nothing. I mean what is there to describe? It was just there, and it's like it was right.
- Question: What were you thinking of before you stabbed her? Answer: Nothing. I wasn't thinking about anything.
- Question: What was your reason? Answer: I don't understand what reason is. Everything is done because it's done.
- Question: Why did you murder? Answer: I don't know why. It just was. I have no feelings for those people.

Krenwinkel would later say:

> *". . . I think it would be quite obvious that a whole lot of things that I said [on the witness stand] were even deliberate lies that were set up to make certain things that, at the time I felt we wanted to say"*[260]

---

258. Atkins, *Child of Satan, Child of God*, p.167; Atkins-Whitehouse, *the Myth of Helter Skelter*, p.175 ff.
259. Atkins-Whitehouse, *The Myth of Helter Skelter*, p.191.
260. Parole hearing, 17 July 1978.

Leslie Van Houten was the next witness. Maxwell Keith's position was distinguishable from the other attorneys because it was known that Keith firmly advised Van Houten not to testify. This advice was rejected, no doubt on Manson's orders. This placed Keith in a predicament. He had to either adhere to Manson's game plan and conform with Van Houten testifying or he could try to cease acting for her. It was unlikely the latter would be permitted at this late stage. So, realistically, Keith had no choice but to continue acting. He might have contemplated refraining from asking her questions as the others had previously done, but he chose not to follow that path. My interpretation of Keith's conduct is that he thought it best to proceed with the questioning and try to keep control of the evidence and minimise the damage Van Houten was bound to do to herself. Damage minimisation would be possible. As will be seen, it didn't work out very well, but I am persuaded that was Keith's intention. In fairness to Fitzgerald and Shinn, they may have had this in mind too.

Unsurprisingly, Van Houten's testimony went disastrously. She falsely claimed Atkins had killed Hinman. And as for remorse:

- Question: Do you feel sorrowful for it? Answer: Sorry is only a five letter word. It can't bring back anything. I don't feel bad about helping to kill Mrs LaBianca.

- Question: I am trying, Leslie, to discover how you feel about it. Answer: What can I feel? It has happened. She is gone.

- Question: Do you wish it hadn't happened? Answer: I never wish anything to be done over another way. That is foolish. It will never happen that way. You can't undo something that is done.

- Question: Do you feel as if you wanted to cry for what happened? Answer: Cry? For her death? She is not the only person who has died.

- Question: Do you think about it from time to time? Answer: Only when I am in the courtroom.

In cross-examination, Bugliosi took the risk of exploring what Van Houten had said to Marvin Part in the interview set out previously. This was risky because it meant going into areas where Bugliosi could not be sure what her answers would be. In any event, the cross-examination might be unproductive because it would stray into areas protected, on the face of it, by client/lawyer privilege. Bugliosi's cross-examination started like this:

> Q. *Isn't it true Leslie that before the trial started you told someone that Charles Manson ordered these murders?*
> A. *I had a court appointed attorney Marvin Part who was insistent on the fact that I was —*

Maxwell Keith objected at this point on the ground that the question would elicit material protected by the privilege. Kanarek joined in Keith's objection. Bugliosi pressed the question. Then Van Houten, feeling she knew better than Keith and Kanarek, butted in and waived her privilege:

> A. *Mr Kanarek will you shut up so I can answer this question? . .*
> Q. *Did you tell Mr Part that Manson ordered these murders?*
> A. *Sure I told him that.*

Van Houten would later concede Copycat had been fabricated. She would also say: "*Charlie was conducting the courtroom [and] telling us what to say*" and:

> "*After the trial started, Charlie suggested that we try to, we meaning the three women, try to carry the load of the case so that he could be released, you know, so that he could further carry on his works to save the world*"[261]

---

261. Interview with Barbara Walters, ABC TV, January 1977.

The defence now turned to calling a number of psychiatrists to the stand. Evidently, Manson had relaxed his ban on psychiatric evidence, presumably emboldened by the girls already having testified to his innocence. It is difficult to get the thread of this evidence accurately because much of the available transcript is illegible, and some of the media reports of it tend to conflict with Bugliosi's account in his book.

It is important to emphasise that none of this psychiatric evidence went to the question of guilt or innocence under the *M'Naghten Rules* previously discussed. By omitting to call psychiatric evidence in the guilt phase, the girls had forfeited the defence of insanity and their guilt and convictions could not be disturbed in any way by any findings about their psychiatric state in the penalty phase. Nevertheless, the jury was entitled to take it into account in their determination of penalty.

The first psychiatrist was Dr Andre Tweed who had examined Patricia Krenwinkel. Dr Tweed testified that LSD could cause brain damage and people may perform homicidal acts under the influence of LSD. Dr Tweed also testified Krenwinkel showed signs of mental illness. As far as I can tell from the available sources, the effect of Dr Tweed's testimony was largely extinguished by Bugliosi's cross-examination.

The next psychiatrist was Dr Keith Ditman. Ditman testified that Leslie Van Houten's use of LSD together with Manson's influence could have been significant factors in her participation in the LaBianca homicide. Again, the effect of this evidence was diluted by effective cross-examination by Bugliosi. Ditman had not actually examined Van Houten, but seems to have based his opinion entirely upon reading the transcript of her earlier evidence. Eventually Ditman agreed that apart from drugs and outside influences, some people simply have greater aggression and hostility and capacity for violence.

Dr Joel Fort was the next psychiatrist called by Van Houten's attorney, Maxwell Keith. Dr Fort testified that Manson's influence played a very significant role in the commission of the murders. And Dr Fort minimised the role of LSD, testifying that most people on LSD tend not to be violent.

Dr Joel Simon Hochman, psychiatrist, was the next witness and he was also called by Maxwell Keith. Curiously, Dr Hochman proceeded to cause considerable harm to the defences of Van Houten and the other two women:

- All three female defendants had evidence of alienation, anti-social and deviant behaviour, even before joining the Family.
- All three had a remarkable lack of remorse. They actually did believe there was no right or wrong.
- Atkins herself now thinks that even without Manson she would have ended up in jail for manslaughter or other violence. There was an absence of a conventional sense of morality or conscience in Atkins.
- Krenwinkel had intense guilt over a sexual liaison at age fifteen. Manson eradicated that guilt and gave her acceptance which she desperately craved.
- Van Houten had more emotional problems than the average teenager. There was something seriously wrong with her. She had been a spoiled little princess unable to suffer lack of gratification. She had extreme difficulty with impulse control and she went into rages when she couldn't get her own way. She was a psychologically loaded gun which circumstances later triggered.
- Van Houten was a very angry girl for a long time, angry with her parents and the establishment, and Mrs LaBianca was a blank object or screen upon which she could project her rage.
- Manson's ideas, presence and relationship with her served to reinforce her feelings and attitudes of hostility and rage. They reinforced her social alienation. Manson had influence which contributed to the lowering of her restraints on her impulsiveness.
- By way of example, say someone says *'let's eat the whole apple pie'*. You are tempted by the suggestion. But your

final decision comes down to you. So the other person is influential, but is not the final arbiter or decider. Someone can tell you to shoot someone, but your decision to do that comes from inside you. It is the personal decision of the person who does the shooting or stabbing.

Dr Hochman's evidence was damaging to all three girls. It is not known why Maxwell Keith called Dr Hochman as a witness. Perhaps he hadn't interviewed the doctor and was taken unawares by what he said. Or perhaps he had finally fallen in line with the general defence of saving Charlie, although nothing else he did conformed with the "save Charlie" defence.

Paul Fitzgerald exacerbated the overall damage to the women's defences by asking this question:

> *"So, really, all you are saying is that (a) Manson could possibly have had some influence and (b) if he did have influence it would only contribute to the lowering of [Van Houten's] restraints on her impulsiveness, is that correct?"*

Whilst the question was framed in terms of only Van Houten, in reality it was pertinent to all three girls and it invited an answer which minimised Manson's role and maximised the girls' culpability. The answer to Fitzgerald's question was "*Yes*". Thus, the defences of all of the girls, including Krenwinkel, were damaged. The next question was even worse:

> *"So any influence Manson had on Leslie Van Houten [read all three girls] . . . is tenuous at best, is that correct?"*

This question was too negligent to be true. After anxious consideration, I have formed the view it could only have been designed to save Charlie and send his own client to her execution in the gas chamber. Fitzgerald was doing more prosecution of his own client than even the prosecutors.

Dr Hochman's testimony was the high water mark of the evidence that the girls were highly culpable and Manson's influence was "*tenuous at best*". However, there are several observations that need to be made about Dr Hochman's testimony and reports. He interviewed the women at a time when they themselves were acquiescing in Manson's plan for them to take the rap. It is plain Dr Hochman's testimony and reports were coloured by the false premise of the girls actively seeking to absorb culpability. Associated with this, it is clear from the testimony and reports that Dr Hochman was not made aware of any of the information now available that points to Manson's autocratic control over the Family members. For example, he appears to have had no information about the violence at the Ranch. He had none of the information from the California Institute for Women. He did not have Watson's memoir. And so on. I doubt Dr Hochman would have found Manson's influence "*tenuous at best*" if he knew the whole story.

Another Family member Catherine Gillies testified that on the night of the LaBianca murders she asked Krenwinkel if she could join in. Gillies was told she wasn't needed. She also testified she would have killed that night if she had gone.

The attorneys' closing arguments on penalty commenced on 18 March 1971. Bugliosi went first, and was brief, asking the jury to impose the death penalty. Kanarek tried forlornly to rebut the notion of Manson's leadership. Keith (for Van Houten) described Copycat as "*nonsense*".

On 23 March 1971, whilst an adjournment (recess) was being taken, events took another strange turn. Manson had been heard yelling from his detention cell that there would be a "*bloodletting*" if he got the death penalty. Assistant prosecutor Steven Kay told the media outside court about Manson's outburst. Paul Fitzgerald was asked by reporters about Kay's apparent breach of the publicity order. Fitzgerald obliged, himself breaching the order. Although it didn't concern his client Krenwinkel, Fitzgerald exclaimed:

"*. . . you only have one side of the story. Mr Manson can't answer these allegations, that Mr Manson's being held*

*incommunicado [sic]. Minimal standards of fairness would
require that you get both sides of the story. Furthermore . .
. no defence attorney knew anything about this until 2:00
in the afternoon. Yet the material was disseminated to the
media at 10:00 in the morning by virtue of a release by the
District Attorney's office"*[262]

Once again, Fitzgerald gave the appearance of acting for Manson.
It defied reason that Fitzgerald, whose client Krenwinkel had an
interest in implicating Charlie, would take up Charlie's cause so loudly
and righteously.   Logic suggested that, as Krenwinkel's attorney, he
should have been happy for things to go against a co-defendant.
Fitzgerald's response is only susceptible to an interpretation that he was
using these incidents as an excuse to get in front of the cameras – great
publicity, and nothing to be paid for it.   And, of course, he was in
reality acting for Manson and against Krenwinkel.

The Manson threat was followed by Bugliosi's submissions in reply.
This time Bugliosi addressed himself to Copycat.   There were many
reasons that Copycat was implausible.   The following are some of the
matters highlighted by Bugliosi, plus others which discredit Copycat.
The list is not exhaustive.   This requires consideration because it was
the central plank of the plan to save Charlie, and Mansonites continue
to promote Copycat to this day.

First, according to the proponents of Copycat, Linda Kasabian was
its author and indeed the instigator and leader of the murder spree.
But she had only been a member of the Family since 4 July 1969.   It
is difficult to pinpoint Beausoleil's movements between 4 July and
6 August (when arrested) but there was no credible evidence that he
and Kasabian had developed a close relationship, or any relationship
at all.   It was crazily implausible that a newcomer such as Kasabian
would be leading the Family on a two-night frolic of wild murders for

262. KTLA 5 Los Angeles news broadcast, date unspecified, presumably on or shortly after 23 March
1971, sourced at www.mansonsbackporch.com.

the purpose of freeing Beausoleil. (Of course, Kasabian denied in her evidence in rebuttal that she ever heard of Copycat and she also denied the other allegations).

Second, Copycat was not put to Kasabian when she gave evidence in the guilt phase. It might be expected to be put if it was true, because it would have been the most exculpatory evidence in Manson's possession. Manson's attorney, Kanarek, spent an incredible seven days cross-examining Kasabian and put nothing to her about Copycat or Beausoleil. It defies belief that Kanarek left the single most important plank of his client's defence out of his marathon cross-examination[263].

Third, if Tate or LaBianca were copycat killings, why weren't the same words scrawled in blood as were scrawled at Hinman? The scribe at Tate (Atkins) knew exactly what had been written at Hinman. She was there. And she testified before the Grand Jury that seeing *"political piggy"* [sic] written on the wall at Hinman *"stuck very heavily in my mind"*[264]. The fact that the words used at Tate/LaBianca were not copies, and the paw print was not duplicated suggests Tate/LaBianca was not a copy of Hinman. It was, however, consistent with a series of murders which have some sort of anti-"pig" theme, which in turn was consistent with Helter Skelter.

George Stimson has argued the writing was different because it was different people who wrote at the respective houses (Beausoleil at Hinman, Atkins at Tate)[265]. But doesn't this just beg the question? If they were really doing this as a copy, wouldn't they make sure they got this simple part of it right? Even allowing for possibly being stoned, and usually pretty vacant, one would expect them to get the copying part of the copycat exercise right. They only needed to reproduce two words and a palm/paw print from the Hinman scene. And Atkins knew exactly what those words were.

---

263. This point might be subject to consideration of the defendant's right to silence: see *MWJ v. the Queen* [2005] HCA 74.

264. Grand Jury testimony, 5 December 1969.

265. Stimson, *Goodbye Helter Skelter*, p.253.

And that Hinman/Beausoleil had nothing to do with LaBianca tended to be confirmed by Krenwinkel's evidence, in particular the following:

"*Q. . . . did you have in mind as you wrote on the wall at the LaBianca residence the words 'political piggy'?*
A. I had nothing in mind."

Fourth, the words "Helter Skelter" written on the LaBiancas' refrigerator door and "WAR" on Mr LaBianca's stomach and the other words on the walls were only consistent with Helter Skelter. The words "Helter Skelter" were not just consistent – the door <u>was</u> Helter Skelter!

Fifth, implicit and central to Copycat was that Manson was unaware of it. This is unbelievable. Manson was a micro-manager. He wasn't just the leader, he was a dictator. It defies belief that the Tate murder mission, involving as it did four of Manson's disciples leaving the Ranch late at night with changes of clothing and with Manson's rope and Manson's gun could have escaped Manson's knowledge.

Sixth, if micro-manager Manson did not know what was going on (as Copycat would have us believe), it would be expected that, upon the return of Watson, et al, to the Ranch, he would be curious as to where they had been (with his gun and rope), what they had been doing, and why they had done whatever they had done. It is now 47 years since the murders as this book is written, and there has been no shortage of air time given to Manson, and not once has he, or anyone, said that he asked even these basic questions of his acolytes upon return to the Ranch.

Seventh, it is difficult to believe that anyone could have thought that committing a copycat murder would have the desired effect. The police had Beausoleil with the murder weapon and Hinman's car and they had his fingerprints at Hinman's house. Even assuming they linked Tate and Hinman, would they just drop the charges against

Beausoleil and let him out? Not likely, to say the least. Indeed, the most natural thing for the police would have been to suspect Beausoleil had accomplices still at large, and that line of enquiry probably would have led them to Spahn Ranch. The proponents of Copycat acknowledge that, yes, the plan was poorly thought out, but they argue that that does not invalidate it. But it was worse than poorly thought out. It was positively crazy to commit such a series of murders – arguably the wildest and most savage in the annals of crime - as part of such a plan. It was so crazy that it made Helter Skelter look positively sane and rational.

Eighth, Copycat was torpedoed by its own dishonesty when advanced by the witnesses. When a fact is lied about, it tends to prove the fact does not exist. The dishonesty of the witnesses, and the suspicious way in which their evidence unfolded, exposed Copycat as a lie.

George Stimson argues in his book that Copycat was the true motive for the Tate/LaBianca murders. However, what is conspicuously absent from his book is any reference to the cross-examination of the witnesses who testified about Copycat. Stimson claims all of these witnesses testified Manson had nothing to do with Tate/LaBianca[266]. Yes, they testified to that effect in their direct examination, but it was exposed as a lie in cross-examination. Writing about the testimony of these witnesses without writing about the cross-examination is a bit like writing about the invincibility of the Titanic but omitting to tell readers it sank. Whether Stimson's statement is calculated to mislead, or is simply a product of his misunderstanding the significance of cross-examination, is not known. Either way, it produces a hugely misleading picture of what actually happened at the first Tate/LaBianca trial.

Unsurprisingly, the jury rejected Copycat. Doubtless chilled by the defendants' lack of remorse, the jury returned death verdicts for all four.

---

266. Stimson, *Goodbye Helter Skelter*, p.318.

On 19 April 1971, Judge Older confirmed the death penalty:

"It is my considered judgment that not only is the death penalty appropriate, but is almost compelled by the circumstances. I must agree with the prosecutor that if this is not a proper case for the death penalty, what would be?"

The death penalty was abolished in California in 1972 whilst the defendants were on death row. All were given life sentences. All subsequently mounted appeals against their convictions, which will be considered in the next chapter.

The Plan to Save Charlie

The plan to protect Charlie had failed. But it would be remiss not to say more about it, in particular the conduct of the lawyers.

It is firstly appropriate to deal with the suggestion, advanced faintly by some commentators, that the defence lawyers were deliberately inept in order to create an appeal point. Counsel's incompetence is a recognised appeal ground, although it is difficult to sustain[267]. To feign incompetence in one of the highest profile trials in American history, in order to save one's client, would be extreme altruism, to say the least. It would be soul destroying and career destroying. It doesn't ring true. As it transpired, despite being foreshadowed in some of the appeal papers, no such argument was put at the hearing of the appeals. Another factor that militates against deliberate incompetence is that in all likelihood the appeal court, if satisfied there was incompetence, would return the matter for a re-trial. The exercise of feigning incompetence would be futile. The defence lawyers would have known this. This leaves the plan to save Charlie as the most plausible explanation of their peculiar conduct at the trial. This was certainly

---

267. *R v. Birks* (1990) 19 NSWLR 677.

deliberate, but it was aimed at a different, more sinister, end which was self-promotion at the expense of the girls going to the gas chamber.

It is impossible to escape the conclusion that Fitzgerald, Shinn and Hughes all agreed to facilitate the plan to save Charlie. This meant each of them acted for Charlie and against the persons for whom they were supposed to be acting. It did not matter that the women instructed the attorneys to do whatever Charlie said, implying that their interests coincided. Their interests did not coincide. No matter how much they loved each other, and how determined the women were to take the rap for Charlie, objectively, they had an interest in putting it on Charlie, and he had an interest in putting it on them.

The result was the women were left with no legal representation. To be left without legal representation, in a case involving the death penalty, was a terrible thing to be inflicted upon them, no matter how awful they were, or how guilty they were, and no matter their coalescence in the plan. The right to independent legal representation is one of the most fundamental rights of a citizen in a modern democracy.

Furthermore, not only were the women without legal representation, the lawyers who were supposed to be acting for them were positively acting against them by their objections, questioning, submissions, and so on.

It didn't end there. Manson also used the plan to engineer that none of the women would investigate or mount a psychiatric defence. Fitzgerald, Hughes and Shinn all participated in this injustice against their own clients. The girls were also deprived of the fundamental defence of blaming Charlie. In short, they were deprived of all means of defending themselves.

For defendants to go into a murder trial, where the prima facie penalty was death by execution, and not be permitted a lawyer or a defence, and have their own lawyers positively acting against them, was incredible. That Manson designed this debacle does not surprise. What was truly shocking was that, of all people, it was a group of lawyers who facilitated it.

The lawyers should have rejected Charlie's plan, withdrawn from the case and reported the plan to the judge or other relevant authorities, even if it meant losing the gig. It might be said that, even if these lawyers withdrew, others would have taken their place. However, if someone had gone public, it is hard to escape the conclusion that Manson's caper would have been up – he would have been ordered off to a separate trial and more stringent measures could have been taken to curtail his influence on the other defendants and on the proceedings generally.

I have given consideration to whether anybody else could, or should, have done something about the situation. This begs the question: did anybody else know? I suspect Bugliosi knew, or suspected, there was wrongdoing on the part of Manson and the girls' attorneys. It might be suggested Bugliosi owed a duty in the interests of justice to say or do something. However, without going into the detail of the ethical obligations of public prosecutors, which are onerous, I doubt a prosecutor's duty extends to the saintly perfection of alleging on behalf of the girls that they were victims of their own lawyers' wrongdoing. It might be different if Bugliosi had firm evidence of wrongdoing, but he could not have had such evidence. For example, the revelation of Fromme's statement that Shinn seemed prepared to go along with the plan to protect Charlie only emerged in Tex Watson's memoir in 1978. It might have been different if the girls' guilt was not so clear. But these were not borderline convictions. I doubt very much in these circumstances that Bugliosi owed some sort of duty to identify and correct the injustice.

There is also the question of whether Judge Older could, or should, have done something. I doubt it. It probably occurred to him there was something not right about the defendants' representation, but his position was not that of inquisitor into such matters. The judge was entitled to assume the lawyers were acting bona fide. It was not his place to go fishing around behind the scenes to work out the peculiarities of the defences. In fact it would be contrary to the impartiality of his office to do so. The system depends, as it must, on the honour and trustworthiness of the lawyers. That is the lifeblood of the oath they swear when they become lawyers. They swear, inter alia, to always assist the court. The system works well, except when lawyers act dishonourably.

Finally, I have wondered whether the appeal court could, or should, have done anything. But this is doubtful. For one thing, the girls were mostly represented by the same lawyers as at the trial, so there was unlikely to be any revelation to the justices of the appeal court about such irregularities and conflicts of interest. The appeal court is largely, if not wholly, in the hands of the parties as to the issues to be resolved on appeal. The justices do not have unlimited terms of reference to enquire into all and any of the rights and wrongs of the trial. They adjudicate what they are asked by the parties to adjudicate. Because none of the defendants' lawyers sought any adjudication of the conflict issues (unsurprisingly), there was no reason for the justices to go there. Sometimes, appellate courts do pick up things which are not strictly issues between the parties, but it is unusual, and unlikely in a case involving nine months of testimony and hundreds of exhibits. It might have been different had the convictions been borderline, and it might have been different had a new line-up of lawyers appeared for the defendants.

All of that said, there is one matter in respect of which, arguably, the trial court erred. It was not trial Judge Older, but rather the arraignment Judge Dell who, back on 6 January 1970, may have erred in not paying sufficient regard to Marvin Part when he stated that Van Houten was "*insane in a way that is almost science fiction*". It is impossible to escape the suspicion that the three women were simply incompetent to plead (stand trial)[268]. The leading American case on this subject at the time was *Dusky v. United States*[269]. There is an Australian case, to the same effect, which is a better factual

---

268. The terms "competence to plead", "fitness to plead" and "fitness to stand trial" all mean, essentially, the same thing. The terms tend to be used interchangeably across various common law jurisdictions.

269. (1960) 362 US 402; 1960 US LEXIS 1307.

vehicle for making the point. In *Kesavarajah v. The Queen* the High Court considered the case of an accused person who claimed to be the reincarnation of God (Vishnu) and that he could control the sun and the planets. The High Court re-stated a number of well established principles including that the accused person must be able to sufficiently understand the proceedings so as to be able to make a proper defence[270].

Some of the delusions of Atkins, Van Houten and Krenwinkel, for example the beliefs in becoming miniaturised and finding the fantasy land of the bottomless pit and the underground river, and Atkins' statements about doing what they did out of love for their victims, do not seem that far removed from the delusions of the defendant in *Kesavarajah*. Where you have defendants who plead not guilty, but are purporting to waive their rights to even investigate the obvious defence of diminished capacity, and effectively waive their rights to legal representation, it might be expected that you have a question about fitness to stand trial. It may have been, upon consideration, that the women <u>were</u> fit for trial. But what was of concern was that their fitness was not even investigated by the court, notwithstanding Part's submission on 6 January. The defendant in *Kesavarajah* was examined by two psychiatrists before a decision was made about his fitness by the trial judge. These girls never even got as far as having their fitness considered by a psychiatrist, let alone by the court. The test for fitness is less demanding than the test for acquittal on the ground of insanity. That is to say, the *M'Naghten Rules* of insanity do not apply to fitness to plead. Even though these defendants were never found insane, they may nevertheless have been unfit to plead. If I am right about this, then this was another right foregone by the female defendants.

Sceptics might argue that, when Van Houten was later given a re-trial (discussed in a later chapter), by this time de-programmed from Manson and presumably free of any question of fitness, and equipped with an independent lawyer (Keith) and a defence (she would plead

---

270. (1994) 181 CLR 230.

diminished capacity), that she was still convicted of murder in the first degree. So much is true and correct. And the argument has force. However, I cannot dismiss as a reasonable possibility that, had the first trial been conducted properly for Van Houten, including consideration of fitness to plead, she may have had better sentencing and parole prospects. (The nature and circumstances of the offence and the matters proved at trial are relevant factors in an inmate's parole entitlement.)

Others might reasonably ask: what does it matter if Van Houten committed the crime anyway (as she has since admitted)? This argument also has force. To be sure, she was an active participant in the conspiracy to commit horrendous murders. However, in the face of this, it matters that there can be such an affront to the rule of law as to disarm a citizen's rights to legal representation and a defence in a trial. The rule of law is the fabric of a modern mature democracy. It should never be disturbed in the way it was in this trial, no matter how guilty the accused, nor how heinous the crime. It is trite to say everyone deserves a fair trial – no exceptions. As the English Court of Appeal observed in *Jones v. National Coal Board*:

> *"There is one thing to which everyone . . . is entitled, and that is a fair trial at which he can put his case properly to the judge . . . No cause is lost until the judge has found it so; and he cannot find it without a fair trial"*[271]

Despite Judge Older's impeccable fairness, justice was disturbed sufficiently by events outside of his control that Van Houten (and Atkins and Krenwinkel) did not get a fair trial.

This begs the question of how the attorneys allowed this state of affairs to develop. This requires a closer look at each attorney.

It is clear Fitzgerald was enamoured of Manson. To confound things, he had been threatened by the Family. It seems that Fitzgerald

---

271. (1957) 2 QB 55, at p.67.

was caught in the same bind as the female Family members – he adored Manson but feared him too.

There was also the problem of having surrendered his job with the PDO. On the one hand, if he disobeyed Manson, he faced dismissal from the case, and to some extent professional oblivion. On the other hand, if he obeyed Manson, he stayed in and got the publicity he craved, with the potential for great professional acclaim (and free sex). But there was a price to pay for obeying Manson and staying in – he would have to comply to the letter with Manson's plan. Fortunately for him, nobody noticed much, or if they did they were unprepared to say anything.

Fitzgerald was not highly experienced, only five years out of law school. It is perhaps conceivable he did not appreciate the vice of the plan to save Charlie. It is evident he became very stressed as the trial progressed. In an interview filmed after the guilty verdict, but before commencement of the penalty phase, he rambled and appeared exhausted, fraught and spent[272]. (The transcript also reveals that around this time he was actually ill, one suspects run down by the stress, sleepless nights etc.) None of this was conducive to sound judgment making.

Prior to the trial, in the course of working up the media hype, Fitzgerald was busily circulating his theory that the defendants were on LSD and the crazy murders were explained by their LSD addiction. He sought to publicise the trial as the first of a series of landmark "acid trials". He made quite a play for media attention about this. The problem was the evidence never came close to proving the crimes were precipitated by LSD, except in the indirect sense discussed earlier. However, Fitzgerald seems to have been unable to divorce himself from his LSD case theory and was still touting it in his final submissions. According to writer Ivor Davis, it was also Fitzgerald who was spruiking the story about serving a subpoena upon John Lennon to

---

272. Unattributed, undated but clearly after jury's guilty verdict on 25 January 1971 and before commencement of penalty phase of trial on 28 January 1971, sourced from www.mansonsbackporch.com.

testify about the lyrics in the song "Helter Skelter"[273]. This was purely media grandstanding by Fitzgerald. There was no way the defence would be calling Lennon for the reasons set out earlier.

My research has left me astounded about the extent of Fitzgerald's self-promotion and publicity seeking. Flying in the face of Judge Keene's publicity ban, he seems to have run a line for the nearest camera every time he left court. He was quoted most (or many) days in the newspapers. According to Ivor Davis (himself a journalist at the time), Fitzgerald was "*a great source of inside information to the media during the trial*" and "*the press corps became bosom buddies with the defense lawyers, hanging out with them at local bars, socializing with them on weekends and communing with them during the trial – simply because that was where the leaks and the backstage information was coming from*"[274]. It has to be wondered when any of the defence lawyers had time to work on the case[275]. Perhaps this explains the bizarre mistakes they kept making.

Hughes was not much different to Fitzgerald, except he was even less experienced. Hughes was so inexperienced that it might be understandable if he did not appreciate the ethical problems. At the outset of the trial, Hughes saw Manson and the Family as kindred spirit, militant hippies, people he had much in common with, so much so he had socialised with them. Hughes agreed with the revolution, if not Manson's precise version then a generic one. This type of strident personal common ground between lawyer and client(s) is never healthy, especially for an inexperienced attorney. Hughes had little or no professional detachment. In fairness, as the trial progressed, he displayed increasing signs of insight and seems to have tried to distance himself and his client from Manson. At one point, Hughes asked that he and Van Houten be excused from court whilst evidence pertaining only to the Tate murders was heard. Juror William Zamora noticed

---

273. Davis, *Five to Die*, p.201.

274. Ibid, pp.200, 196.

275. Kanarek seems to have been the exception. From other things said by Ivor Davis, Kanarek was not involved in the socialising.

increasing animosity between Hughes and Manson, with Manson at one point yelling abuse at Hughes[276]. Assistant prosecutor Steven Kay would later recall a spat between Manson and Hughes on Hughes' last day in court before his disappearance: *"Manson was upset about the suggestion that Van Houten be tried separately . . . Charlie pointed across the counsel table at Hughes and with that steely stare of his said, 'I don't want to ever see you in this courtroom again'"*[277].

There was a tension in the defendants' camp which positively leaps out of the transcript pages when it came to a head on 20 November 1970. Since the start of the trial, when Krenwinkel had protested Fitzgerald was supposed to be her voice, the defendants believed and claimed the lawyers were to be their mouthpieces. That is to say, the lawyers, so the defendants believed, were simply supposed to relay what they wanted to the court, and have no independent mind or voice. This was fundamentally wrong. A lawyer must never allow himself to be an unthinking mere mouthpiece of his client. By dint of the force of the defendants' personalities, plus the lawyers' obsession with involving themselves in the "greatest trial of the century", the lawyers allowed themselves to become, in particular, Charlie's mouthpiece. They in fact became more than just part of his plan. By virtue of their positions as the trial attorneys, they inevitably became its active facilitators.

It surprises, and saddens, that the defence lawyers did not tell Manson to go and jump in the proverbial lake. But I can conceive of inexperienced lawyers being intimidated by him, not to mention the women who were aggressive themselves. In a perfect world, lawyers would never be intimidated by their clients, but it does happen. It also has to be factored in that the Family was issuing death threats to the lawyers.

I have so far confined matters to Fitzgerald and Hughes. Daye Shinn appears to have had no idea what he was doing, to the extent

---

276. Zamora, *Blood Family,* p.306.
277. Quoted in Davis, *Five to Die,* p.204.

he completely failed to understand conflict of interest issues. As mentioned, the Family was satisfied that Shinn was willing to go along with the plan to protect Charlie. The apparent ease with which he fell in line with Manson meant the case was stress free for him. It didn't seem to trouble him that he was acting against his own client's interests. And the icing on the cake for Shinn was that he was being paid for his services. Manson had quickly sized him up as pliable, amoral and incompetent, someone he could control and depend upon to implement the plan to save himself.

Kanarek's conduct can be distinguished to some extent. He was Manson's lawyer. Therefore, his role, properly understood, and broadly stated, was to implicate the women. Kanarek was more experienced than the others and there could be little doubt he was cognisant of the collective wrongdoing. He was also more skilful and effective than the other defendants' counsel. He would eventually resign from legal practice in 1990 whilst disciplinary charges were pending for an alleged offence, the nature of which was unknown.

Figure 6 Susan Atkins outside the Grand Jury room with her then attorney Richard Caballero, 5 December 1969. (Getty images)

Figure 7 Charles "Tex" Watson. (Getty images)

Figure 8 The female defendants during the first Tate/LaBianca trial. From left, Susan Atkins, Patricia Krenwinkel, Leslie Van Houten. (Getty images)

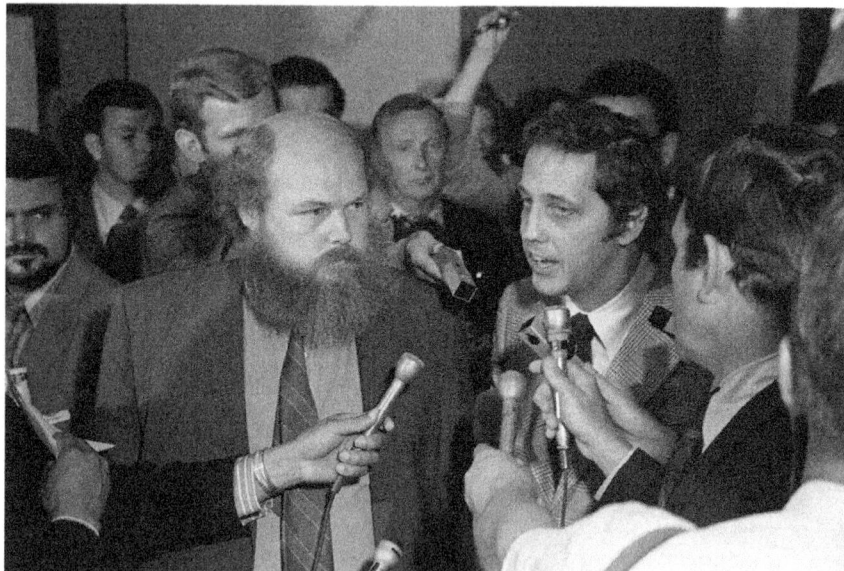

Figure 9 Hippie lawyer Ronald Hughes, bearded. To his left, Paul Fitzgerald. Hughes acted for both Manson and Van Houten at various times. Fitzgerald acted for both Manson and Krenwinkel at various times. In reality, both men were receiving their instructions from Charles Manson and became part of the hideous plan to send the female defendants to their executions in an attempt to have Manson acquitted. (Getty images)

Figure 10 Bruce Davis, centre, in handcuffs. To his left, attorney Daye Shinn. Shinn was a close confidante of Charles Manson. He represented Susan Atkins, all the while taking his instructions from Manson, a gross conflict of interest, one of many. (Getty images)

CHAPTER 8: TATE AND LABIANCA – AFTERMATH

"You are next, all of you. There's a revolution coming."
Sandra Good to media outside court, Tate/LaBianca trial.

Post Trial - June 1971 – Manson's Private Confession to Bugliosi

On 14 June 1971, Manson was back in court, on trial before Judge Raymond Choate and a jury for the murders of Gary Hinman and Donald Shea, the latter being the subject of the next chapter of this book.

Bugliosi was not prosecuting on this occasion. But he dropped in to watch proceedings. Manson asked to speak to him after the finish of court business. Talk got around to Tate/LaBianca. Manson admitted to Bugliosi he knew the murders were going to happen and *"I said to them; 'Here do you want this rope? Do you want this gun?' And later I told them not to tell anyone about what happened"*[278]. These admissions were tantamount to a confession[279].

Manson also effectively conceded Helter Skelter was behind the murders. Bugliosi asked him when he thought Blackie was going to

---

278. Bugliosi, *Helter Skelter*, p.609.
279. A confession is not the same as an admission. Every criminal offence (crime) consists of a number of elements, which are established by the prosecutor proving facts relevant to each element. An admission occurs when an accused person admits one, or some, of the alleged facts or elements of the crime. A confession occurs when the accused admits concedes all of the alleged facts or elements of the crime.

take over. Manson replied: *"I may have a put a clog in them"*. Bugliosi asked: *"You mean the trial alerted whitey?"*. Manson replied *"Yeah"*[280].

August 1971 - Trial of Charles "Tex" Watson

Watson's trial commenced on 2 August 1971. Many of the same witnesses who had testified against Manson and the girls were called against Watson. However, he admitted the killings. The real issue was his plea of insanity.

Watson testified in his own defence. He added another link between Manson and the murder scenes – one that the prosecution had been unable to nail down at the first trial – the bolt cutters. He identified cutters taken by police from Manson's dune buggy as those he had used to bring down the telephone lines at Cielo. Therefore, the links between Manson and the murder scenes now comprised:
1. Disciples.
2. Gun.
3. Rope.
4. Thong.
5. Scripture.
6. Houses.
7. Bolt cutters.

The jury rejected Watson's insanity defence. He was convicted on seven counts of murder and one of conspiracy. On 21 October 1971, the jury sentenced him to death. He was saved from that fate by the abolition of the death penalty

1976 – Disposition of Appeals

Watson's appeal against conviction was unsuccessful[281]. He is still in custody as this book is written.

---

280. Bugliosi, *Helter Skelter*, p.609.   Manson himself, and a court officer Mr Burrell, both subsequently corroborated Bugliosi as to the content of these conversations.
281. *People v. Watson* 2d Cal. Crim. No. 22241.

Appeals by Manson, Atkins, Van Houten and Krenwinkel were heard together. It appears much of the argument on appeal was taken up by Kanarek, again representing Manson. Whether Kanarek himself, or Manson, came up with the appeal points is open to conjecture. They were characterised by the appeal court as, variously, *"specious"*, *"silly"*, *"frivolous"*, *"superfluous"*, *"patently ridiculous"* and *"absurd"*. It is quite an achievement to get any type of court proceeding to that level of hopelessness.

Despite showing no reluctance to run any conceivable argument, no matter how *"silly"*, there was nothing of any consequence said by Manson about Helter Skelter in the appeal. If Manson genuinely disputed Helter Skelter, and given his propensity to argue anything, one would expect him to contest Helter Skelter somewhere in his appeal. And if ever there was something which had the inflammatory potential to propel a jury into reversible error, it was Helter Skelter, so it would have made forensic sense to say something about it, especially if he genuinely disputed it. But effectively, as far as I can tell, he said nothing about it. The appeal court judgment was the most authoritative assessment of Charles Manson's involvement in Tate/LaBianca, and you wouldn't know from reading it that Manson ever disputed the authenticity of Helter Skelter as his motive in the slightest[282].

The appeals of Manson, Atkins and Krenwinkel were dismissed. Van Houten's appeal succeeded on the ground that she was prejudiced by the disappearance of Ronald Hughes. Van Houten's convictions were set aside, and she was granted a new trial.

Van Houten's Re-Trials and Second Appeal

Leslie Van Houten's re-trial took place in 1977. She was again represented by Maxwell Keith. I have been unable to source the

---

282. There may be arcane legal considerations involved in what I have said. It might be argued on Manson's behalf that in accordance with his undoubted right to silence he was not obliged to say anything against Helter Skelter at his appeal. However, for various reasons, I doubt this applies without qualification and my present view is that enough had been said against him on the topic by this stage that there arose some sort of expectation that he take steps to rebut it, especially in the circumstance that the appeal court was bound to take his case at its highest. Alternatively, even if not for forensic reasons, in the circumstances that had developed in this case, I would have expected him to say something if he genuinely disputed its authenticity as a suggested motive.

transcript of this trial, but it was clearly a close contest. After 27 days of deliberation, there was a hung jury, seven jurors voting for first degree murder and five voting for manslaughter. A manslaughter verdict would have resulted in her immediate release on account of time already served.

Van Houten's new trial commenced in March 1978. On 5 July, the jury brought in a conviction for first degree murder. On 15 December 1980, the appeal court rejected Van Houten's appeal against conviction[283]. She has been incarcerated ever since.

1977 – Susan Atkins' First Book: *Child of Satan, Child of God*

In 1977, Susan Atkins published her first book *Child of Satan, Child of God* in which, surprisingly, she sought to resurrect the Copycat argument, albeit tentatively:

> *"to the best of my understanding, the copycat plan was the primary motive behind [Tate/LaBianca]"*[284]

The language of "*to . . . my understanding*" was not convincing. It suggested Atkins did not in fact know Copycat was the motive – rather it was something she had pieced together from other sources.

The book does not address any of the improbabilities about Copycat that have already been set out. Moreover, Atkins did not say why she failed to make any mention of it in 1969 either with her lawyers or at the Grand Jury hearing, which was when it would have been expected had it been true.

Furthermore, the book descended into significant error. Atkins wrote that on Wednesday 6 August 1969 word was received at the Ranch that Beausoleil was in jail and the knife had been found in the car. This much was correct. But then she said the following:

---

283. *People v. Van Houten* (1980) Cal App 3d 283.
284. Atkins, *Child of Satan, Child of God*, p.134

". . . we all were affected by Charlie's obsession with getting Bobby out of jail . . . Charlie was possessed with the need to prove his loyalty to his 'brother', to die for him if necessary.

'He's our brother' Charlie almost shouted to a small gathering of the core group. 'Our enemy has him in its territory and we have to get him out!'

. . . Charlie's loyalty touched a similar spark in me, and I forced myself to join the round-the-clock sessions *to find a way to free Bobby"*[285] [emphasis added]

However, as we have seen, Charlie did not learn about Beausoleil's arrest until he returned to the Ranch on the afternoon of Friday 8 August. Charlie's "*obsession*" could not have commenced until then and it was that night that the first murder mission went out. So there was not even time for one "*round-the-clock session*", let alone a number of them.

Furthermore, this version hardly sits well with the other passage (already mentioned) from the same book, in fact only two pages before, in which Atkins declared that, after Hinman, Manson had spent "*hours and hours, nights and nights . . . lecturing*" that Helter Skelter was coming down faster and faster[286]. Between the "*round-the-clock sessions*" thinking of ways to free Bobby and, on the other hand, the "*hours and hours, nights and nights . . . lecturing*" about Helter Skelter, there couldn't have been time to catch breath. Having been indoctrinated to not think about anything, Family members were now being implored to brain-storm 24/7. It must have been a shock to the system. It sounds highly unlikely.

---

285. Atkins, *Child of Satan, Child of God,* p.133.
286. Ibid, p.131.

1980 – Clara Livsey: *The Manson Women*

In 1980, Dr Clara Livsey published *The Manson Women*[287]. It is important to review this book because it was the first earnest attempt to discredit the Helter Skelter motive, and also discredit Manson's conviction. Some of Manson's followers have held this book up as a rallying cry for their protests about Manson's conviction.

Livsey was a medical doctor, with special interest or expertise in family psychiatry. The theme of her book was that Van Houten, Atkins and Krenwinkel were spoiled brats whose only interest was in delaying the onset of immaturity. Watson was included, but the emphasis was on the females. Livsey argued that too much attention had been given to Manson's brainwashing of the girls and not enough to their innately violent and self-aggrandizing tendencies. Livsey took it so far as to suggest that, far from Manson being the dominant manipulator, in fact he may have been the victim of their manipulations[288]. Associated with this, Livsey set about downplaying the significance of Charlie's Helter Skelter in the overall scheme of things, describing its *"acceptance"* by the prosecution as *"absurd"*, and asserting that *"[I]f one were to accept that [the defendants] truly believed the helter-skelter fantasy and that it really motivated these murders, one would have to conclude that they were psychotic (a hole in the desert, where thousands or people would live?). But they were not psychotic, clinically or legally"*[289].

There may have been force in what Livsey said about the innate predispositions of the girls, but the discussion of Helter Skelter was ill-informed and out of kilter with the evidence at the trials. The reference to Helter Skelter being *"accepted"* by the prosecution was another example of the mistaken perception that the prosecution somehow had ownership of the theory of Helter Skelter, or did actually believe it. It was not *"absurd"* for the prosecution to advance Helter Skelter at the

---

287. Livsey, C., *The Manson Women*, Richard Marek Publishers, 1980.
288. Ibid, p.115.
289. Ibid, pp.49 to 50.

first Tate/LaBianca trial, no matter how fantastic or out of proportion it may have seemed. There was an immense body of evidence from which, irrespective of its fantasy, it could be inferred that it was a motive. It would have been negligent of the prosecutor to not present that evidence. By my count, no less than 32 people, including Manson himself, represented or heard things consistent with Helter Skelter being the core of Charles Manson's manifesto. Almost all of these communications had occurred before the end of 1972. There was so much evidence of it that Bugliosi could afford to pick and choose which witnesses to call about it. This is a rare luxury in litigation. Ultimately, 10 persons testified under oath at the first and second Tate/LaBianca trials, and were tested by cross-examination. And that cross-examination was unable to contradict any of those witnesses, nor expose any reason whatsoever to doubt their testimony. It was far-fetched and fanciful nonsense of the highest order to suggest Helter Skelter was not a motive for the murders.

Furthermore, the statement that the killers were not clinically or legally psychotic was misleading. First, the clinical. True it was that evidence came out from clinicians in the penalty phase of the first Tate/LaBianca trial that the girls were not insane. However, I have already touched upon the slap-dash nature of this evidence. It was adduced in the vacuous context of the girls never having pleaded or run an insanity defence in the guilt phase. As such, it is impossible to convert this evidence into a finding that the girls were not insane under the *M'Naghten Rules*. Furthermore, whilst none of the killers attracted clinical findings of insanity or psychosis, there was equally no doubt - clinically - that, at the time of the murders, each of the killers had some sort of mental illness - maybe not insanity or psychosis - but some sort of mental disturbance. Dr Hochman testified the girls had histories of anti-social or deviant behaviour. Van Houten was mentally unbalanced and a psychologically loaded gun. Atkins had an hysterical personality[290]. Dr Joel Fort reported that, while Tex Watson was not so mentally ill as to be unable to form the intent to murder, nevertheless

---

290. Interestingly, Bugliosi pointedly commented on Atkins in his book: *"She was crazy. I had no doubt about it. Probably not legally insane, but crazy nonetheless"*: Helter Skelter, p.234.

"his specific and general behaviour and life style are not such that they would be considered normal, mature, or healthy in terms of psychiatric standards"[291]. It would become virtually common ground between the medical experts on both sides at Watson's trial that there was some sort of psychological disturbance – the issue was whether it was severe enough, or of such a nature, to qualify him for the defence of insanity. Even without this expert evidence, it would be difficult to accept that people who relentlessly plunge knives into other human beings, and then remorselessly gloat over it, and even talk of it as sexually gratifying, are in a healthy frame of mind, even if they are not full blown insane.

Secondly, as to <u>legal</u> insanity, at the first Tate/LaBianca trial, none of the defendants ran an insanity defence, so there was no legal judgment, one way or another, about whether they were insane. True it was that Watson and Van Houten, in subsequent trials, both unsuccessfully ran insanity defences. But Manson, Atkins and Krenwinkel had never run insanity defences. Therefore no judgment was ever made as to their (legal) sanity. For all we know, they may well have been legally insane, or legally of diminished capacity, but it was never tested, much less actually adjudicated.

The other problem with the argument that Helter Skelter was too fantastic to be believed was that it created the inference that, for a motive to be accepted by a jury, it had to be <u>not</u> fantastic. That is to say, the argument implies that the prosecution has to prove not only that the defendant had a motive, but also that that motive was rational and reasonable. None of this represents the law, nor does it equate with good sense. For one thing, it would involve the prosecution cutting across its own case and arguing, in effect on behalf of the defendant, that the motive for the crime was rational and reasonable. That it does not represent the law was confirmed by the appeal court:

> *"<u>The characterization of Helter Skelter as a fanatical fantasy</u> <u>is of no consequence</u>. The gist of the conspiracy was the*

---

291. Report of Dr Joel Fort, undated but based upon an interview with Watson on 8 July 1971.

comprehended common design, however bizarre and fanciful.
It is not necessary that the object of the conspiracy be carried
out or completed"[292] [emphasis added]

Livsey missed the point. The question was not whether Helter
Skelter was so "fantastic" that no-one <u>would</u> believe it. The real
question was whether anyone in fact <u>did</u> believe it (despite its
obvious fantasy). The answer was emphatically "yes". Watson
was a true believer in Helter Skelter. Krenwinkel was too, for she
thought it central enough to her murderous activities on 10 August
1969 to leave it emblazoned on the LaBiancas' refrigerator door.
Van Houten and Atkins believed in it as they told their lawyers and
others in late 1969. The three girls continued to believe in it so
much that they had to be educated and counselled in an attempt
to unravel it when incarcerated. Even the relatively articulate and
intelligent Kasabian truly believed it. Unquestionably the killers,
and almost certainly the rest of the Family, were committed true
believers in Helter Skelter.

Therefore, Livsey was wrong. There <u>was</u> something unhinged
(even if not full blown insane) about the killers, the extent of the
fantasy of Helter Skelter was irrelevant and most importantly these
killers <u>did</u> very much believe it, just as they believed everything Charlie
told them. And it should never have to be proved by the prosecution
that the motive contended for is a somehow rational or reasonable one.
No doubt the plausibility or rationality of the motive might enhance
the prosecution's chances of proving it, but absence of rationality
cannot rule out the motive contended for.

The final irritant about *The Manson Women* was that Livsey left
it until well into the book before disclosing she had had an interest
in Van Houten's litigation. She had acted in a consultative capacity
for the prosecution in the second re-trial of Van Houten (1980)[293].

---

292. *People v. Manson & Ors.* [1976] 61 Cal. App. 3d 123, at pp. 155 to 156.
293. Livsey, *The Manson Women*, p.211.

To be clear about it, the prosecution's case in that re-trial was that Van Houten had capacity for killing independent of Manson's influence and independent of Helter Skelter. The prosecution agenda was anti-Van Houten, anti-Helter Skelter, and (ironically) pro-Charlie. Thus, Livsey had an interest in the litigation having an outcome which was anti-Van Houten, anti-Helter Skelter and pro-Charlie. To this end, she came out with some significant inaccuracies and/or errors in her book:

- *"Manson did not have a history of violent behaviour"*[294].
- *"Anyone was free to go"*[295].
- the women stayed in the group of their own free will[296].
- *"it is simply untrue that the women were afraid of Manson"*[297].

2012 - Susan Atkins' Second Book: *The Myth of Helter Skelter*

In her second book, Atkins made another attempt to resurrect Copycat. This time, 40 years after the events, Atkins proffered (for the first time) a more elaborate version. She now claimed that, after learning of Beausoleil's arrest, Manson had actually sent people to talk to Bobby in custody. Then she wrote it *"can only be imagined that Bobby gave them an earful to report back to Manson"* [emphasis added][298]. This was not very convincing. Now, rather than known facts, the reader was being asked to imagine things. Then, readers were told what Bobby *"probably"* said[299]. But if an envoy visited Bobby in jail, and given Atkins was an inner-circle Family member, how come she doesn't know what Beausoleil actually said? As was often the case with Susan Atkins, it sounds more like conjecture than fact.

---

294. Ibid, p.35.
295. Ibid, p.105.
296. Ibid, p.147.
297. Ibid, p.148.
298. Atkins-Whitehouse, *The Myth of Helter Skelter*, p.83.
299. Ibid.

Also, there were again timing problems. Atkins says the envoy visited Beausoleil when he was transferred to Los Angeles County Jail, which was probably the day after his arrest i.e. 7 August[300]. Then she says that "*immediately*" Beausoleil's "*messages*" were received, Manson drew the Family together and issued the battle-cry about getting brother Bobby out of jail. But this was unlikely because Manson did not return to the Ranch until the afternoon of Friday 8 August.

It is useful to look at the remarks of Atkins when she was questioned about these issues in a Parole Hearing in 1985:

> "*Officer Aceto: And which [of Copycat or Helter Skelter] — which would be the most accurate then?*
>
> *Atkins: In my opinion [Copycat] . . . it's really difficult, Mr. Aceto, to assess what Mr. Manson's thoughts and feelings were, but that's what I had heard at the time. My personal belief is the former, the Copycat killings was more in touch with what was really happening*"

The problems are immediately obvious. Copycat was something she "*heard*" at the time, rather than something she knew. And it was her "*opinion*" or "*belief*" that Copycat was more likely – again not something she knew for a fact herself. As with Tex Watson, Atkins has mostly only been able to talk about things she has heard or otherwise opined rather than things she knew as facts. This was consistent with the Family ethos that nobody but Charlie really knew what was happening or why it was happening.

Furthermore, Atkins spends a large part of the book vigorously adopting her Grand Jury version of events and claiming it was her truthful version. And yet it was the Grand Jury version that embraced Helter Skelter. Thus, on the one hand, she refutes Helter Skelter and, on the other hand, urges readers to accept her version of events which embraced Helter Skelter.

---

300. Ibid, p.84.

Furthermore, Atkins specifically confirmed in her book that her evidence at the trial, which included evidence in support of Copycat, was "*a joke*"[301].

Furthermore, as already discussed, it was Atkins (in her first book in 1977) who revealed that as late as late 1972 the other girls were only just beginning to doubt Helter Skelter was going to happen. Although not explicit, the tenor of the passage written by Atkins was that she herself had not yet reached the same early stage of doubt about Helter Skelter as the other two had reached. This suggested that she, Atkins, was even more inculcated with Helter Skelter than they were. This alone makes her later refutation of Helter Skelter unconvincing.

In the result, Atkins' purported rebuttal of Helter Skelter ought to be disregarded.

Manson's Continuing Arguments

Manson has supporters who write and speak on his behalf. The scheme of much of the argument is that when the murders are assembled, collectively, it can be seen they all have a common denominator, namely that they were all committed pursuant to the code of honour, brotherhood and loyalty within the Family, rather than pursuant to the "far out" Helter Skelter:

- Crowe shooting – Manson did it to protect Watson.
- Hinman – Beausoleil did it to protect Manson (from inevitable loss of parole for his assault on Hinman).
- Tate/LaBianca – Watson did it because he owed Manson (for Crowe).
- Shea – dealt with in following chapter – Manson, Watson, et al, did it because Shea was snitching on the Family.

All honourable motives. We've already discussed Crowe and Hinman. Let's review Tate/LaBianca.

---

301. Ibid, p.191.

First, as to Tate, Manson claims through Stimson's book, as I understand it, that on Friday 8 August he knew that Tex, et al, were going out. But he thought they were going on a garbage run[302]. This story actually got an airing at the first Tate/LaBianca trial when Sandra Good tried it on in the penalty phase. She testified that the changes of clothing taken by Watson and the others were necessary in case, after the garbage run, they needed to go to a supermarket to buy cigarettes in which case they needed to have "*nice*" clothing on hand. And the knives were necessary because they had to cut up the fruit at the dumpster so excess garbage would not accumulate at the Ranch. Knowing what we know about life and conditions at the Ranch, it seems a joke that anyone thought they needed "*nice*" clothes for the supermarket or that sanitation was such a pressing issue. There were other matters that rendered the garbage run story implausible. For example, the garbage runs were not a night-time activity. Nancy Pitman testified before a Grand Jury that the she had not seen the garbage runs happen at night, and they would happen "*in the daytime*"[303].

Manson also claims that when Watson and the others were leaving the Ranch he gave them a pair of glasses and told them to drop the glasses[304]. But if this was a garbage run, why would Manson be giving them a pair of glasses to drop (in the dumpster)? We do know glasses were found at the Tate murder scene, otherwise unaccounted for. The suspicion arises that these were the glasses Manson was talking about, and they were destined to be left at the scene as a false clue. Manson more or less confirms the suspicion by saying the glasses were to be left to "*create confusion*" which can't be a reference to leaving them in a dumpster[305]. If this is correct, as it surely must be, then the glasses become another connection between Manson and the murder scene.

302. Stimson, *Goodbye Helter Skelter*, pp.157 to 158.
303. Evidence to Grand Jury 8 December 1969.
304. Stimson, *Goodbye Helter Skelter*, p.158.
305. Ibid.

Therefore, the links between Manson and the Tate/LaBianca murder scenes now comprise:

1. Disciples.
2. Gun.
3. Rope.
4. Thong.
5. Scripture.
6. Houses.
7. Bolt cutters.
8. Glasses.

Talk about leaving calling cards. Charlie may as well have sent signed confessions with Watson and told him to pin them on the front doors of Cielo and Waverley.

For much of Stimson's book it is difficult to work out whether the arguments are Stimson's own arguments or, instead, are reproductions of statements by Manson. This needs to be kept in mind during the following discussion.

George Stimson's book mounts many arguments in favour of Manson. The first that drew my attention was, as I understood it, an argument that the three essential elements of a crime are motive, means and opportunity[306]. This is incorrect. It amounts to saying that if a person <u>wants</u> to commit a crime, and perceives he <u>can</u> commit a crime, that he must be guilty – even if he didn't do it. In fairness, Mr Stimson may not have been intending to define the (legal) elements of a "crime" as such. But the trouble is that "crime" is inherently, and only, a legal concept. Crime depends upon law for its meaning. When crime is spoken about in anything but a legal context, the level of abstraction becomes elusive. At the very least, without wishing to offend Mr Stimson, the language is clumsy and apt to confuse and mislead.

Another point made by Stimson is that, contrary to popular opinion, the murders were not bizarre and people are bludgeoned to

---

306. Stimson, *Goodbye Helter Skelter*, p.203.

death "*all the time*" and mutilation such as carving words into a body is "*fairly common*"[307]. This is impossible to accept. Sharon Tate and her unborn child were executed. Frykowski was stabbed 51 times. And so on. It was small by the standards of international war atrocities like Katyn or My Lai. But for civilian peacetime killing in the suburbs, it was incredible.

Stimson also indulges in other questionable statements about the Tate/LaBianca murders. He says that "*most of the people involved in the murders refute [Helter Skelter] as the motive*"[308]. In fact, as we have seen, <u>most</u> of the people (Watson, Van Houten, Krenwinkel and Kasabian) <u>support</u> rather than refute Helter Skelter as the motive (to the extent they actually knew the motive). This is the polar opposite of what Stimson says. Only Susan Atkins has moved away from Helter Skelter over the years, but when it counted – at the time and in private conference with her lawyer – she embraced it totally. And we have seen the problems with her purported later rebuttal of it. Stimson's statement is completely wrong. In truth, all of the participants supported Helter Skelter as the motive. And despite premising his book on the supposed flaws in the prosecution's case about the Helter Skelter prophecy, Stimson avoids the 10 witnesses who gave uncontradicted sworn evidence about Helter Skelter at the trials, avoids the cross-examination of the Family witnesses which demolished Copycat and ignores Manson's admissions about Helter Skelter. For a book that holds itself out as presenting "*the first realistic examination of the murders*", the failure to even acknowledge, let alone confront or engage with, these incontrovertible matters is astounding. I have given anxious consideration to using such intemperate language. However, I find myself unable, in the interests of fairness and justice to all parties, to shirk from making harsh calls on these types of statements. I must add that I have communicated with Mr Stimson during the preparation of this book and, despite knowing I intended

---

307. Ibid, pp.229 to 230.
308. Ibid, p. 252.

to criticise him, he has been nothing but gracious and decent and has wished me luck with my project. He promptly answered several questions I asked of him.

Stimson then proposes *"premises"* for investigating Manson's guilt, all of which conveniently seem to be factual assumptions devoid of Manson's involvement in any of the murders[309]. As best as I can understand it, Stimson then proceeds to analyse the question of Manson's guilt on the basis of these assumptions. This is misconceived and, frankly, silly. What Stimson is proposing is that we make an assumption that Manson was not involved in the murders, and then proceed to analyse whether or not he was involved. In other words, we are going to assume he was innocent, and then analyse whether he was innocent. This is terrifically convenient for Manson, because such analysis can only have one result – innocence.

Stimson then turns to the previously mentioned direction (instruction) given to the Tate/LaBianca jury on proof of guilt beyond doubt and, as I understand it, takes this direction to mean that the jury must acquit the defendant if there is another more rational motive (inconsistent with the defendants' guilt) besides the motive contended for by the prosecution (consistent with guilt)[310]. Stimson argues that Copycat was a more rational motive than Helter Skelter and, therefore, Manson should have been acquitted. But there are several difficulties with this. First, Stimson's basic premise is wrong. The ultimate inference of guilt depends upon proof of the essential elements of <u>intent</u> and <u>killing</u>. If there are rational alternatives to the prosecution's versions of <u>intent</u> and <u>killing</u>, then the jury must acquit the defendant. Motive is different. Presentation of a more rational alternative <u>motive</u> does not mandate an acquittal. Motive is not an essential element of any crime. A rational alternative motive just means there was another motive. It is difficult to see how, as a matter of logic, it could even derogate from the motive contended for by the prosecution (even if

---

309. Ibid, p.290.
310. Ibid, pp.319 to 320.

it is more likely or "rational"). And it would plainly do nothing to negate the mountain of other incriminating evidence against Manson (admissions, links, and so on). Secondly, upon analysis, Copycat was not rational in any event. When it was offered to the jury in the penalty phase of the trial, the jury rejected it. So why would the jury have accepted it had it been offered in the guilt phase instead of the penalty phase?

Stimson's assumption of the role of de facto lawyer for Manson is a matter of some concern. I cannot find anywhere in his book any account of qualifications, experience or expertise in law. The few questions which remain about these murders are quintessentially forensic questions about which Stimson appears to have no experience or comprehension. Some of his arguments seem to have an instant appeal but upon analysis the appeal is lay and superficial. Almost all of his arguments remind me of the ill-conceived arguments put forward by unrepresented litigants I have opposed in trials. It is a bit like a person submitting a thesis on surgery to a medical symposium, or an article on cures for cancer to the Lancet, without ever having studied or practiced medicine. It is self-evidently unsatisfactory. Furthermore, trial law and advocacy are technical sub-specialties of general law. And prosecution is a further sub-specialty of trial advocacy. Prosecutors are subject to unique duties and responsibilities that have no bearing on other advocates.

Another of Stimson's assertions is that Manson could have severed his trial from the other defendants and escaped with a lighter sentence but chose to stick by his friends, "*even if it meant dying [in the gas chamber] with them*"[311]. This claim is erroneous. The last thing Manson wanted was a severance of the trials – he had fired Charles Hollopeter immediately upon Hollopeter moving for severance. He even had a temper tantrum about it. He then instructed Ron Hughes to immediately withdraw the severance motion. He had both Part and Reiner fired when they pursued severance on Van Houten's behalf. It was abundantly clear Manson wanted the trials heard

311. Stimson, *Goodbye Helter Skelter*, p.403.

together because he wanted to keep control of the women's defences. Manson knew his control would be diluted if they were hived off to separate trials, as it had been when Atkins was separated out during her initial custody and started talking to anyone who would lend an ear, as it was when Krenwinkel was off in Alabama and implicated him to Dr Brown, and as it was when Van Houten implicated him to Marvin Part. He didn't want that control for their benefit - he wanted it for the most evil purpose of protecting himself at the expense of sending them to the gas chamber. Apart from the actual murders, this was one of the worst aspects of this story. Manson went out of his way to protect himself at the girls' expense. His plan to save himself at their expense depended upon the trials being heard together. The plan had little or no chance of success if there were separate trials[312].

Stimson's claim of Manson sticking by his friends is incorrect. There was no doubt the girls were 100% loyal to Manson, but it was a one-way street. Charlie was the epitome of disloyalty to the extent of positively engineering the plan for the girls to falsely testify to his innocence, so they would face execution and he would survive. In this way, Charles Manson actively set about killing the girls. And Fitzgerald, Hughes and Shinn joined in.

George Stimson appears to be a friend and confidante of Charles Manson. His loyalty to Manson is, on one view, commendable. The book is dogmatically pro-Manson. Loyalty has its place. However, scholarly objectivity and enquiry, based on genuine expertise, would be preferable.

Ultimately, there were no debts owed to Charlie, nor were any favours granted by Charlie. The crimes cannot be explained by codes of brotherhood or loyalty within the Manson Family. Charlie's "IOU's" were fictions created by Charlie, and propagated by Stimson,

---

312. Manson would have another tantrum in the Hinman/Shea prosecution when Judge Raymond Choate separated his trial from the trials of Bruce Davis and Steven Grogan. Manson tore a button from his shirt and threw it at the judge. Charlie most certainly didn't like any of his followers' trials to take place without him there: Guinn, *Manson*, p.386.

in an attempt to mitigate the crimes which were in fact calculated and cold-blooded executions, almost all based upon the Helter Skelter prophecy. The code of honour was, and still is, a deception perpetrated by Manson. He used it get his acolytes to be willing to kill, or be killed (*"will you die for me?"*). But there was no way he was ever going to kill, or be killed, for them.

Vincent Bugliosi

It is appropriate that I make some comments about prosecutor Vincent Bugliosi. My research has revealed he has had detractors from time to time. He ran unsuccessfully for public office. He certainly was not a person who charmed people. He could be abrasive and obviously made enemies. However, the only judgment I can make about Bugliosi, from a trial lawyer's perspective, is that he was proper in his conduct of the Tate/LaBianca trials. I cannot recall finding a single improper question, objection or submission by Bugliosi in the thousands of pages of transcript.

Stimson alleges Bugliosi unfairly pre-judged the evidence against Manson and, essentially, set out to get him at all costs. This notion of Bugliosi's preconception of Manson's guilt mistakenly informs much of Stimson's book. One could readily understand this complaint if it was the judge or jury who had a preconception of guilt. But Bugliosi was the prosecuting lawyer. The very thing for which he was paid by the people of California was, as a public prosecutor, to form preconceptions of guilt and then take them to a jury for a decision. He was obliged to form judgments about potential guilt so he could carry out his duty of selecting who should, or should not, be prosecuted in respect of alleged criminal acts. It is not hard to imagine the chaos that would ensue if nobody was assigned the task of discriminating between possible defendants in respect of suspected criminal acts.

Furthermore, it does not appear to me that Bugliosi was over-reaching for a conviction to conform with police or public expectations. He had been independent enough to stand up to Police Chief Ed Davis and try to stop Davis going public prematurely in December 1969 with an announcement that Manson and the others were suspects[313]. And on 1 January 1970, he was independent enough to warn District Attorney Younger that, without Atkins' evidence, the Tate case was "*anaemic*" and the LaBianca case was "*non-existent*"[314]. During the penalty phase he refrained from objecting to inadmissible material being tendered on behalf of Krenwinkel. He also refrained from cross-examining the parents of Krenwinkel and Van Houten. He also backed off objecting to Paul Fitzgerald's clearly improper argument to the jury about the ghastly way in which people expire in the gas chamber. He was decidedly cautious about indicting Steven Grogan for LaBianca, some would say too cautious (see Appendix 2 for further discussion). None of this was the sort of language or conduct one would expect of a prosecutor who was over-reaching. My overall impression of Bugliosi is that, if anything, he tended to err on the conservative side in his management of the Tate/LaBianca prosecutions.

In the final analysis, this book is principally concerned with events at court. Bugliosi did nothing improper in my assessment of his conduct of the case in court. There were things I would disagree with, and things I would not have done, but I find it impossible to fault his conduct of the case in terms of either skill or integrity.

313. Bugliosi, *Helter Skelter*, pp.219 to 220.
314. Ibid, p.285.

CHAPTER 9: THE MURDER OF DONALD "SHORTY" SHEA

"And after the crimes we went out and looked for the hole"
Leslie Van Houten[315]

"I've told my people to start killing you"
Charles Manson turns and addresses the press in court
during the Shea trial[316]

Events at the Ranch After LaBianca

Donald "Shorty" Shea was a ranch hand at the Spahn Ranch. About one week after Tate/LaBianca killings, on 16 August 1969 (same day as the police raid on Spahn Ranch), Shea separated from his wife and told her he was going to stay at the Ranch for a while. The next day, Shea's wife noticed his possessions, including two suitcases and a footlocker bearing the stamped words "Donald Jerome", were gone.

Shortly after the 16 August raid, Manson told various people, including Family member Barbara Hoyt, that Shea had been responsible for the police raid and wanted to have the Family evicted from the Ranch.

315. Record of interview with Marvin Part, 29 December 1969, sourced from www.cielodrive.com.
316. Bugliosi, *Helter Skelter*, p.605.

Between 27 August and 1 September, Shea's wife tried to contact him at the Ranch by telephone but was unsuccessful. On one occasion, she was told by a female voice that he had gone to San Francisco.

Around 30 August, Ranch Manager Ruby Pearl was in her car and stopped and talked to Shea. As she drove away she saw a car drive up to Shea "*real suddenly*". Pearl saw Manson, Watson, Grogan and Davis get out of the car and spread around Shea. Pearl was the last non-Family member to see Shea alive.

On 9 December, Shea's car and other possessions were found in Chatsworth. In February 1970, Shea's suitcase and brief case were found under some bushes in Goler Wash. By the time of the trials of Manson, Davis and Grogan, Shea's body had not been found[317].

Trial of Manson for Murder of Shea – Prosecution Case

Manson, Davis and Grogan were indicted for the murder of Shea. I have been unable to find any record of Watson being indicted for Shea. Nor have I been able to find anything which explains why he was not indicted. Manson's trial was severed from the Davis and Grogan trials. Manson was again represented by Irving Kanarek.

This was a wholly circumstantial case. The absence of a body was problematical for the prosecution, but not insurmountable. It became necessary for the prosecution to prove other circumstances consistent with guilt. This was, potentially, a case where motive might be important, depending on the strength of the other proved circumstances.

Shea's wife testified that she last saw her husband on 16 August 1969. Shea had owned a matching set of .45 Colt revolvers of which he was very proud. They had been kept in a case bearing the words "Reverend Donald Shea".

---

317. It would be located in 1977 with the help of Grogan.

Robert Bickston testified that Shea was to commence employment with him on 15 September 1969. However, Bickston hadn't seen Shea since June. Victor Lance had gone to the Spahn Ranch in August or September to see Shea but hadn't been able to find him. Jerry Binder testified that he loaned money to Shea in July and Shea had not repaid it. The last time Binder had seen Shea was at the end of July.

Frank Retz testified that he was in the process of purchasing Spahn Ranch and wanted the Family off the Ranch. It was apparently agreed between Retz and Shea that Shea would become a watchman at the Ranch.

Ranch hand Johnny Swartz testified that Manson had told him after the (16 August) raid that Retz had purchased one half of the Ranch and had offered the watchman job to Shea. At the end of August, Swartz asked Manson if he had seen Shea. Manson said Shea had gone to San Francisco. Swartz also testified he had seen Danny DeCarlo and Bill Vance at Spahn Ranch in possession of Shea's revolvers.

Ruby Pearl testified about seeing Manson and the others surround Shea.

Barbara Hoyt testified that Manson said Shea was a snitch and he was trying to get the Family kicked off the Ranch. Hoyt also testified that one night in late August, as she was going to sleep, she heard screams from the nearby creek. She recognised the screams as coming from Shea. The next day she overheard Manson telling Danny DeCarlo: "*Shorty committed suicide, with a little help from us*". Manson said they cut him up in nine pieces. Hoyt then heard Manson ask DeCarlo if lye or lime would get rid of the body, to which DeCarlo replied that lye would, but lime would preserve it. Hoyt also testified that Manson had talked to various Family members about having killed Shorty:

> "*Charlie said that they had killed Shorty. Uh they cut him up in nine pieces. And first they asked him . . . if he would like to see something and . . . then he got in the dune buggy*

*and they took him away. And then, they hit him in the head
with a pipe. Uh, they pulled him out . . . and they started
stabbing him. And then, um, they kept stabbing him . . .*

*And . . . Shorty said 'Why Charlie why?' and Charlie said
'Why? This is why' And then he stabbed him again.*

*And . . . he said that it was very hard to kill him until
they brought him to now. And when they brought him to
now, he said that [Steven Grogan aka Clem] chopped his
head off."*

Brooks Poston testified that in September 1969 Manson had told
Family members:

*"You remember Shorty don't you? You know, we had to
do him in. He was badmouthing the Ranch and calling
the Man on us, and scheming with Frank Retz to get the
Ranch. And we warned him two or three times to stop, but
he didn't. So we hit him on the head, took him for a ride.
And when he started to come to, we stuck him with knives.
And when he started to get to now, he was really hard to
kill, because he wouldn't give it up. So Clem had to cut his
head off"*

Paul Watkins testified that on 1 September 1969 Manson had said:

*"We had to kill Shorty. Clem cut his head off [with a
machete]. He's been badmouthing the Ranch and . . . calling
the man on the Ranch"*

Other circumstantial evidence included:
- The discovery of Shea's car with his footlocker in the trunk.
- Bruce Davis' fingerprint on the footlocker.
- Evidence of sale of the revolvers by DeCarlo.
- Evidence of attempts by police to locate Shea's body.

The jury began its deliberations on 21 October 1971 and returned a verdict of guilty for Manson on 2 November 1971. Davis and Grogan were convicted in separate trials. Appeals by all three men were unsuccessful[318].

More Revelations – Davis and Grogan Parole Hearings

Davis and Grogan have since both confessed and revealed more details about Shea's murder at parole hearings. I shall deal with each in turn.

Davis has stated that he and Grogan and Tex Watson asked Shea to drive them to get some spare car parts. Shea got in the driver's seat. Watson sat next to him. In the rear was Grogan (behind Shea) and Davis. After setting off, Watson told Shea to pull over. Shea refused. Watson pulled his knife and stabbed Shea in the eye. Shea pulled over. Grogan hit Shea in the head with a pipe wrench. Watson and Grogan hauled Shea out of the car and dragged him down a ravine. Davis remained in the car.

Manson then pulled up behind and handed Davis a machete and told him to chop off Shea's head. Davis said he couldn't do that. Grogan and Watson and Bill Vance were standing around with bloodied knives. Manson handed Davis a knife and said *"well, do something"*. Davis slashed Shea's shoulder, from the armpit across to the collarbone. Davis does not know whether Shea was dead before he slashed his shoulder, and concedes his blow could have been fatal. He described the knife and the blow at his 2008 parole hearing:

". . . I cut him right across the shoulder. I cut him with this knife. Boy this knife was sharp. It laid him open. I don't know if he was dead or not."[319]

---

318. *People v. Manson* 71 Cal. App. 3d 11; *People v. Davis* Cal. 2d Crim 22505, unpublished, 31/3/76; *People v. Grogan* Cal. 2d Crim. 21932, unpublished, 19/1/73.

319. Parole hearing 15 September 2008.

Grogan told a parole hearing in 1981:

"[Manson] handed me like a pipe wrench. He told me to hit Shorty in the back of the head as soon as Tex gave me the go ahead or gave the signal. At that point Tex and I entered the back seat behind . . . Shea, and Tex was on his right hand side. We proceeded down Santa Susanna Pass toward San Fernando Valley. And about a quarter of a mile down from the ranch there was like a turn off where cars, you know, like a rest area. And Tex mentioned he had some spare parts over there that he had to get . . .

Then we pulled off the road. Tex got out. The car was still in gear. I think he just had his foot on the brake, and they got out and they looked around the bushes like he was looking for some parts.

In the meantime I was supposed to hit this guy in the back of the head . . .and Tex was urging me, you know, come on hit this guy, I kept hesitating. . . . I just hit the guy . . . there was no accurate shot or nothing like that . . .

Well the blow knocked him forward so he hit the steering wheel . . . he had already been stabbed. I imagine Tex [stabbed him]. [I] came out of the car and [Shea] was laying on the ground in a semi-conscious state. He was already going or something. At that point Manson arrived on the scene with another person . . .

And I was handed a knife and told to stab him. I stabbed him twice in the chest. And some others were told the same . . . [Manson] might have slashed him. I don't recall if he stabbed him. . . . I think Bruce might have stabbed him in the arm"[320]

---

320. Parole hearing 1981.

When the revelations of Grogan and Davis were added to the evidence adduced at the trial, Manson's guilt was beyond question.

Stimson's Book – Manson's Defence

Stimson writes a whole chapter about the murder of Shea but it is difficult to understand exactly what he is trying to convey. He sets out some passages of Charlie's mumbo-jumbo which, if anything, seem to amount to a confession.

Stimson contends there was no physical evidence or direct eye-witness testimony that necessarily connected the defendants to the murder[321]. This is very misleading. True there was no eye-witness evidence. But there was no shortage of other evidence. Ruby Pearl saw Manson and the others surround Shea. Hoyt heard Shea's screams. Davis' fingerprint was on Shea's footlocker. Manson made damning admissions. It was an overwhelming case. The appeal court would later say, as in the Hinman case, that Shea was not even close.

Stimson then claims that *"[F]or a long time, even after the convictions were obtained, there was still some doubt as to whether there had even been a murder"*[322]. This is wrong. There was no doubt amongst the 12 jurors who heard the evidence in 1971. There was no doubt amongst the appeal court judges. Davis and Grogan have never doubted, both having confessed. The autopsy on the discovered remains of Shea's body revealed a missing hand, multiple stab and chop wounds and a severe blunt force trauma to the skull[323]. It's unlikely Shea died of natural causes. Even Manson himself, as best as can be made out, does not doubt his guilt for murdering Shea. Stimson is the only doubter.

---

321. Stimson, *Goodbye Helter Skelter*, p.184.
322. Ibid.
323. Report of Dr Noguchi, Deputy Medical Examiner, County of Los Angeles dated 12 January 1978.

CHAPTER 10: REFLECTIONS

". . . it's the Beatles, the music they're putting out. They're talking about war. These kids listen to this music and pick up the message . . . "

Charles Manson to Vincent Bugliosi[324]

Justice

Justice was done, almost. The female defendants in the first Tate/LaBianca trial did not get a fair trial. Charlie had prevented them being defended by lawyers. He pitted their own lawyers against them. He prevented them running potential defences. He prevented them contesting fitness to plead. It is inconceivable that a fair trial could be had in such circumstances. It is a separate question whether the outcome would have been different had the women got a fair trial. My view tends to be they still would have been convicted, but their sentencing and parole prospects may well have been better had they obtained a fair first trial.

The institutions of judge, jury and prosecutor otherwise withstood Manson's attempts to corrupt the trial. These three institutions were sanctuaries of sanity and fairness in a trial which was otherwise a Charlie-circus and a media circus. These three institutions took the loss of life seriously. The defendants and their attorneys played the loss

---

324. Bugliosi, *Helter Skelter*, p. 497.

of life as if it was a game. They mocked the victims. They did so for the most part in short sighted and greedy pursuit of fame or fortune.

Manson's criminal achievements were incredible. It is remarkable to think what he achieved in two and a half years as a free adult. Quite apart from the nine murders for which he remains in jail, there was a long list of other potential offences for which he escaped charges or trial:

1. Bribery of a public official.
2. Conspiracy to pervert course of justice.
3. Conspiracy to commit perjury.
4. Grand theft auto.
5. Vandalism/destruction of property (destroying earth moving equipment in the desert).
6. Sexual assault.
7. Credit card fraud (multiple counts).
8. Theft (multiple counts).
9. Attempted murder of Bernard Crowe.
10. At least 14 known assaults at Spahn Ranch.
11. Assaulting a judge.
12. Narcotics possession.
13. Contributing to delinquency of a minor.
14. Multiple charges of contempt of court.

That's, say, 30 serious offences in 30 months, or one per month. And that's only those that are known about. Had he not been caught for the murders, he'd probably be in jail for the rest of his life anyway. Other criminals might feel aggrieved that Manson has never been charged or tried for the other offences. He escaped lightly with his nine life sentences!

Other Family members did well too. Tex Watson was never indicted for the Shea homicide, a crime he almost certainly committed. Nor, to my knowledge, was Bill Vance indicted. Steven Grogan was not indicted for LaBianca despite being prima facie party to the agreement to kill that night[325]. Mary Brunner was never indicted

---

325. For some possible explanations of the anomalous failure of the authorities to proceed against Watson and Grogan, see Appendix 2.

for Hinman, although, in fairness, she gave her testimony against Beausoleil in exchange for an immunity from prosecution[326]. The Family members who fabricated evidence in the penalty phase of the first Tate/LaBianca trial, including Share, Good, Atkins, Van Houten, Pitman, Gillies, Fromme and Krenwinkel may also, arguably, have been lucky to escape charges for various criminal offences relating to their false testimony on oath.

Motive

Ultimately, given the strength of the prosecution case, it was unnecessary to prove motive against Manson. However, to understand the broader social questions of how and why these murders came about, it is useful to pay some regard to the question of motive.

Motive is defined by one dictionary as:

"(of **power** or **force**) **causing movement** or **action** "[327]

Most people would think of "motive" as a dynamic that makes a person <u>want</u> to do something. What made Manson <u>want</u> to kill?

At the outset, the Copycat scenario for Tate/LaBianca can be eliminated. On the only occasion Copycat was tested by cross-examination, it was exposed as a fabrication. And it was inherently implausible in any event. And the Family witnesses who testified to it have since conceded, effectively or directly, that it was concocted. Eliminating Copycat is the simple part of the exercise.

The prosecution argued that Manson had three motives:

(i)   His anti-establishment rage.

(ii)   His lust for death.

(iii) Helter Skelter.

---

326. Brunner back-flipped repeatedly on her immunity deal, but ultimately the appeal court confirmed her immunity: *People v. Brunner* (1973) Cal. App. 3d, Vol 32 p.909.

327. *Cambridge Dictionary,* Cambridge University Press Online.

Manson has never stopped advertising his anti-establishment rage. This was truly a motive for these murders. He hated the establishment, and he wanted to kill it. And on Friday 8 August 1969 he was having a very bad day. The role of the "bad day" ought not be underestimated. Charlie Manson was a capricious, moody and unpredictable individual, given to irrational and impulsive behaviour and prone to temper tantrums. Volatile would be an understatement. In no small way, the victims at Cielo and Waverley just happened to be in the way when Charlie was stressed out and having a bad day, against the backdrop of his general desire for revenge against society for the bad hands it had dealt him since childhood and against the backdrop of incitement of himself and the others to wage a revolution.

Manson's so-called lust for death also motivated, or at least facilitated, the murders.

As for Helter Skelter, I contend its true significance was that it provided a means for Manson to persuade his warriors to go out and kill. Consideration was earlier given to the wavering perceptions about whether Manson himself really took Helter Skelter seriously. Bugliosi doubted that he did. I respectfully agree with Bugliosi. This also explains something that is otherwise anomalous about the role of Helter Skelter <u>as a motive</u>: if Manson didn't really believe in all (or any) of it, how could it be characterised as something that motivated him? The answer lays in what Bugliosi says: it wasn't really <u>his</u> motive as much as something that he used to motivate his warriors. In that limited sense, it was <u>a</u> motive for the murders, even if not <u>the</u> motive.

Another layer could be added to what Bugliosi said. It is readily apparent from Stimson's book, which cites more of Manson's exact words than any other publication of which I am aware, that the topic of "war" is usually uppermost in Manson's mind. He repeatedly talks about "war", and associated things such as soldiers, guns, combat, God and country. He introduces it into most conversations. He seems always ready to go to war, and often makes his point by war analogies. He explained Tate/LaBianca in terms of soldiers going into war in a television interview with Dianne Sawyer in 1994[328]. War magazines were found in the Family bus in late 1969. The early statements of Van Houten and Atkins emphasised the war-like nature of their activities. Van Houten regarded herself as a soldier on a *"mission"*. Good and Pitman have repeatedly spoken in similar terms.

Helter Skelter was a means of elaboration and decoration of what was, for Manson, basically a campaign of war against the establishment. Helter Skelter became a rallying war cry. And also it became a hook-line by which Manson seduced his followers. What better hook for a group of teenagers and early 20-somethings in the 1960's than Beatles' songs? This draws support from Manson's own words, as alleged by Bugliosi, in a court room rap: *"Bugliosi, it's the Beatles, the music they're putting out. They're talking about war. These kids listen to this music and pick up the message . . ."*[329].

Helter Skelter sceptics often read too much, and too literally, into the paraphernalia of Manson's Helter Skelter prophecy. It wasn't really the 12 tribes, miniaturised people, bottomless pits etc, that motivated Manson. It was war that motivated Manson. He called it Helter Skelter and added promotional fluff about the bottomless pit and so on for the sake of the story to seduce the kids.

If Manson ever developed the capacity to reflect, and speak sensibly and honestly, I suggest he would say something like this: *"well yes, the bottomless pit and the 12 tribes and so on, that was just stuff that came up when we were stoned and it was fun just imagining all of that, and the kids all went 'Amen, Amen', but I didn't really have that seriously in mind, what I was serious about was going to war and killing the society that had been killing me since I was born"*. Some of this is borrowed from things Manson actually has said, and so it may not be far from the truth of what was in his mind at the time.

The Family overwhelmingly embraced Helter Skelter. They fell for the trappings of war –knives, guns, Armageddon, armed dune

---

328. *A Turning Point,* 1994, ABC TV.
329. Bugliosi, *Helter Skelter,* p.497.

buggies, "us against them", the establishment pigs, and so on. Manson himself glorified war. He regarded Helter Skelter as an ancillary thing – "confusion" is a term he has used – but with all of its trappings (plus Beatles) it was an ideal vehicle for sucking in disengaged and disaffected 1960's teenagers. Manson ultimately engaged in so much seduction about war that he indulged himself and actually kick started it by sending his soldiers out to kill.

To summarise on Helter Skelter:

1. Despite being a far-fetched and fanciful prophecy, the evidence was overwhelming that the Family members, in particular the participants in the murders, intensely believed in it.

2. Charlie may or may not have believed in all of the paraphernalia of Helter Skelter, but he certainly believed in waging war against the Establishment. He wanted to kill it.

3. Helter Skelter was a motive in the sense that Manson used it to work his acolytes up into a lather of violence. It was not the motive. It was part of the motive equation.

4. Whilst these matters help explain why, as a matter of fact, the Manson Family committed the Hinman/Tate/LaBianca murders, the way in which the respective trials unfolded made it unnecessary for the prosecution to prove motive. This was simply because there was so much other evidence, against Manson especially. Helter Skelter did serve other forensic purposes, the most important of which was that it afforded links between Manson and the murder scenes. It effectively put Manson at the scenes. This was how it was seen by the appeal court who commented (in the context of the Kasabian corroboration issue):

"The consistency of the statements [of the witnesses who testified about Helter Skelter] reveals an intense obsession on Manson's part to see the fulfilment of his prediction. The similarity between the Helter Skelter prophesy and the

*manner in which the Tate-LaBianca murders occurred is
sufficiently great to be characterized as strong circumstantial
evidence . . .*"[330]

The question remains: how did Manson get his soldiers to kill?
It is trite to say Manson was a dictator of sorts, a Messiah and the
Second Coming of Christ to his followers. But this much is not such
an unusual phenomenon. All cults worship their Messiahs. What
<u>was</u> unusual about the Manson Family was that Charlie was able to
persuade his minions to kill other humans for him. Military leaders do
this in wars. But Charlie did it with teenagers and 20-somethings in a
civilian peacetime setting. How?

The Cult of Charlie

Cults are psychologically and socially destructive forces. Some are
violent, but rarely to the extent of Manson's random savage violence
inflicted upon strangers. Manson took cultism to another level. He
added military method and homicidal madness to the brew.

Popular images of the killers in their pre-Charlie lives focus on
Watson as the school athletic champion, Atkins in the local choir, Van
Houten as the homecoming queen and Krenwinkel as the compliant
child. Their average suburban childhoods are highlighted. However,
on scratching below the surface, it becomes obvious their lives were
not so straightforward. Watson was immature. Atkins was getting in
trouble in her mid-teens. From age 15, Van Houten was wayward. She
was a drug user, and had a pregnancy. Krenwinkel was unhappy and
by age 18 was holed up with a heroin addicted sister. None of these
people were mature enough or capable enough to lead independent
adult lives. My impression of these people is that, although three of
them had reached their early 20's, they were so immature and incapable
that emotionally and intellectually they were in their early teens.

---

330. *People v. Manson & Ors.* 61 Cal. App. 3d 102, p.140.

All of that said, in Watson, Atkins, Krenwinkel and Van Houten, Manson had four potentially good soldiers. Each was pliable, obedient, loyal and ripe for violence. Others in the group rejected Manson's overtures to violence, but not these four. But more work would be needed to turn them from potential soldiers into killing machines. Beyond calling it brainwashing, there has been little or no scholarship about the precise means used by Charles Manson to move his minions from potential soldiers to actual killers. It is important to try to de-mystify this dynamic.

This is where social science takes over and leaves law behind. Science takes over for the hard part – working out <u>why</u> something happened. Although I have formally studied sociology, I have no experience or true expertise. I have rudimentary knowledge of mental health issues from having conferred with, examined and cross-examined professionals in those areas. What follows should not be regarded as an authoritative set of findings. What follows merely represents my observation of the remarkable similarity between what I have read in the literature about cultism and what I have learned about the Manson Family. I have tried to keep in mind the previously mentioned strictures about the risks inherent in crossing over into other areas of expertise. In these circumstances, I apologise in advance for any inaccuracies which follow.

Cultish Behaviour

Margaret Singer has defined cults by reference to their relational structures:

> *"A cultic relationship is one in which a person intentionally induces others to become totally or nearly totally dependent on him or her for almost all major life decisions, and inculcates in these followers a belief that he or she has some special talent, gift, or knowledge."*[331]

---

331. Singer, M.T., *Cults in Our Midst*, Jossey-Bass, 1995, p.7.

A reader of the literature on cults could be forgiven for thinking he was reading the story of the Manson Family. All of the following have been identified as psychological manipulations deployed by cult leaders to entice and hold their followers. All are self-evidently laced with notions of brainwashing or, to use Singer's term, thought reform. There will inevitably be overlap between some of these matters. I apologise in advance for undue repetition:

- The leader offers pathways to fantastic prizes such as: "God", "the Truth" or the "*revolution*"[332]. Manson went further than most by using drugs to make it seem he could perform magic and miracles (Good's fantasies about bringing birds back to life etc). And new recruits are often people whose lives are in transition. A typical follower is in late adolescence and is bewildered by the range of pressures that the adult world presents. He craves help and guidance but is unable to find that in the normal family structure. The leader offers just what the follower is seeking. The follower wants to be brainwashed.

- There is a demand for purity. You're either with us, or against us. Outside elements need to be eliminated lest they contaminate the group.

- Critical and evaluative thinking and independent choice are discouraged, if not prohibited – "no-think"[333].

- Cults have a double set of ethics. Members are supposed to be open and honest with each other, but deception of outsiders for the advantage of the group is tolerated, if not encouraged[334].

- The hierarchy is rigid and dictatorial. The leader has the final say on everything. The leader descends into the followers' lives in detail – he dictates what the followers wear, where and when they eat and sleep, who they

---

332. Ibid, Introduction, p.xxvii.
333. Ibid, Introduction, p.xxvi.
334. Ibid, p.9.

have sexual relations with, and so on. The followers are relieved of responsibilities and, in the case of transitional teenagers and adolescents, are relieved of the burden of confronting the stresses of the adult world. Patricia Krenwinkel would later say: "... *when I was 19 years old, I had not really at any time ever been forced to make a decision in my life for myself, and I found it very easy to let someone make my decisions for me continuously*"[335]. Leslie Van Houten has also spoken of the relief she felt at having someone else do her thinking for her. Watson could only explain the omission to kill Mr and Mrs Weber (almost immediately after leaving Cielo) on the basis that they didn't live on Cielo Drive. It was as if he was an automaton, switched "on" for Cielo, and "off" elsewhere. It is hard to conceive of any other explanation of the omission to kill Mr Weber.

Research scientist Kathleen Taylor is one of the few writers on thought reform and associated topics who has focused to some extent on the Manson Family. She wrote about the phenomenon of diffusion of responsibility:

"Group membership can provide two comforting sensations: that the member is not alone, and that he or she is not responsible. For highly cohesive groups, the group can become an entity in its own right with its own power of action, often personified by the leader, who takes on the role of supernatural protector and relieves the individual of the need to make his own decisions. This diffusion of responsibility through the group can be one of the most dangerous phenomena in strong groups, as it can lower the threshold for violent action by reducing the normal social constraints (e.g. fear of being blamed and punished) which would deter most individuals. Knowing intellectually that there are people out there who

---

335. Parole hearing 17 July 1978.

would disapprove of what one proposes to do is very different from living among people who are clearly showing their disapproval. The closed nature of the Manson Family in effect isolated its members from the immediate sensations of disapproval which they knew intellectually they could expect to receive if they committed murder. That stored information about what society would think of them, as killers, was outweighed by the message from their environment: that murder would gain them social credit and group benefits, that the prospective victims were not real humans (not one of us), and that they were not really, individually, responsible for the murders"[336]

Associated with this, the leader is given control of the fate of the followers. He can decide whether they live or die. He purports to exercise his discretion for the good of the group. Hence Manson's chilling explanation to Van Houten of the plan for her to go to the gas chamber so that he could continue the group's work. Taylor wrote: *"the primacy of doctrine over person coexists with the dispensing of existence – the right granted to many cult leaders to determine the fate of their followers"*. Taylor then wrote that Manson did not actually kill his Family, whereas Jim Jones made a choice which ended the lives of his followers[337]. But we now know this wasn't for want of trying on Charlie's part. He tried to kill the girls by getting them to take the rap for him, and would have killed them, but he didn't get away with it. Taylor need not have conceded the Manson Family as exceptional to her thesis.

- Gossip is forbidden so that doubts and misgivings have nowhere to breed.

336.Taylor, K., *Brainwashing: The Science of Thought Control*, Oxford University Press, 2004, pp.42 to 43.

337. Ibid, p.43.

- The language is loaded. A group-speak is developed[338]. Some Mansonites struggled to understand Charlie-speak. When Charlie persuaded Atkins to drop her deal with the District Attorney (and recant her Grand Jury testimony and sack her lawyer), this was how he did it (bearing in mind the lawyer and a police sheriff were in the room):

  "He . . . launched into a sort of doubletalk, with real words dropped in every now and then. The others had practically no idea what he was talking about, but I grasped most of his meaning I believe"[339]

- Directives are delivered indirectly. This was a classic Manson strategy. Most ex-Family members have spoken about the way Charlie's orders were couched in indirect language. As Susan Atkins told her lawyers, Charlie controlled everything but he always said *"you do what you want to do"*. Charlie didn't order the girls to steal credit cards. Rather he would comment that we need this or we could do with that. When Charlie asked Van Houten *"Are you crazy?"*, she knew it meant *"are you crazy enough . . . to kill someone?"*. In this way, according to Singer, followers come to believe they are not being ordered to do anything, rather everything they do is of their own initiative. They can deny to family and friends that they are being ordered or unduly influenced to stay in the group. And, importantly, the leader can deny it too. Singer cites these examples:

  - *"No one is ordered or forced to do anything against their will . . . Dederich may advocate it – yes, he's a great advocate. But he is very careful not to order it"*.
  - *"I had never been directly told to kill my father, but I knew that if I should see the need to save the group, I would do it without any direction beyond what I knew I must do"*.

---

338. Ibid.
339. Atkins, *Child of Satan, Child of God*, p.163.

- *"Our leader never told me to whip my son, but I knew that when he didn't smile when I told him to be quiet that I must spank and spank him until he smiled . . . I just knew I must do it"*
- *"It was his words and how much I wanted him to like me. I saw myself as doing as he would. He didn't have to be there, he didn't have to tell me when or who or where. I wanted to do just what he wanted, so I began to shake and slap one woman"*[340]

  A code of physical signs is also developed. The rub of an ear lobe. Stroking of the beard. A particular stare is an order to quieten down. All members understand each action.
- The cult leader claims to offer innovative and unique solutions to the world's problems[341]. And he focuses the followers on thinking about the future. Hannah Arendt wrote that *"there is a hardly a better way to avoid discussion than by releasing an argument from the control of the present and by saying that only the future can reveal its merits"*[342]. What is said about the future cannot be tested. However, because doomsdays tend not to happen, some cult leaders have found themselves in a predicament[343]. Catherine Share was probably right to suppose that Charlie was staring this predicament in the face. And Charlie's Helter Skelter doomsday, being a bit more elaborate than most, was about to be usurped by the new Beatles album, which might discredit his prophecy. Unless, that is, he could lend

340. Singer, *Cults in Our Midst*, p.161.

341. Ibid, p.9.

342. Arendt, H., *Totalitarianism*, Harcourt, Brace and World, 1951, p.44.

343. Festinger et al looked at a cult whose doomsday passed uneventfully. After the initial disappointment, the group swept itself up into a new wave of enthusiasm, but eventually this faded and the group fell apart: Festinger, L., Riecken, H.W., Schacter, S., *When Prophecy Fails: A Social and Psychological Study of a Modern Group That Predicted the Destruction of the World*, Harper and Row, 1964.

an apocalyptic interpretation to the Beatles' new album, although songs like "Octopus's Garden" on *Abbey Road* hardly seem to have the same apocalyptic or revolutionary gravitas as "Helter Skelter" or "Revolution 9".

• The followers are programmed away from their previous lives and families. Isolation forces followers to become dependent upon the cult[344]. There is a reinterpretation of the follower's life history so as to accept a new version of reality. The sense of self is destabilised and ultimately extinguished. These changes are gradual and imperceptible. They eventually take over the follower to the point where even material vestiges of the former self, such as wallet, driver's license etc., are done away with[345]. Schein has referred to this as *"unfreezing"*[346]. It often involves forms of criticism so as to make the member undecided about his past (destabilised). Manson took it even further, inflicting violence and justifying it as necessary to bring about the required "changes". Singer cites the case of "Harry", who had been in the army, and was reasonably well adjusted. He joined a Bible cult. They criticised him for not learning to speak in tongues quickly enough. He was resisting change, they told him over and over. Convinced he was a bad person for not adjusting well enough, Harry started confessing to a past which included alcoholic parents and a prostitute sister, none of which was true. He began, slowly, imperceptibly, doing what he was told in order to impress the leadership. He began to engage in illegal behaviour which he would have previously found abhorrent[347]. Family member Leslie Van Houten would later say: *"It was an honor to be that close to a chosen person*

---

344. Singer, *Cults in Our Midst*, p.10.
345. Ibid, p.62 ff.
346. Schein, E.H., Schneier, I., Barker, C.H., *A Socio-psychological Analysis of the 'Brainwashing' of American Civilian Prisoners by the Chinese Communists*, W.W. Norton, 1961.
347. Singer, *Cults in Our Midst*, pp. 75 to 76.

of God, but he made me feel stupid, and it was clear by his behaviour that I had a lot of 'giving up' to do, to be worthy of my position and closeness to him"[348].

- A paradox is created. The cult leader engages in the ultimate manipulation of power. He makes his followers fear him and love him at the same time. Two of the strongest emotions experienced by human beings are synthesized. The followers become disciples.
- Followers give up their possessions and money for the advancement of the cult.
- There is a "flirty fishing" policy whereby female followers are used as prostitutes to lure males to join the group[349].
- There is a cadre of second-level helpers to assist with recruiting, convincing members to stay and perpetuating the behaviour the leader wants. In the Manson Family this included, at various times, Krenwinkel, Watkins, Davis and Fromme[350].
- Physiological manipulations are engaged, for example, chanting, swaying, and hyperventilation (producing a dizzy high). Van Houten has spoken repeatedly about Charlie's motions and his exhortations to Family members to mirror his movements. Manson spoke in his soliloquy in court about using Indian motions to explain his feelings to the jury. The Family engaged in lots of this stuff, chanting "Amens" to Charlie's preaching, and so on. Brooks Poston told Sheriff Don Ward: *"And one of the songs is a repeat-after-me song in which he will start the song and say 'Who's God?'. And the people around him will answer back 'Who's God?'. And he'll say 'You're God'. And they'll answer back 'You're God'. And then he'll say 'I'm God?'. And they'll say*

348. Correspondence between Van Houten and Karlene Faith, cited in Faith, *The Long Prison Journey of Leslie Van Houten*, p.72.
349. Singer, *Cults in Our Midst*, p.12.
350. Ibid, p.81.

'I'm God?'. And then he'll say – as in a statement 'I am God'. And they'll answer back the same way. And he gets them into a emotional frenzy [sic], *and this is supposed to lead to sex"*[351].

- Dietary changes and vegetarianism. Charlie preached vegetarianism and eschewed the killing of animals for meat. Charlie was so gentle he wouldn't even kill a chicken, as he himself proclaimed to reporters in Independence. That was what he said publicly. Privately, when holed up in the cells at Independence, out of sight of the Family members, he wolfed down a hamburger. The hungry acolytes, *"fearful of the master's wrath should they break a loyalty-proving vegetarian oath, sat nervously picking at their plates"*[352].

- There is a tendency to violent finales and self-destruction. Most humans and human groups are born, then grow, stabilise, and gradually decline. But cults tend to end in catastrophe. Taylor writes: *". . . their death agonies bring them into the public gaze. The Manson Family's killings, the mass suicides and murders of Jonestown, the Ugandan 'Movement for the Restoration of the Ten Commandments of God', Waco, and the Order of the Solar Temple all made world headlines; all were largely unknown outside directly affected communities until they, in Waco's case, literally, went up in flames"*[353]

The cultish characteristics of the Manson Family did not go unrecognised at the time. Professor Gerald Aronson, psychiatrist, was interviewed for a magazine article in January 1970:

". . . there follows a peculiar operation in the minds of [cult members]. They deny the shortcomings of their group. They assert that everything about it is wonderful and that their leader is super-marvelous.

351. Record of interview 3 October 1969.
352. Bishop, *Witness to Evil,* p. 37.
353. Taylor, *Brainwashing,* p.35.

They cannot stand to tell themselves the truth. Manson's followers, for example, could not afford to realistically assess this ridiculous little guy who had spent most of his life behind bars, who was relatively unlearned, unloved, and filled with tremendous hostility. They could not permit themselves the luxury to judge him honestly. Because once they permit doubts to creep into their minds, then the value of their group starts to crumble and eventually they crumble themselves.

Thus, they eventually become fanatics. Everything connected with their group is good, everything outside their group is bad. Once you have established that belief, everything becomes permissible, murder included. There is an idealization of your group and the denigration of the other. The whole world becomes polarized.

If [the killers] did not do what Manson offered or suggested, they would feel themselves disconnected from everything which heretofore had given them a sense of value, a feeling of worth, a pleasure of belonging. That's why they carried out his orders. They dared not chance what would happen within themselves if they said no"[354]

Research has shown that most people who leave cults usually rediscover, and merge back into, their former selves. Watson, Atkins, Van Houten and Krenwinkel were not violent people before joining Manson. (Atkins and Van Houten had displayed troubling tendencies, but hadn't actually done anything violent). Then they became vicious killers for the brief periods of their lives with Manson. Then they left Manson and reverted to their former abstinence from violence. To be sure, some of them carry flaws, for example they have at times had varying degrees of lack of insight into their crimes, and from time to time other foibles have been held to disentitle them to parole. But indisputably, each have been model prisoners. Krenwinkel has

---

354. Shearer, L., "The 'Manson Family' Murders", *Parade* magazine, 11 January 1970, p.8.

astounded some prison authorities and has never in 47 years even had a write-up for any sort of misdemeanour, let alone violence. As counter-intuitive as it might seem, this suggests that the persons who did the killing – Tex, Sadie, Lulu and Katie – were different human beings to the ones that we identify as the killers – Watson, Atkins, Van Houten and Krenwinkel.

Total personality transfusion seems an alien and elusive concept. And yet researchers and psychologists have recognised it at least since the 1950's. During the Korean War, an American soldier, Colonel Frank Schwabble was brainwashed by the enemy into signing a confession that the American military was engaging in bacteriological warfare. Later before a military board of enquiry he testified:

> *"I was never convinced in my own mind that we . . . had used bug warfare. I knew we hadn't but the rest of it was real to me - the conferences, the planes, and how they would go about their missions.*
>
> *The words were mine but the thoughts were theirs. That is the hardest thing I have to explain: how a man can sit down and write something he knows is false, and yet, to sense it, to feel it, to make it seem real"*[355]

Dr Charles Mayo stated to a United Nations enquiry into brainwashing:

> *". . . the tortures used . . . are not like the medieval torture of the rack and the thumb-screw. They are subtler, more prolonged, and intended to be more terrible in their effect. They are calculated to disintegrate the mind of an intelligent victim, to distort his sense of values, to a point where he will not simply cry out 'I did it!' but will become a seemingly*

---

355. Cited in Meerloo, J., *The Rape of the Mind*, Martino Publishing, 2015, first published 1956, pp.19 to 20.

willing accomplice to the complete disintegration of his integrity and the production of an elaborate fiction"[356]

When Watson and the girls said weird things to various people about killing being for love and being right and so on, they weren't just mouthing hollow words. They really, deeply, believed those things. They weren't just <u>claiming</u> the rightness of what they had done – they were so twisted and distorted that they were <u>feeling</u> it. Before Manson, they had never felt such things. Since Manson, they have never felt such things.

Singer articulates the cult exit phenomenon in the context of supplying hope to the survivors of cults. It may also emphasise the pervasive realness of the experience for the cult member:

"We might ask ourselves – and surely many former cult members have – how a person can display reprehensible conduct under some conditions, then turn around and resume normal activities under other conditions. The phenomenon has been variously described as doubling or as the formation of a pseudopersonality (or pseudoidentity), a superimposed identity, a cult self, or a cult personality. What is important about these labels is that they call attention to an important psychological and social phenomenon that needs to be studied more carefully – namely, that ordinary persons, with their own ideas and attitudes, can be rapidly turned around in their social identity but later can recover their old selves and move forward.

By this, I am not saying that people in cults or groups that use thought reform processes are just faking it by role-playing, pretending, or acting. Anyone who has met a former friend who's been transformed into a recruiting zealot for a New Age transformational program, for example, knows that something

---

356. Ibid, p.20.

*more profound than role-playing is operating as that old
friend defends her or his new self and new group, speaking
single-mindedly, spouting intense, firmly stated dogma. This
is not play-acting. It is far more instinctive and experienced
as real"*[357]

Caution is needed. The study of cultism is laced with political
and legal considerations. Brainwashing has been used by and against
nation states for propaganda purposes. And people sue, and get sued,
over it. Singer herself was involved in litigation. That said, I do not
read Singer's work as other than conveying that cautious objectivity is
required.

The 1960's

Several commentators have attempted to draw meaning from
the context of the times in explaining Manson, but most of it is
directionless and does not go much beyond stating the obvious, that
the murders happened against the backdrop of some violent times of
political assassinations, the Vietnam War and student unrest.

My research has left me with the impression there was an unusually
large confluence of homeless teenagers and an exploitative criminal
class that converged on San Francisco in 1967, of which the Manson
Family was a microcosm. Vincent Bugliosi referred to the turmoil of
the times when interviewed in 1976:

*". . . the late sixties, which were filled with ferment – race
riots, discontent over Vietnam, campus violence, the sex and
drug revolutions – probably provided a much more fertile soil
for someone like Manson to blossom in. In a way, it can be*

---

357. Singer, *Cults in Our Midst*, p.79.

compared to post-World War 1 Germany, whose social climate
was right for an Adolf Hitler to emerge"[358]

Probably the most convincing explanation of the significance
of the times was provided by Singer. She argued that the volatility
of the 1960's lent to increased alienation, bewilderment and
destabilisation for transitional adolescents, all of which ripened them
for exploitation by master cult manipulators who typically prey on
these circumstances[359]. This has force. Family member Bruce Davis
would later say:

"Peace and love. The 60's . . . That's the kind of thing that
would get [Manson] an entrée into the most vulnerable
market. If he'd have thought he could control some other
group, he would have got their nomenclature down, and
went there. But this was the most vulnerable. It was
obviously the most vulnerable because it was morally
deficient, it was young and inexperienced, it was a great
vacuum of what to do, where to go, a very good opportunity.
So he learns to say peace and love . . . it's the right bait for
the fish"[360]

Dr David Smith would later comment:

"[Manson] was a very charismatic person, and there was no
reality testing, people were taking LSD and Charlie would
use LSD to reinforce that he had magic, that he was this all
powerful person that could make things move, that could
read people's minds and know what their thoughts were. So
that was all part of that psychedelic drug counter culture
then. If you back up and say 'well that's crazy' . . . reality

---

358. "Vincent Bugliosi", *Penthouse*, Vol.7, No.10, June 1976, p.101.
359. Singer, *Cults in Our Midst*, p. 29ff.
360. *Charles Manson: The Man Who Killed the Sixties*, Channel 4, 2004.

test, but the whole community was like that because there were so many susceptible young people that came [to San Francisco] that were looking for something to believe in, and Charlie's philosophy was very appealing to a lot of these young people"[361]

Method in the Madness

There was, in fact, military method about the way lives and events unfolded within the Family during 1969. It is not known whether all of the matters which follow came about by Manson's design, or by chance. The former can probably be assumed.

Manson needed to activate the military potential in his soldiers. This was not unlike the task confronting any conventional military leader – the task of persuading unlikely or reluctant soldiers to become capable of killing other human beings. But Manson took it further than a conventional military stratagem. He worked his children up to a level of intensely self-satisfied barbarity.

No-think

The no-think edict had a place in Manson's strategy, as has been the case in other military settings: *"Good soldiers don't think. They simply follow orders . . . It never occurred to me during those days of euphoria that I had been carefully programmed all through that wonderful time in the [Hitler Youth]. Fuhrer befeil! Wir folgen! Leader give orders! We follow!"*[362]. No-think was the starting premise of a variety of Manson's psychological manipulations. It is helpful to explore some of this psychology in more detail.

---

361. Ibid.
362. Holz, R., *Too Young to be a Hero*, Harper Collins, 2000, pp. 45, 216.

Authorisation and Obedience

In 1961, Stanley Milgram conducted experiments aimed at working out the extent to which ordinary people will follow orders to commit acts of cruelty to other human beings. Milgram was inspired by the Nazi mantra: *"I was just following orders"*.

It is useful to consider the detail of Milgram's best known experiment. The subject of the experiment was under the supervision of the experimenter. They were together in the same room. A confederate of the experimenter was in another room. The subject was instructed to administer what he believed were real electric shocks to the confederate who feigned painful responses. The experimenter instructed the subject to increase the voltage. At any sign of reluctance by the subject, the experimenter said things like *"please carry on"*. The fake pain increased to the point of extreme anxiety and cries to the effect of *"I've got a heart condition"*, *"please stop the experiment, I can't stand this"* and so on. The confederate started punching the walls and screaming. The experimenter continued to instruct the subject to increase the voltage with instructions to the effect of *"It is essential to complete the experiment, you must continue"*. Milgram found that 65% of his subjects continued to follow orders despite the apparent suffering of the confederate:

> *"Ordinary people, simply doing their jobs, and without any particular hostility on their part, can become agents in a terrible destructive process. Moreover, even when the destructive effects of their work become patently clear, and they are asked to carry out actions incompatible with fundamental standards of morality, relatively few people have the resources needed to resist authority"*[363]

---

363. Milgram, S., *Obedience to Authority,* Harper and Rowe, 1974, p.6.

Herbert Kelman confronted the same question in the context of the My Lai massacre in 1968 in which over 500 innocent civilians were killed by American soldiers. The same defence was offered up: "*we were told to do it*". Kelman undertook a survey of American citizens and found, incredibly enough, that 51% of respondents would have obeyed such an order, and only 33% said they would disobey[364].

Authorisation and the innate human tendency to obey orders are, of themselves, powerful psychological tools. Professor David Livingstone Smith states: "*Where persons in positions of authority endorse acts of violence, the perpetrator is less inclined to feel personally responsible, and therefore less guilty in performing them*"[365].

Authorisation and obedience feed into routinisation. Making a task routine tends to remove the need for thought and judgment-making, which in turn assists moral and intellectual disengagement from the task. Disengagement is a fundamental pre-requisite of killing. The removal of the need for thinking and judgment making made it easier for the Manson killers to accomplish their task. The murder school and the intensely repetitive banter about death, killing, no wrong, no guilt, and so on, desensitised the acolytes sufficiently that killing was not a difficult or even unwanted task. It was routine, it was easy, even fun, for some.

Group Conformity in the Military Context

Group think is a central military theme and strategy. It was the subject of research, in the military context, by medical doctor and later lecturer in psychopathology at Cambridge University, John MacCurdy. MacCurdy studied World War 1 soldiers and identified the notions of group solidarity and loyalty, which were two major themes in Mansonism, as a dangerous paradox:

---

364. Kelman HC, *Violence without moral restraint: Reflections on the dehumanization of victims and victimizers*. Journal of Social Issues. 1973;29 (4) :25-61.

365. Smith, David Livingstone, *Less Than Human: Why We Demean, Enslave, and Exterminate Others*, St Martin's Press, 2011, p. 127, reprinted by permission of St Martin's Press. All Rights Reserved.

"Here we have what is perhaps the greatest paradox of human nature. The forgetting of self in devotion to others, altruism or loyalty, is the essence of virtue. At the same time, precisely the same type of loyalty that makes man a benefactor to all mankind can become the direst menace to mankind when focused on a small group"[366]

Group conformity and cultism leads to a tremendous sense of self-righteousness about the group. It is difficult to find two groups who have exalted so much in the rightness of killing than the Nazis and the Mansonites. Heinrich Himmler said this at the notorious Poznan conference on 4 October 1943:

"I am referring to . . . the extermination of the Jewish people . . . most of you men know what it is like to see 100 corpses lying side by side, or 500 or 1,000. To have stood fast through this and . . . to have stayed decent, that has made us hard . . . We had the moral right, we had the duty to our people to destroy this people . . . we can say that we have carried out this most difficult of tasks in a spirit of love for our people. And we have suffered no harm to our inner being, our soul, and our character"[367]

Lynette Fromme would later say killing was *"a difficult thing to imagine doing, and but* [sic] *I still believe they were right because they felt right, they felt that despite the ugliness of it that it was the right thing to do"*[368]. Sandra Good thought the same way. Van Houten thought what she was doing was *"perfectly right"*[369]. Professor Faith would later write:

366. MacCurdy, J.T., *The Psychology of War,* John W. Luce and Coy, 1918, p.40.
367. Charny, I.W., *Encyclopedia of Genocide, Vol. 1,* ABC-CLIO, 1999, p. 241.
368. *The Manson Women,* Biography Series, Entertainment Channel, 2004.
369. Record of interview with Marvin Part, 29 December 1969, sourced from www.cielodrive.com.

> *"As [Atkins, Krenwinkel and Van Houten] saw it for the first several years of their incarceration, if they hadn't been caught they would have triggered the race war that guaranteed justice to black people. Early in our association I sensed that they were consoled with the belief that they were right for having at least tried"*[370]

In some ways, this sums up the madness and the tragedy. The Manson Family did what they <u>felt</u> was right. They took the rule of law into their own hands and, without judge, jury or process, but because they felt like it, commenced passing sentence on people as "pigs" and executing them. It was an abject lesson in the terrible dangers inherent in ignoring, or even taking for granted, the rule of law, and the folly of seeing the end as justifying the means. As well, there was hedonism, misanthropy and violence, all of which thrived in the Manson Family. Thus was created the perfect homicidal storm.

Dehumanisation

Group conformity leads to the thesis of Livingstone Smith's book – dehumanisation – the denigration of "them" as sub-human. Dehumanisation was front and centre of life at the Ranch during the summer of 1969. The enemy comprised the pigs of the establishment. The rhetoric was all about the pigs. The murder school and the talk about death and killing took aim at the pigs.

Livingstone Smith cited Austrian biologist Irenaus Eibl-Eibesfeldt who wrote:

> *"Cultures mark themselves off from each other as if they were different species . . . To emphasize their differences from others, representatives from different groups describe themselves as human, while all others are dismissed as*

---

370. Faith, *The Long Prison Journey of Leslie Van Houten*, p.75.

nonhuman or not fully equipped with all the human values."[371]

Dehumanisation promotes, or accompanies, moral disengagement. Morality is a powerful inhibition against violence. When morality is disengaged, inhibitions against violence are weakened or removed.

Livingstone Smith later took up Eibl-Eibesfeldt's treatment of dehumanisation:

"Eibl-Eibesfeldt also recognised a connection between dehumanisation and war, in primitive cultures as well as the developed world. [Dehumanisation] has a special role to play in war. For war to take place, [Eibl-Eibesfeldt] notes, human beings need to find ways to overcome biological inhibitions against lethal aggression. Dehumanizing the enemy is a means for doing this.

'In tribal societies as well as western civilisation this is done through attempts to 'dehumanize' the enemy. . . . In both cases, indoctrination transfers the aggressive act to a context of being directed against another species. The opponents are degraded to inferior beings. War is primarily a cultural institution, even though it utilizes some innate dispositions"[372]

Livingstone Smith himself developed it this way:

"This is a subtle, multilayered analysis. We are innately biased against outsiders. This bias is seized upon and manipulated by indoctrination and propaganda to motivate men and women to slaughter one another. This is done by inducing men to regard their enemies as subhuman creatures,

371. Smith, *Less Than Human,* p.69.
372. Ibid, p.71.

which overrides their natural biological inhibitions against killing. So dehumanization has the specific function of unleashing aggression in war"[373]

Livingstone Smith described a number of unspeakable atrocities committed by Japanese soldiers upon civilians in the Chinese city of Nanjing in 1937 and asked:

"How can ordinary men (and they <u>were</u> ordinary men) do such things? Yoshio Tshuchiya, [a] Japanese veteran, tells us the answer. 'We called the Chinese 'chancorro' . . . that meant below human, like bugs or animals . . . The Chinese didn't belong to the human race. That was the way we looked at it'. Tshuchiya describes how he was ordered to bayonet unarmed Chinese civilians, and what it was that enabled him to comply with this order. 'If I'd thought of them as human beings I couldn't have done it' he observed. 'But . . . I thought of them as animals or below human beings'"[374]

The history of genocide is replete with the dehumanisation of the enemy as pigs and other entities traditionally not cherished by the human race:

"In most genocidal events the perpetrators devalue the humanity of their victims, often by referring to the victims as animals, diseased, or exceptionally filthy . . . notably pigs, rats, maggots, cockroaches, and other vermin."[375]

---

373. Ibid.
374. Ibid, p.18.
375. McCauley, C., and Chirot, D., *Why Not Kill Them All? The Logic and Prevention of Mass Political Murder,* Princeton University Press, 2006, p.80.

The merger of dehumanisation into propaganda was recognised as long ago as the 1930's in a speech delivered by Aldous Huxley:

> *"Most people would hesitate to torture or kill a human being like themselves. But when that human being is spoken of as though he were not a human being, but as the representative of some wicked principle, we lose our scruples . . . . All political and nationalist propaganda aims at only one thing; to persuade one set of people that another set of people are not really human and that it is therefore legitimate to rob, swindle, bully, and even murder them"*[376]

Dehumanisation was a constant feature of Family life. It wasn't just the imagery of pigs. Atkins testified about Sharon Tate sounding like an IBM computer or a *"mannequin"*. Watson testified about his victims seeming like *"blobs"*. Bugliosi challenged him about this in cross-examination:

> *"Q. . . . You testified yesterday that the people you murdered were like blobs to you. What do you mean by that?*
> *A. Well, it was kind of . . . in between, like I said, a dark and a light . . . It was hard to tell what they were, really. It was hard to tell what they were in a lot of ways.*
> *Q. You knew they were human beings didn't you?*
> *A. The thought of anything like that just didn't occur, you know. The only thought in my head was just what Manson said.*
> *Q. Are you saying, then, that these people whom you killed were just objects to you?*
> *A. Yes, I guess so.*
> *Q. Didn't you testify yesterday that the woman on the front lawn – No. 1, it was woman, it wasn't an object, it was a woman – and didn't you testify that she was covered with blood, yesterday?*

---

376. Unpublished speech, cited in Lifton, R.J., and Humphrey, N., *In a Dark Time*, Cambridge, MA:Harvard, 1984, p.10, cited in Smith, *Less Than Human*, p.21.

A. *She was covered with blood, yes.*

Q. *And it was a woman?*

A. *The best I could tell, because she had on a gown, had on a piece of cloth like; it must have been a woman.*

Q. *Well, now, a woman with blood on her, that's not a blob, is it, Tex?*

A. *Well, that's what it appeared to me to be, you know; that's what it looked kind of like.*

Q. *You also testified yesterday that there was a man inside – again, not a blob or an object, but a man, and he was wearing blue jeans?*

A. *Right; that's right.*

Q. *Is this what you mean when you say 'blobs', men with blue jeans and women with blood on them? . . .*

A. *I don't really mean anything, you know, really mean that much. I don't know, I just know they were kind of in between, like I said."* [emphasis added]

This was an interesting exchange. Bugliosi was seeking to convey that Watson was cold and insensitive, and that he knew his victims were human beings. In order to overcome Watson's insanity plea, Bugliosi had to prove Watson knew he was doing the wrong thing. Bugliosi sensed that the "blob" version was fabricated by Watson in an attempt to show he did not appreciate the wrongness of his actions. But it was almost as if cross-examiner and witness were at cross purposes. Arguably at least, Watson was not trying to show failure to appreciate wrongness. There was a gormless naiveté about the way he dealt with the cross examination which suggested he literally had convinced himself his victims were other than human. That was how Watson was able to do what he did. Later in his book, Watson would write: *"[T]hat night and the night after, [the victims] were so many impersonal blobs to be dealt with as Charlie had instructed"*[377]. And at a

---

377. Watson, *Will You Die For Me?*, p. 139.

parole hearing, Watson would say: *"At the time of the crimes, the people we killed weren't human beings to us"*[378].

The dehumanised have not always been depicted as animals. They have also been depicted as disease organisms that require cleansing. This was also a notion with which the Family ran. Van Houten thought she and her cohorts were cleansing the world with their revolution. So were the Nazis cleaning away the disease carrying Jews. The Pol Pot genocide emphasised cleaning. Following a massacre of approximately 250,000 Khmer, Pol Pot declared: *"The party is clean. The soldiers are clean. Cleanliness is the foundation"*[379].

Livingstone Smith wrote:

". . . there is no better way to whip up enthusiasm for genocide than by representing the intended victims as vermin, parasites, or disease organisms that must be exterminated for the purpose of hygiene.

The architecture of our minds makes us vulnerable to these forms of persuasion. Images like these speak to something deep inside us."

and then ominously:

"If you still believe you are the exception, and are immune from these forces, I hope that by the end of this book you will have embraced a more realistic assessment of your capacity for evil"[380].

Livingstone Smith mounted a strong case that the power of these psychological manipulations would probably overwhelm many otherwise moral and right-thinking people into the capacity for cruelty.

---

378. Parole hearing 4 May 1990. This drew an incredulous response from one of the presiding board members: *"I'm sorry but you talk as if you're from another planet"*. This response was understandable, but it might not have been so incredulous had more recent learning about dehumanisation been available.

379. Quoted in Kiernan, B., *Blood and Soil: A World History of Genocide and Extermination from Sparta to Darfur,* Yale University Press, 2007, pp.549 to 550.

380. Smith, *Less Than Human,* pp.130-131.

Others who have written about brainwashing (sometimes called "thought reform" or "menticide' – mind killing[381]) share Livingstone Smith's perception that most anyone can be a victim of these psychological manipulations. Joost Meerloo wrote in 1956:

> *"When during the enquiry into the Schwabble case, I was called upon to testify as an expert on menticide, I told the court of my deep conviction that nearly anybody subjected to the treatment meted out to Colonel Schwabble could be forced to write and sign a similar confession.*
>
> *'Anyone in this room, for instance?' the colonel's attorney asked me, looking in turn at each of the officers sitting in judgment on this new and difficult case.*
>
> *And in good conscience I could reply, firmly: 'Anyone in this room'"*[382]

Most theories about dehumanisation dwell on the dehumanisation of the <u>enemy</u> so as to enable easier killing. The Manson Family had a twist. There was a touch of the dehumanised about the Mansonites themselves. Bugliosi wrote about his first encounter with Good, Fromme and others in late 1969:

> *". . . there was a sameness about them that was much stronger than their individuality. I'd notice it again . . . in talking to other female members of the Family. Same expressions, same patterned responses, same tone of voice, same lack of distinct personality. The realization came as a shock: they reminded me less of human beings than Barbie dolls"*[383]

---

381. Meerloo, *The Rape of the Mind*, 2015.
382. Ibid, pp. 34 to 35.
383. Bugliosi, *Helter Skelter*, p.185.

Bugliosi was not the only one to recognise the Village-of-the-Damned vibe put out by the Mansonites. David Dalton and Karlene Faith would later refer to it as well[384].

Conclusions

Group-think. No-think. Conformity. Obedience. Desensitisation. Routinisation. Dehumanisation. The Family members were subjected to an incredible battery of psychological manipulations. It becomes unsurprising that they killed for the leader who drummed into them that they were at war. What was surprising was there weren't more killers and killings. And they were queuing up. Catherine Gillies wanted to be involved. Ruth Ann Moorehouse couldn't wait to get her first pig. Van Houten wanted to be asked to go. Watson reckoned it was only his mother's chance phone call that stopped the slaughter.

Some Family members resisted. Kasabian was by nature a peaceful person, a true hippy if there ever was one. And even if she had been otherwise, she had only been with the Family for a month or so, and had much less exposure to Manson's manipulations than the others. The moral disengagement that overtook the others took more than one month. Watkins had been intelligent and independent enough to get away when he saw the Family's perilous direction. Ella Jo Bailey left after the Hinman murder. T.J. Walleman wanted nothing to do with snuffing people. It remains an open question whether the ability of these people to resist Manson's manipulations meant that resistance was, in fact, not hard. Barbara Hoyt has recently suggested it wasn't difficult to get away from the Family, and says she left three times. But it is not clear how much can be drawn from this. Doubtless some soldiers in military wars are able to avoid, or minimise, their roles in violence and killing. No amount of psychological manipulation will change some. But that does not alter the fact that others will be affected, some deeply so.

---

384. Dalton, D., *If Christ Came Back as a Con Man*, Gadfly, October 1998; Faith, *The Long Prison Journey of Leslie Van Houten*, p.62.

Another matter that has troubled me during this project has been the ages of the killers. Their biological ages were, essentially, early 20's. But as I have said, their emotional and intellectual ages were something different. I venture to suggest, admittedly without the relevant expertise, that they were more like 13 year olds than 20 year olds. Thirteen year olds inside adult bodies. I continue to feel a slight reluctance to judge the killers as if they were adults. I have a commensurate flicker of sympathy for them, even Watson. On the other hand, my judgment of Manson has hardened considerably during the journey of writing this book.

Did Manson know all of this stuff about manipulating people and so on? It seems unlikely it all happened just by chance. Furthermore, the effect of all of this on Manson's own mind ought not to be underestimated. Whatever vestiges of morality Manson may have retained in 1967 had been totally disengaged by mid-1969. It is evident he had lost all inhibitions against amoral or criminal undertakings. Furthermore, he was positively empowered by his knowledge that (a) his underlings would commit criminal acts for him and (b) they would even take the rap for him. Once he recognised this empowerment, the death sentences were pronounced for those who would be his victims.

There is not a shred of doubt that Manson orchestrated and masterminded murder and mayhem. He made it all happen. It might reasonably be doubted that any of the killers, in particular the females, would have come to killing in their lifetimes, but for Charles Manson. The foreman of the first Tate/LaBianca jury, Mr Herman Tubick, told a media conference on 1 April 1971 that *"[Manson] was leader"* and *"if he wasn't there, nobody would have done what they did"*. Whilst the popular view of Manson seems to be that he was evil, not many people really know the half of it. One can only imagine the destruction he would have caused had he been in 1930's Germany with the resources and backing of the state to do what he wanted to do. As it was, with a small bunch of runaways, drop outs and petty criminals, he was able to wreak havoc.

Manson was a con-man. He had a knack for knowing what to say to make people feel happy. He could disarm people with his sense of humour. He could vary his use of language. He could turn his affable charm on and off like a tap. He was a master of ingratiation. He actually became better at this than most con-men. His superficial charm was seductive and addictive. He was even able to fool relatively mature adults and lawyers such as Paul Fitzgerald. Lawyers are not immune to this sort of thing. They are human beings. But most would see through Charlie, especially when they donned their professional caps. That Charlie was able to choose and manipulate the girls' lawyers in the way he did through the first Tate/LaBianca trial, and have people such as Fitzgerald still lauding him as a nice, thoughtful guy many years after the trial, is an impressive indication of his powers of manipulation. Disaffected teenagers would have been easy pickings for Charlie. But what set Charlie apart from the average con-man was his delusional megalomania and his appetite for war and death. Most con-men stop at defrauding people. Charles Manson went beyond that into a vortex of death, war, murder and destruction.

All court cases have an element of tension between, on the one hand, the appearance of certain characters and events and, on the other hand, the reality. The practice of trial law is often the art of breaking down appearances, or at least keeping the distinction in mind. Appearances can be dangerously deceptive. Manson often appeared nice and harmless, but he wasn't. The girls appeared like hippies, but they weren't. The murders appeared (to some people) drug related, but they weren't. Helter Skelter appeared to be something the law would not recognise as a motive for murdering people, but it was. The defence lawyers said, for the record, they were acting for the girls, but they weren't. I can't recall seeing a case in which there so many deceptive appearances.

Manson murdered the nine primary victims and he also tried to murder his own acolytes, Atkins, Krenwinkel and Van Houten, by conspiring with their attorneys to send them to the gas chamber in order to save his own life. To the earlier list of crimes for which

Manson escaped charges could be added "Attempted murder of Atkins, Krenwinkel and Van Houten".

I have fallen short of quantifying with much precision the extent to which the killers were brainwashed as opposed to being possessed by their own evil. However, I consider the evidence favours the former to an extent that has not been sufficiently recognised and was unable to be recognised by the courts that dealt with these cases in the 1970's. I am inclined to agree with Mr Tubick to the extent that Van Houten, Krenwinkel and Atkins, probably would not have done what they did without Charles Manson's extreme and evil influence. As for Watson, I do not know. I sympathise and agree with the words of Mr Anthony DiMaria, nephew of Jay Sebring, at Watson's 2016 parole hearing: "*[Watson] was an angry individual who identified with an organization bent on mayhem and destruction. His actions . . . define him as a cruel hearted sociopath, a determined killer*". That said, my research has left me doubtful that Watson would have become what he became without Manson. Watson was destined for lawlessness in his life before he met Manson, but it was Manson who made him into a monstrous killer.

To the surviving families and friends of the victims, I apologise for re-opening memories and stirring up thoughts of these crimes. I sincerely extend my condolences and hope I have restored some perspective and accuracy so that the events, and some of the social and psychological factors underpinning them, are better understood.

I also hope I have not brought the law, or legal profession, into disrepute by what I have said about the defence lawyers in this case. The way these people practiced law in 1970/71 was not a way with which I am familiar. The law and legal profession are not immune from vice. But the majority of legal practitioners with whom I am familiar practice law decently and honourably. I know they will be appalled by some of the things they read in this book. They will find it hard to believe as I did when I wrote.

Finally, a reflection about the historical intersection between Manson and the Beatles. In the summer of 1969 the Beatles were reported in the press to be searching for accommodation in the Bel Air district of Los Angeles. The article was written by Anne Moses: "*The Beatles are house-hunting in Los Angeles. Our smog may not suit Frank Sinatra, who sold his house here saying it was no good for his health, but it's good enough for the Beatles. Ron Kass, head of Apple Records, arrives in town this week to scout out a six to seven bedroom house in the Bel Air-Beverley Hills area at up to $250,000 dollars. Beatles new album is expected to gross 22 million dollars in the United States alone, so they can afford it!*"[385]. The clipping is undated, but appears to have preceded *Abbey Road*, thus before 1 October 1969. It will never be known how close the Beatles came to being Manson's next random victims.

---

385. Barratt C., *The Beatles in the News 1969*, Lulu Press Inc., 2015.

APPENDIX 1

MEMORY AND OTHER FACT FINDING CONSIDERATIONS

"what has been forgotten can rarely be shown"
United States Supreme Court[386]

Quality of Evidence – Fading Memories

The Manson murders occurred almost 50 years ago. Memories fade and inevitably there is a deterioration in the ability of witnesses to speak accurately about events.

In *Brisbane South Regional Health Authority v. Taylor,* the Australian High Court considered the effluxion of time in the context of a civil application for extension of time within which to sue:

> *". . . it must often happen that time will diminish the significance of a known fact or circumstance because its relationship to the [events in question] is no longer as apparent as it was when the [events occurred]"*[387]

---

386. *Barker v. Wingo* [1972] USSC 146; [1972] 407 US 514 at page 532.
387. [1996] 186 CLR 541; [1996] HCA 25, per McHugh JA.

The problem is not unique to court cases. Parole boards are routinely required to evaluate events many years and, in this case, decades, after they have occurred:

> "... *things are* ... *sanitised eight to ten years later when [the parole] hearing is held, persons sitting right there before you and they look just like Mr Middle Class, and they have plenty of time to prepare, and they have an attorney and they've been coached* ... *a lot of it gets lost in the telling and the re-telling* ... *as the years go by*"[388]

The reference to coaching may be unduly cynical, but there is no doubt that many years of telling and re-telling of stories is undesirable. There would be few cases with more re-telling, to lawyers, doctors, television interviewers, for books and so on, than the Manson cases. Leslie Van Houten, for example, has had three trials, two appeals, 19 parole hearings and several television interviews.

On reading some of the parole hearings of the killers, one is struck by the air of unreality of interrogating people about events that occurred so long ago. Take Van Houten again as an example. At her parole hearing in 2016, she was asked how many times she stabbed Rosemary LaBianca. Her answer was to the effect the Coroner's report said between 14 and 16 times. In other words, she can't remember.

And there are lots of answers which are obviously the result of years of reflecting upon the crimes. In so many years of reflecting, it is inevitable there will be reconstruction. And reconstruction upon reconstruction.

Psychological Research

Psychological research in Australia has yielded results that may surprise. This research was in the context of the admissibility of evidence and, as

---

388. Robert L. Carter, former member Californian Board of Prison Terms, television interview, undated, unattributed, internet.

such, it imposed stricter requirements on "freshness" of memory than are perhaps appropriate for the purposes of this book. Nonetheless it is instructive. The research was the basis of the enactment in Australia of the then section 66(2) of the *Evidence Act 1995* (Cth.) which was considered by the High Court of Australia in *Graham v The Queen*:

> *"The word 'fresh', in its context in s.66, means 'recent' or 'immediate'. It may also carry with it a connotation that describes the quality of the memory (as being 'not deteriorated or changed by lapse of time') but the core of the meaning intended is to describe the temporal relationship between 'the occurrence of the asserted fact' and the time of making the [statement]. Although questions of fact and degree may arise, the temporal relationship required will very likely be measured in hours or days, not as was the case here, in years"*[389]

and:

> *"While it cannot be doubted that the quality or vividness of a recollection will generally be relevant in an assessment of its freshness, its contemporaneity or near contemporaneity, or otherwise, will almost always be the most important consideration in any assessment of its freshness . . . There may be cases in which evidence of an event relatively remote in time will be admissible pursuant to s.66, but such cases will necessarily be rare and requiring of some special circumstances or feature"*[390]

Depending on the circumstances, it might be a fine line between memory that is fresh and memory that is unreliably stale. In *R v*

---

389. (1998) 195 CLR 606, per Gaudron, Gummow and Hayne JJ at page 405.
390. (1998) 195 CLR 606, per Callinan J, Gleeson CJ concurring, at page 410.

Adam, the New South Wales Court of Criminal Appeal ("NSWCCA") considered that a statement made 49 days after the events in question was made when fresh in the memory of the maker of the statement[391]. However, in *Langbein v The Queen,* a differently constituted NSWCCA thought 66 days was not fresh[392].

Section 66(2) has since been amended to reflect later psychological, and other scientific, research which suggests that the subjective importance of the event to the maker of the statement is a reason to relax the requirement of contemporaneity[393].

However, there is no doubt that contemporaneity remains important. Its precise importance will depend upon the circumstances. It is doubtful that even the more relaxed notion of freshness of memory would, generally, allow that statements made years or decades after the events in question would qualify as being made when fresh in the memory. It is impossible to draw a bright line as to when statements by witnesses started to become tainted by unreliable memories. It will vary from witness to witness.

None of this means that evidence which is less than contemporaneous should be dismissed out of hand. It just means it requires extra scrutiny and caution.

In my research, I have noticed a tendency of people to assume that contemporaneous statements in this case are actually less useful than later statements on the basis that the makers of the statements were drug addled in 1969 but they were later drug free and, so the argument goes, had more clarity of mind. This is mistaken. The evidence about drug use at Spahn Ranch is equivocal, at best. In any event, there can be no question that all of the Tate/LaBianca participants (Atkins,

---

391. (1999) 47 NSWLR 267 at 281-2.

392. [2008] NSWCCA 38, at paragraphs 83 to 85.

393. The Australian Law Reform Commission reported (ALRC 102) that the more recent research tended to show that *"the significant central actions of an emotionally arousing event are likely to be better remembered than ordinary non-emotional events",* that memory is likely to be lost rapidly after an event is less true for a remarkable event than for something unremarkable and *"how quickly something is forgotten depends upon its subjective significance, both at the time it was witnessed, and in the days, weeks and months following the event".*

Van Houten, Krenwinkel, Watson, Kasabian) were free of the effects of drugs by the time they gave their various statements to lawyers and others in late 1969. Atkins was interviewed by her lawyers on 1 December, some six weeks after arrest. Van Houten's interview with Marvin Part took place on 29 December, some 10 weeks after arrest. And so on. These people were not under the influence of drugs, but they were very much still under the influence of Charles Manson, as some of them would remain for quite some time.

Reliability of Evidence – Credit

Credit was a serious issue with many of the witnesses in the subject trials. It is difficult to rely upon anything said by some witnesses, unless independently corroborated. A person's propensity to lie does not necessarily deprive all of their evidence of probative value. It is permissible for courts to take into account, and act on, such evidence where it is independently corroborated or otherwise plausible.

A brief excursion into some of the basic principles about evidence is helpful. In most common law jurisdictions, the touchstone of admissibility of evidence is relevance. Evidence is relevant if it is probative of the issues between the parties. If the evidence is not probative, it is irrelevant and, therefore, inadmissible. But not all evidence that reaches the admissibility threshold, and is admitted into evidence, is necessarily of the same weight. Some admitted evidence has great weight, some doesn't. Some types of evidence that are generally recognised by judges and trial lawyers as having weight include (without being exhaustive):

(i)   statements made against interest (admissions);

(ii)   statements made without embellishment;

(iii)   contemporaneous statements;

(iv)   statements made independently of litigation. Associated with this, evidence from witnesses who are truly independent, that is to say, witnesses who have no association with any interested party;

(v)   answers which are directly responsive to questions;

(vi)   communications between lawyers and clients. Records of client/lawyer communications are very rarely accessible by anyone other than the client and the lawyer. However, if and when they do become available, they are prima facie invaluable sources of truth. What is unique about this case is that, over time, the client/lawyer privilege has been waived in a number of instances, and the communications are therefore available for consideration;

(vii)   business records. There is a strong incentive for accuracy in the recording of the affairs of a business. True it is that errors and inaccuracies, both accidental and deliberate, occur from time to time in the recording of the activities of a business, but this is the exception rather the rule[394];

Conversely, some types of evidence tend to be regarded as having relatively little weight. They include:

(i)   self-serving statements;

(ii)   out-of-court statements (hearsay);

(iii)   opinion evidence;

(iv)   character evidence;

(v)   evidence of propensity or tendency;

These types of evidence have long been regarded by the law as of so little probative value that, in general, they should not be admitted into evidence. However, the tendency in recent decades in most common law jurisdictions has been to water down these exclusionary rules. Thus, some of these types of evidence are now regarded as admissible. But even if admitted into evidence, they will generally carry less weight than, say, admissions or any of the types of evidence previously enumerated. (One notable exception is opinion evidence given by witnesses who possess relevant qualifications and expertise, e.g. doctors, engineers, such evidence often having considerable weight.)

---

394. *Albrighton v. Royal Prince Alfred Hospital* [1980] 2 NSWLR 542.

APPENDIX 2

(i)   Why was Tex Watson not prosecuted for the Shea homicide ?

I have not found any explanation of the failure to prosecute
Watson for the Shea murder.

Watson's trial for Tate/LaBianca commenced on 2 August 1971.
At that time, Manson's trial for Shea was still underway in a different
court.   It would be logistically impossible to prosecute Watson for
Shea at the same time Manson was being prosecuted for Shea.   The
witnesses and exhibits could not be shared between the two separate
courts.   I suspect a decision may have been made by the District
Attorney to defer the prosecution of Watson for Shea and indeed only
proceed with it in the event that Watson escaped conviction for Tate/
LaBianca.

This is speculative, albeit informed by legal experience.

(ii)   Why was Steven Grogan not prosecuted for the LaBianca homicide ?

The omission to prosecute Grogan for the LaBianca murders is
perplexing.

There are reasonable arguments to the effect Grogan escaped
prosecution simply because the case against him was never strong
enough.

In the part of his book devoted to the state of investigations at 19 to 21 November 1969, Bugliosi stated the prosecution had virtually nothing on Grogan, which would be hard to disagree with. Moreover, it was learned that Grogan's brother was a police officer, and it was hoped that the brother might be able to influence Grogan to cooperate with the prosecution[395].

On 5 December 1969, Susan Atkins testified to the Grand Jury and, as a result, all of the participants – bar Grogan – were indicted. Atkins omitted to testify about the events of 10 December after leaving Watson et al at Waverley, in particular the other failed plans to kill people. Atkins merely spoke about Grogan being in the car that night. It is clear Bugliosi considered that was insufficient to indict Grogan[396]. And there was still a "*slim hope*" Grogan would be persuaded by his brother to cooperate. I think it is understandable that Bugliosi refrained from seeking the indictment against Grogan at this point, although there might be other prosecutors more bullish.

Over a few days in late February/early March 1970, Bugliosi interviewed Linda Kasabian and discovered the exact extent of Grogan's involvement in LaBianca. Bugliosi had earlier mentioned in his book that if he had known back in November/December 1969 of the matters described by Kasabian that he would have added Grogan to the indictment. However, curiously, now that he did know about them, he took no steps to add Grogan to the indictment.

One difficulty with indicting Grogan in March 1970 might have been the necessity to hold another Grand Jury hearing, which would have been an unwelcome distraction from the prosecution's otherwise intense preparation for the upcoming trial due to start in June. Another possibility is that Bugliosi still hoped Grogan's brother

---

395. Bugliosi, *Helter Skelter,* pp.187 to 188.
396. Ibid, p.248.

may be influential. Another possibility is that Bugliosi simply lost sight of prosecuting Grogan. Another possibility is that Bugliosi feared Grogan's apparent insanity might somehow influence people to consider his leader, Manson, must have been insane, thereby creating a defence for Manson[397]. I'm not sure that any one of these possibilities, by itself, adequately explains the omission to prosecute Grogan. But I find it impossible to take any further. I am inclined to the view that Grogan should have been indicted.

---

397. Bugliosi, *Helter Skelter,* p.188. See also www.mansonblog.com, *"So Manson Didn't Kill Anyone",* 6 February 2017.

BIBLIOGRAPHY

** Recommended reading.

BOOKS

Aes-Nihil, J., and Ors., *The Manson File*, Feral House, 2011.

Arendt, H., *Totalitarianism*, Harcourt, Brace and World, 1951.

Atkins, S. and Slosser, B., *Child of Satan, Child of God*, Menelorelin Dorenay's Publishing, 2005 (first published 1977).

Atkins-Waterhouse, S., *The Myth of Helter Skelter*, Menelorelin Dorenay's Publishing, 2012.

Baer, R., *Reflections on the Manson Trial: Journal of a Pseudo Juror*, World Books, 1972.

Barratt, C., *The Beatles in the News 1969*, Lulu Press Inc., 2015.

** Bishop, G., *Witness to Evil*, Dell Books, 1971.

Bravin, J., *Squeaky: The Life and Times of Lynette Alice Fromme*, St. Martin's Press, 1997.

Brown, P., and Gaines, S., *The Love You Make: An Insider's Story of the Beatles*, New American Library, Penguin Group, 1983.

** Bugliosi, V. and Gentry, C., *Helter Skelter*, W.W. Norton & Co., 1974 (Afterword 1994).

Chandler, D., *Voices From S-21: Terror and History in Pol Pot's Secret Prison*, University of California Press, 1999.

Charny, I.W., *Encyclopedia of Genocide, Vol. 1*, ABC-CLIO, 1999.

Davis, I., and LeBlanc, J., *Five to Die*, Thor Publishing, 1ˢᵗ Rev., Edn., 2009.

Didion, J., *The White Album Essays*, Simon and Schuster, 1979.

Emmons, N., *Manson in his Own Words, As Told to Nuel Emmons*, Grove Press, 1986.

** Faith, K., *The Long Prison Journey of Leslie Van Houten*, Northeastern University Press, 2001.

Festinger, L., Riecken, H.W., Schacter, S., *When Prophecy Fails: A Social and Psychological Study of a Modern Group That Predicted the Destruction of the World*, Harper and Row, 1964.

Gaines, S., *Heroes and Villains: The True Story of the Beach Boys*, Da Capo Press, 1995.

Gilmore, J., and Kenner, R., *Manson: The Unholy Trail of Charlie and the Family*, Amok Books, 2000.

Goldhagen, D.J., *Worse Than War: Genocide, Eliminationism and the Ongoing Assault on Humanity*, New York: Public Affairs, 2009.

** Guinn, J., *Manson*, Simon & Schuster, 2013.

Hendrickson, R., *Death to Pigs*, Tobann International Pictures, 2011.

Holz, R., *Too Young to be a Hero*, Harper Collins, 2000.

Howard, C., *Criminal Law*, Law Book Company Limited (Australia), The Carswell Company Ltd., (USA), 3ʳᵈ Edn., 1977.

Hunt, D., and Devallis Rutledge, J.D., *California Criminal Law Concepts*, Pearson Learning Concepts, 2013.

Kiernan, B., *Blood and Soil: A World History of Genocide and Extermination from Sparta to Darfur*, Yale University Press, 2007.

King, G., *Sharon Tate and the Manson Murders*, Barricade Books, 2000.

Lewisohn, M., *The Complete Beatles Recording Sessions*, The Hamlyn Publishing Group Limited/EMI Records Limited, 1988.

Lifton, R.J., *Thought Reform and the Psychology of Totalism: A Study of Brainwashing in Red China*, W.W. Norton, 1961.

** Livingstone Smith, D., *Less Than Human: Why We Demean, Enslave, and Exterminate Others,* St Martin's Press, 2011.

Livsey, C., *The Manson Women,* Richard Marek Publishers, 1980.

MacCurdy, J.T., *The Psychology of War,* John W. Luce and Coy, 1918.

Marynick, M., *Charles Manson Now,* Cogito Media Group, 2010.

McCauley, C., and Chirot, D., *Why Not Kill Them All? The Logic and Prevention of Mass Political Murder,* Princeton University Press, 2006.

Meerloo, J., *The Rape of the Mind,* Martino Publishing, 2015, first published 1956.

Milgram, S., *Obedience to Authority,* Harper and Rowe, 1974.

Moyer, N., *Escape From the Killing Fields,* Zonervan Publishing House, 1991.

Nelson, W., *Manson Behind the Scenes,* Pen Power Publications, 1997.

Sanders, E., *The Family,* Penguin Books USA Inc., 1989.

Sargant, W., *Battle for the Mind: A Physiology of Conversion and Brain Washing,* Malor Books, 3rd Edn., 1997 (1st Edn., Wm Heinemann Ltd., 1957).

Schein, E.H., Schneier, I., Barker, C.H., *A Socio-psychological Analysis of the 'Brainwashing' of American Civilian Prisoners by the Chinese Communists,* W.W. Norton, 1961.

Schiller, L., *The Killing of Sharon Tate,* The New American Library Inc., 1970.

** Singer, M.T., *Cults in Our Midst,* Jossey-Bass, 1995.

Stimson, G., *Goodbye Helter Skelter, A New Look at the Tate-LaBianca Murders,* The Peasenhall Press, 2014.

Taylor, K., *Brainwashing: The Science of Thought Control,* Oxford University Press, 2004.

** Watkins, P., *My Life With Charles Manson,* Bantam Books Inc., 1979.

** Watson, C., as told to Chaplain Ray, *Will You Die For Me?,* Revell, a division of Baker Publishing Group, 1978, used by permission.

Watson, C., *Manson's Right-Hand Man Speaks Out,* 2012.

Wells, S., *Charles Manson Coming Down Fast*, Hodder & Stoughton Ltd., 2009.

Zamora, W., *Blood Family*, Zebra Books Kensington Publishing Corp., 1976, first published as *Trial By Your Peers*, 1973.

ARTICLES

David E. Smith and Alan J. Rose (1970) *The Group Marriage Commune: A Case Study*, Journal of Psychoactive Drugs, 3:1, 115-119, DOI:<u>10.1080/02791072.1970.10471368.</u>

"The Love and Terror Cult", *Life* magazine, 19 December 1969.

Dalton, D., "If Christ Came Back as a Con Man", *Gadfly*, October 1998.

Dalton D., Felton, D., "Year of the Fork, Night of the Hunter", *Rolling Stone*, no.61, 25 June 1970.

Kelman, H.C., *Violence Without Moral Restraint*, Journal of Social Sciences, Vol.29, No.4, 1975

"Vincent Bugliosi", *Penthouse*, Vol.7, No.10, June 1976.

INTERNET

<u>www.cielodrive.com</u>
<u>www.genocidewatch.org</u>
<u>www.themurdersofaugust69.freeforums.net</u>
<u>www.mansonsbackporch.com</u>
<u>www.mansonblog.com</u>

VIDEOS/FILMS

A Turning Point, ABC TV, 1994.

ABC Evening News, Leslie Van Houten Interviewed by Barbara Walters, ABC TV, January 1977.

ABC Evening News, Leslie Van Houten Interviewed by Barbara Walters, ABC TV, January 1977, unedited version.

Charles Manson: The Man Who Killed the 60's, Channel 4, 2004.
Charles Manson: Serial Killer, Entertainment Channel, 2000.
Hard Copy, 1997.
Larry King Live, Paul Watkins Interviewed by Maureen Regan, CNN, 1988.
Most Evil: Charles Manson, Discovery Channel, 2006.
NBC News Archives, 1971.
The Manson Women, Biography Series, Entertainment Channel.

TRANSCRIPTS

People v. Beausoleil, 1969.
People v. Beausoleil, 1970.
Grand Jury Proceedings (various)
People v. Manson & Ors, 1970, 1971.
People v. Watson, 1971.
Parole hearings: Beausoleil, Davis, Watson, Manson, Atkins, Krenwinkel, Van Houten, Grogan
Records of Interview: Poston, Brunner, Schram, Van Houten, Atkins, DeCarlo.

AUTHORITIES

Alister v. R (1984) 154 CLR 404; [1984] HCA 85.
Barker v. Wingo [1972] USSC 146; [1972] 407 US 514.
Darwiche & Ors. v. R [2011] NSWCCA 62.
De Gruchy v. R (2002) 211 CLR 85; [2002] HCA 33.
Dietrich v. The Queen (1992) 177 CLR 292; [1992] HCA 57.
Kesavarajah v. The Queen (1994) 181 CLR 230.
Martin v. Osborne [1936] 55 CLR 367; [1936] HCA 23.
Mutual Life Insurance Coy. Of New York v. Moss (1906) 4 CLR 311; [1906] HCA 70.
Miranda v. Arizona 384 US 436.
MWJ v. The Queen (2005) 80 ALJR 329; [2005] HCA 74.

People v. Aranda (1965) 63 Cal. 2d 518.

People v. Beausoleil Cal. 2d Crim 22232, unpublished.

People v. Blye (1965) 233 Cal. App. 2d 143.

People v Coefield 37 Cal. 2d 865.

People v. Davis Cal. 2d Crim 22505, unpublished, 31/3/76.

People v Ford 60 Cal 2d 772.

People v. Grogan Cal. 2d Crim. 21932, unpublished, 19/1/73.

People v. Guillen (1974) 37 Cal. App. 3d 976

** *People v. Manson & Ors.* [1976] 61 Cal. App. 3d 123.

** *People v. Manson* [1977] 71 Cal. App. 3d 11.

People v. Miller 121 Cal. 343.

People v. Robles (1970) 2 Cal. 3d 205.

People v Thomas 41 Cal 2d 470.

People v Ulsh (1962) 211 Cal. App. 2d 258.

People v Washington 62 Cal 2d 777.

Plomp v. R (1963) 110 CLR 234; [1963] HCA 44.

Pointer v. United States [1894] USSC 38; 151 US 396.

R v. Birks (1990) 19 NSWLR 677.

R v. Mobbs [2005] NSWCCA 371.

Shepherd v R (1990) 170 CLR 573, [1990] HCA 56.

MISCELLANEOUS

Archives of District Attorney for County of Los Angeles

INDEX

Y

Younger

Z

Zamora

CPSIA information can be obtained
at www.ICGtesting.com
Printed in the USA
BVOW06s2006010817

490860BV00023B/371/P

9 780648 125204